MIDDLE ANDZIA

A Memoir
by
Anda Meisels Rosen

MIDDLE ANDZIA

A Memoir

For more information direct your web browser to:
www.middleandzia.com

ISBN1-4196-3811-4

Library of Congress Control Number:

2006904529

Publisher: BookSurge, LLC
North Charleston, South Carolina

Cover design and book layout by Mark Rosen

CONTENTS

Contents

Shavuot 2005

Dear Children,
Tonight is the start of the holiday Shavuot. It was on this holiday, 62 years ago, that the last three thousand Jews of the Sambor Ghetto were machine-gunned by the Nazis into a ditch. Sambor was my home town in Poland.
Last night, in my dream I was there. Please keep memorial candles lit for the two nights and days of Shavuot and a few days beyond.

Words cannot resurrect the past and heal it, so that we could move on, unshackled by it. However, words can make the past come alive within our hearts and minds, when we share them with others in order that we may learn from it and create a better future. The past must not be ignored. It is the rest of the "iceberg" lurking beneath the surface of each present moment, our present experience being merely its tip. And even though each "Here-Now" is the point of departure to whatever else will later happen in our life, it is our past that brings us there and then comes along on the journey to the future.

History should be taught to young and old, so that they can learn from it and figure out how to prevent genocide like the one that was taking place in Europe, in the midst of twentieth century Western civilization. But nothing will be learned by distortions, denials and amnesia. Without awareness of history the cycle of violence will continue. Our beautiful earth, which, for better or worse, binds us forever to each other in a constant exchange of molecules, energy and consciousness, is being polluted by the chemistry of hatred, violence and suffering. History should be taught not only in terms of conquests, defeats, dates and famous military and political leaders but also in terms of human suffering brought upon the human race by evil men, and those that tolerate them; and it should be taught in terms of the triumphs of the human spirit over evil and injustice.

Now, years after WWII, there is a somewhat popular interest in the Holocaust; new generations want to know what happened. And there are now those who deny it. Films are being made, books written, but many of them are told not directly by survivors, but through second hand representations that are politically correct and commercially viable.

We, the few remaining survivors are getting very old, and many of our personal histories are being lost daily. These are not the histories of military events and war statistics. They are the personal histories of the lives, thoughts and feelings of ordinary human beings who experienced an extraordinary mass genocide that was thrust upon them by other ordinary human beings who felt themselves superior. The overwhelming majority of Germans between the years of 1933 to 1945, and their many active and passive collaborators all over the world, did not find it necessary to measure their ideology, their politics, and their actions against known civilized standards of justice, decency and compassion. To them these standards did not apply to people they considered inferior to the Germanic Aryan race or even their dogs. The result was the systematic murder of six million European Jews and the enslavement and death of millions of Gentiles.

The Holocaust affected me personally and profoundly. Having lived through it, I carried inside, for the rest of my life, not only emotional scars, but also a legacy and a mandate. The history of the Jewish people and my personal experience as a Holocaust survivor is my legacy. It has affected my perspective on the totality of human history. My mandate is to remember and recount my own history and that of the people I knew, the few who survived and the many that did not. I also want to encourage my children to listen to the accounts of other Holocaust survivors.

In response to the Holocaust, one could drown in hatred, anger and depression, or one could wake up to become a few notches more human. Thus one could become more sensitive to the corrosive potential of prejudice and hatred and the immense suffering to which innocent beings are still being subjected, in all corners of the world, near and far.

In response to evil, we can take a stand. Sometimes we can respond with small acts of kindness and honesty, but sooner or later we are called by our conscience to take a courageous and active stand, be it on the battlefield, in courts, in the classroom, or in a voting booth.

After the war, while facing an indifferent world, remembering and recounting episodes from the Holocaust years was unbearably painful. Although after WWII, which ended in 1945, I was no longer condemned to die and was not living in hiding, I remained emotionally stuck in the past for many years. I was confused, sad, mistrusting, fearful and very angry. Although outwardly I seemed to adjust well to postwar situations, inside my war was not over.

There were many questions I had about the war, and there were many things I needed to express and tell others. But no one

I came across wanted to hear what I had to share, and no one was there to give me any answers to my questions. Now, sixty years after WWII, my questions still remain unanswered. How could this kind of genocide have happened in the midst of twentieth-century Europe? Why and how could a fate of such blatant murder -an attempt at total extermination- have befallen a whole ethnic group of peaceful, non-violent people? After all, Jews had lived in Europe for many hundreds of years, and had contributed so much in every field and in every country they had lived in. Why did their fellow human beings, their Christian fellow citizens, particularly in the Ukraine, in Poland and in Germany, allow it to happen? Why did so many of them perpetrate it? Were these Christians not acting against the teachings of Jesus?

Did those who had actively or passively collaborated with Hitler in bringing about the Holocaust, still call themselves Christians? Did they still feel one hundred percent human? Did they pray to God? Did they love? Were they able to see beauty in the world? Did they experience joy? How could they listen to Mozart or Schubert? How could they dance to the joyful music of Johann Strauss? How could they read Goethe, Schiller, or Lessing and still be so barbaric? These were the questions that I was seeking answers to.

When I did try to talk about my life during the Holocaust, people were mostly reluctant to dwell on the subject. The usual response was "It's too damn depressing". I understood that it was too jarring and out of sync with life, as we know it today. The topic was out of place at a party, at dinner, at work, on a hike, or during a casual visit when a friend would drop by for a cup of coffee. Besides, people would have only a vague understanding of what I was talking about. Many tend to place events that happened at the time of World War II into the category of ancient history.

The Jews I had met and befriended right after the war who were unscathed by the Holocaust, did not seem to be interested in the stories of survivors. They were too preoccupied with preserving their own safe niche in the Diaspora. Nor were non-Jewish people I met interested in learning about the Holocaust. Had they been open, they would have realized that what I had experienced was not merely a Jewish problem, but a human one.

I found Europeans to be particularly closed to putting their history of intolerance under scrutiny.

Often, I would be complimented on my "charming" accent and some would even make a well-meaning and lighthearted effort to say a few German or Polish words in my honor. People expect me to talk of the lands of my childhood with pride and describe them in glowing terms like an exciting travelogue. Usually, I don't bother to say anything; I just fidget and squirm. But sooner or later, more needs to be said.

I wish I could just say "I love the Polish polkas, landscapes, language, and the music of Chopin. I admire German orderliness, and love Bach, Beethoven, operettas and classical literature. I love the Swiss Alps, chocolate and civility. I love French elegance and sophistication. I love the Italian people, their operas and their movies." Of course, no one would expect me to respond with a serious tirade: "Yes, I was born in Poland, and so were my parents and grandparents, and great, great, great-grandparents, but as a Jew, I was never considered by the Gentile community to be a real Pole while living in Poland." People don't realize that their well-meant compliments on my European background give me a sickly feeling in the pit of my stomach. In Europe, not only did I lose the people who nurtured me since birth, but I also experienced rejection and exclusion from the people and places I grew up with and those who represented the rest of my world.

Living in a democratic and pluralistic society, Americans don't understand that. The Poles said to me, dirty Jew, go to Palestine; the British said, Jew keep out of Palestine; and the Germans said, cursed Jew, go to Auschwitz. There was never a European Abraham Lincoln.

In a way, other's disinterest helped me indirectly to anesthetize myself through day-to-day activities.

That is how we, the survivors, were able to move on in life after liberation and live, at least on the surface, more or less like "normal" people.

Sooner or later, I needed to become reconciled and grounded within a new, post-Holocaust, world. But to do that, I needed to find a meaningful point of reference to regain my bearing as a human being, while becoming reinstated into "the family of man". I needed to accept, not in theory, but deep within my own gut, that I was a legitimate human being after all.

Israel became that point of reference for me. What it did for me, and probably for all victims of anti-Semitism throughout the world, was to make Jews feel like "a normal people" so that henceforth we would relate to others as equals.

Among the people of Israel, we the survivors were not only legitimate human beings, but our survival was celebrated and the loss of the six million was deeply felt and mourned. In Israel our miraculous survival became an important part of the miraculous rebirth of a great people as a nation in their ancient homeland. Before that, my Jewishness meant being condemned to death; then it meant sadness, homelessness and isolation. It gave me a sense of not belonging, no matter where I went. It also reminded me of the fear, the anger and the mourning I carried within me since childhood.

For me, it was not easy to recover a trust I had lost, and to believe that living with mutual respect among people of different racial, religious, and ethnic backgrounds was possible. Living in the USA, I soon came to understand that not only was this possible, but that is what this country is all about. Although this society is far from perfect, at least we have an opportunity to work together towards mutual respect and equal rights and opportunities. When I received my American citizenship I was afforded the American credo that the pursuit of a happy life is not only my human right, but also within my reach.

But not until my children were born did some healing on a personal level begin to happen. With each child that I gave birth to, it felt as if I was partaking in an act of resurrection.

My children were precious and fragile gifts that were entrusted to me.

I sometimes questioned whether someone with my history and legacy could raise happy and well-adjusted children.

After my children were born I went about creating, for myself and for my family, a beautiful, new, little world. I surrounded myself with children and with lots of animals. I planted trees, danced with my children, and avoided funerals and cemeteries.

But more than anything else, I avoided angry and petty people.

In the love for my children and in nature, music and dancing I rediscovered joy. In finding kindred friends and getting to know good people, I rediscovered hope.

And yet, even during this time of rebirth and healing, my journals of that time speak of the still open wounds from my childhood. I recently found this old diary entry from the seventies:

"It's a Saturday afternoon; the sky is dark gray. I drive without a destination along Ventura Boulevard as if searching for someone, and yet knowing that anyone I may find on or near Ventura Boulevard in Encino, California, will not fill the void I so often feel. Mind shadows of past living, thousands of miles away, seem more real than this, my new life one block north of mainstreet USA. I am an American, a mother of five healthy American sons. I speak to them in English. I am a grown woman who lives in a big house just around the corner. I have intelligent and loving friends, many interests, and a busy schedule. Within the next few hours I will probably cook a great dinner for my family; I usually do. Yet driving aimlessly on Ventura Boulevard on this gray and drizzly Saturday afternoon, I feel like a homeless child, forever longing for home. Home was some other place, some other time."

Then, I found two more recent journal entries:

"Tarzana, winter, 1997, it's 8 am and it's a beautiful morning. From my window, I see snow in the San Gabriel Mountains and the sky is radiantly blue. I'm hungry, and I'm making breakfast. But just beyond the plate and cup I'm reaching for, I seem to see, off in the distance, scenes and faces from my "other" life. Frozen in time, transparent ghost-like faces. They are there before me whichever way I turn, because they're in my head, within my eyeballs. Yet they are a lifetime away. I see my cousins Zosia, and Big Andzia, and Bunek. How hungry they must have been after they were rounded up by the Germans and kept for five days without food before being taken to the forest to be shot. Weak and emaciated, did they still want to live, did they think about escaping? But where would they go? No one wanted them. Were they all numb and silent? Does one still feel human in such a situation? And the killers, what did they do afterwards; after the executions? Did they go to church or get drunk, beat their kids and rape their wives? Or did they just come home for dinner and eat in silence. There were rumors that the German SS officer in charge of the executions went insane.

Suddenly knowing nothing anymore, like a robot, going through the motions of doing what I set out to do, I sit down to breakfast and ask myself, what would really be important to do today, tomorrow, or with one's short and fragile life? I feed the dogs. Sooner or later someone will call or come over, and I'll jump onto that stage."

Tarzana, CA, undated:

"Tonight I watched a nature program about zebras. It seems that during a certain season the herd gathers in one spot where the pregnant female zebras give birth to their young. The jackals lurk nearby, waiting for a chance to pounce on the newly born zebras. The mother zebras helplessly watch the jackals tear their young ones to shreds. Occasionally a lion shows up and does the same. Soon the herd of zebras gallops away. The new mother-zebras eventually give up circling about their captured babies and they gallop away to join the herd.

After that program, as if by a strange coincidence, looking for news I came upon a documentary about the Nazi era: Kristalnacht, deportations, Auschwitz, the crematoria, the skeletal inmates, and the mass executions in smaller towns. How do I spend the rest of this long night in my beautiful, warm home?

Earlier this evening I had a great dinner, at the end of a great weekend, baking pies and cooking for my visiting children and grandchildren. The day before, on Saturday night I went country western dancing with my friend. He teased me about my inability to sit out a song, and grimaced when he saw me eyeing the handsome young cowboys with their narrow hips, in their tight jeans and big hats. My friend likes the fun loving bubbly me, he knows little of my wartime past, and my occasional dark moods when I am reminded to look back and I am shaken to the core.

After the documentary and the news, I turned off the TV and went to bed but couldn't fall asleep. The documentary took over my mind. My great weekend faded from my thoughts. Instead, events that took place far away and long ago, scenes and sounds from my childhood take center stage, all still flashing so vividly before me: the panic, the cries, the screams, the wailing, the eyes frozen in terror. The eyes of my grandfather Yanche, aunts Dvorka and Laika, and my young cousins are looking at me. I see myself at age ten and little cousin Andzia clutching my hand and not wanting to let go, as I was saying goodbye to her. And I hear myself asking over and over again: why did I let go of her hand and go into hiding without her? Why did I leave without my friend and cousin Zosia? They were both killed three weeks later. My thoughts flashed back to the mother zebra galloping away to join the herd; there was no way she could have saved the baby zebra from being devoured by the jackals."

Today I have decided to gather up my memories and write them down as best as I can and not delay any longer. Some early memories were beautiful, but the memories of my wartime experiences followed me like a giant black shadow, no matter where I happened to be or what I was doing.

Anti-Semitic words still trigger in me intense rage and sadness. I do not want to numb these by escaping into present day-to-day trivia. These emotions are intertwined with a history not yet accounted for, and they keep me connected to its victims and the family I lost. The victims of the Holocaust now live through those of us who remember them and tell their story, in whatever ways we can -be it in words, in the way we live, in the values we hold or in the way we treat others.

The millions of European Jews, so brutally annihilated by the German Nazis in WWII (with incredible cooperation from most of the general populace) should never perish from the world's consciousness or conscience.

The war created a time warp in my mind. In ways I don't understand, it seems that memory is selective. The wartime years I spent between the ages of seven and twelve, imprinted themselves strongest onto my being and they seem to have lasted longer than they actually did. Was that because of the constant threat of death, and by way of contrast to the early happy years? The time after the Holocaust passed quickly.

Being young, curious, and hungry to sample new opportunities that were opening up after the war, I soon blended into the new societies wherever I happened to live. Yet everywhere I felt different from other young people my age.

Recently, I received a letter from a German acquaintance in which she downright denies the German role in the Holocaust. She knows my background. Apparently in Germany they no longer teach about the Holocaust in their history classes. Already history is being twisted and rearranged to comfortably fit current social trends and political expediency. And by now some even deny that the Holocaust ever happened in their midst, or was acquiesced to and perpetrated by their parents and grandparents.

Many people in Europe and the rest of the world want to overlook the ugliness of the Hitler era and forget its not-so-distant history. And when they forget, what moral standards are they to use when confronting new tyrants and hate mongers?

It seems that most perpetrators of past atrocities were not held accountable and the heirs to their twisted minds continue to spout their hatred. So far, the human race is not learning enough from history. But there are many good people who make an effort to build a better world by heeding and teaching the lessons of history and by promoting tolerance and the principles of democracy, freedom and human rights.

By now my children are grown. Now I live alone in a small house on top of a mountain in Tarzana, California. I love being in my quiet little home on a rainy winter day with my three dogs Yogi, Picoush and Shanti and my beloved cat Tommy. Outside in my yard, my old horse, Fiddle, is eating hay under his shelter. The silence in my small house is delicious and sacred. It is a time to stop and ask, who am I?

How shall tell my story? I will begin to tell it in the context of my relationships to the people and events that shaped it. I look at my parents' wedding picture above my desk. How beautiful they looked and how symbolic that picture is of the world of the thirties as I remember it. It is also a reminder of a lost Jewish world in Europe, and for me that was in Sambor, Poland.

I remember to take a deep breath and be a witness to what is. I feel my neck and back, which are by now very tense. I look at the cat, hear the rain outside, and notice the smell of fried onions and the freshly baked pie.

Clinging to this moment for balance, I stroke the cat, clean his litter box, and give the dogs a treat. Once a Kabalistic rabbi told me that the Hebrew word for a dog, kelev, comes from two words: kol lev, which means "all heart".

By now the cat has snuggled up behind my back and my dogs lie down beside me. I look into their eyes and I'm ready to write.

I am not a scholarly historian or a skilled writer, but I will pass on these words, my history to my children and to theirs, because who I am and where I came from had a great bearing on who they became and where they are going. On the road ahead, knowledge of history adds perspective to the way we see life and hopefully it inspires us to evolve and become better humans.

As one of the very few who had survived the Holocaust, I do not take life and freedom for granted.

In the context of my personal history, I was always driven to ask questions, seeking to understand not only our physical universe but also human nature, our relationship to each other and to existence. Who am I? Where did I come from and where am I going? What can I learn, and what can I teach?

Middle Andzia

1

AN EARLY IMPRESSION

On a beautiful Saturday morning, just before the war, when I was almost seven, Mama took me to the park near the railway station. Sitting with Mama on a bench, I saw in the distance a young man being forcefully led by two attendants. He was wearing a straight jacket and was screaming and struggling to free himself. As he came closer, he stopped in front of our bench, looked at me, and became still. Then, in a calm voice, he said to my mother, "Madam, please take the child away, I don't want her to get frightened." I never forgot that man. Although I was a very young child, his concern for me must have touched me deeply. For a long time after, I thought about that man, and worried about him. I worried that someone might be hurting him. The man was being taken to an insane asylum in Lvov. At just about the same time, in Germany and in Austria, two of the most cultured countries in the world, throngs of supposedly sane people were cheering a murderous maniac, and supposedly sane world leaders were shaking his hand and making deals with him.

A recreation of Sambor's historic emblem

2

HOME WAS SAMBOR

I was born in 1932. Until I was twelve I lived in Sambor. Up to the first eight days of September 1939, Sambor was a small town near Lvov, in eastern Poland. Two big rivers, the Dniester and the Strwianc bordered our town. Because of its proximity to several countries, Sambor had a long history of commerce and invasions, and therefore, it was exposed to different cultures and languages. The town has been under Russian rule, under Austrian rule, under Polish rule, under German occupation, and under Soviet rule. Since the thirteenth century, Sambor was repeatedly overrun and destroyed by Tartars, Turks and others. In the Middle Ages, in between hostile invasions, it was under the rule of Polish kings, who even built castles there. Before WWI, in 1902, when my father was born, Sambor was under Austrian rule. Now, since the collapse of the Soviet Union, Sambor is a town in the Ukraine.

In Polish Sambor means "All Forest". Legend has it, that a long time ago, the Polish queen Bona, while hunting in the forest, hit a young deer with a bow and arrow, and in her honor, on that very spot in the forest, the city was built.

To me, my hometown Sambor was beautiful. It had parks, rolling hills, rivers, old churches, and many old cobble stone streets.

A third river, the Mlynoovka, which was a tributary of the Dniester, ran through the town. In the middle of town stood the city hall, which we called the Ratuszss building, with a tall clock tower. On the very top of the tower stood a brass sculpture of a young deer pierced by an arrow, a symbol of Sambor's legendary origin.

Before World War II, Sambor had a population of about thirty thousand. Of these about eight thousand were Jewish. In Europe, very few Jews survived the Holocaust during WWII, and in Sambor less than one hundred survived and I am one of those very few survivors. Today, of those who were born or lived there before the war, there are no Jews left in Sambor. After liberation by the Russian army in August 1944, the few survivors left Sambor and scattered throughout the world. Many have died since.

According to historic records, Jews had lived in Sambor for about six hundred years. Sambor, like the rest of Poland and the Ukraine, had a long history of rabid anti-Semitism. When its Jewish residents suddenly disappeared, life in Sambor went on as if they had never existed. The locals took over Jewish homes and businesses. Since 1939, strangers have been living in my parents' home, the homes of my grandparents, my aunts and my uncles, and my Jewish neighbors.

The town, whose founding symbol was a deer shot in the forest, ceased to exist as far as I was concerned when, one thousand years later, the last remnants of its Jewish community was executed in that same forest, just a few miles beyond the statue atop the Ratusz clock tower. I saw Sambor for the last time in January 1945.

In my dreams I go back, frantically searching among the ruins of the Sambor ghetto, calling out name, after name, after name. No one answers, and I wake up far from home. Home was some other place, some other time. No other place since, felt quite right.

Mama picnicking at the Dniester riverbank (1937).

3

I REMEMBER LOVING LIFE

Here and there, within the flow of an "ordinary" day, beautiful things come my way, and so often they bring up memories from my early childhood before the war; though by now they appear almost dreamlike. Glimpses of grazing horses, the scent of earth and pine, or a crispy winter night, bring back images of beloved native landscapes, of soft faces I once touched, dear hands that once held mine, and of sweet voices I used to hear singing Yiddish, Polish, Ukrainian, and Russian songs.

Things, once known so well, suddenly jump out from across distant continents and time spans and reincarnate into momentary flashes, lighting up an ordinary day with extra-ordinary childish-like joy. And then something within gets reconnected, and something within gets reaffirmed and perhaps resolved and healed. My early years before the war were exciting and happy. Apparently they were also very significant, because many incidents and the feelings they evoked at the time seem to have imprinted themselves on my memory in great detail. I remember things from a time when I still slept in a crib, used a potty, and was riding in a stroller. During the war I must have often looked back to the happy times, clinging to the memories, like someone in a hurricane, holding on for dear life to a deeply rooted tree.

I remember loving the winters of my early childhood. Outside, the softly falling snow was always magical, especially at night. The nights were long and quiet. Here and there one could hear the sound of snow-bells from a passing horse-drawn sleigh.

I remember lying in my white metal crib with brass trim, safe and warm, staring at the windows, which were covered with frost around the edges, and looking at the snow falling outside, until falling asleep. And like a beloved lullaby, the quiet of the winter night would sing me to sleep. At such times it seemed as if time stood still. And like a fossil in clay before it hardens to stone, such magical moments embed themselves in a young heart forever.

In Sambor, as in most of eastern Poland, winters were long and cold. After a snowfall the streets and yard were pure white. The ice on our kitchen windows had the most amazing crystalline frost patterns. I remember one morning, after the first snowfall of the season, our maid Yanka picked me up from my crib and wrapped me in a large fur and took me outside. That winter morning scene awakened in me such joy that I relive it each time I see a first snowfall. And Yanka, who was young, surely must have shared with me its wonder.

My grandparents, Yanche and Tilly Glickman, who were my mother's parents, used to come to visit almost every day. (Yanche is a Yiddish version of Hebrew name Yaakov.) Our little house was cozy and warm, heated by large wood-burning tile heaters in every room. In the kitchen there was a big wood burning cooking stove, tended by our maid Nascia, and there was always some food being cooked or baked. Nascia would bring in the wood and light the stoves first thing in the morning and then help out in the kitchen. Mama did all the cooking, while everybody else would usually sit around the large kitchen table. My maternal grandma, Tilly, would be darning a sock, stretched over a wooden mushroom. Mother's younger sister, Laika, would be knitting or sewing, my sister Genia would be reading a book or playing with me, making clothes for my dolls. Nearby, in the adjoining dining room, my grandfather Yanche would sit in a rocking chair, studying the Talmud and chain-smoking. Often I would sit on his lap and stroke his beard and listen to the singsong with which he would read. His fingers were yellow from nicotine. Sometimes he'd let me try to roll his cigarettes and even let me have a puff. My mother would scream at us when she would catch us. Grandfather would look at me and laugh.

Occasionally during the day there would be a knock on the door, a beggar would ask for food or money, the milkman would deliver milk or the butcher would deliver meat. Sometimes people would drop in for a visit. People talked, told stories, gossiped or sang together. The children listened and learned about the world. We did not have a radio and there were few distractions from whatever was happening in life, as it was unfolding. My life was peaceful and safe and time moved slowly.

I loved winter evenings best. Outside it was very cold, inside our home was warm and comfortable and the smell of food would fill the house. Often it was potato soup with fried onions, sometimes it was goulash, a beef stew full of onions and red paprika. Thursdays were shopping days and on Fridays, my mother cooked and baked all day in preparation for the Sabbath. She cooked chicken soup and gefillte fish (ground fish balls, boiled with onion and sugar), and cholent (meat stew that had slowly cooked all night), and she baked fresh twisted white bread with poppy seeds, called challah. She also baked a sweet raisin, cinnamon and chocolate cake we called buchta.

After the baking was finished, the cholent dish was placed in the hot oven and left to cook all night for the midday Sabbath meal on Saturday. For orthodox Jews it was forbidden to cook on the Sabbath, so all the food had to be prepared in advance. On Friday night there was always a big family feast. It started with a song welcoming the Sabbath, "Shalom Aleihem... Peace be unto you", and a blessing over sweet dark grape wine and the white, twisted bread. The cup of wine and the bread were passed around the table, and everybody said a short prayer praising God for bringing forth food from the earth. After dinner, and a prayer of thanks, "Benching", there was much singing of religious and other songs.

Saturday mornings we children ate the buchta, dunking it in milk. Father dressed in his best clothes and went to the Mizrachi Synagogue for the Sabbath prayers. It was a progressive-ortho-dox Synagogue. He would return at noon and then we had lunch, which was another Sabbath feast. The "cholent " was retrieved from the oven and the table was filled with all sorts of delicacies. After lunch, while the children went for a walk with the maid, my parents went to sleep. When they got up, they went for a walk, or would visit friends and family. Adhering to the strict rules for the Sabbath, we children were not allowed to use sleds outside or play inside with play-dough, pencils, or use scissors until the end of the Sabbath. By dusk, we would all crawl into Mama's big bed with her and sing in the dark until father came back from the synagogue, or three stars could be seen in the sky and it was time to turn on the lights. Sometimes when our cousins Zosia and big Andzia visited us, they would join us in the big warm bed and sing along with us.

In winter, the days were very short. On weekdays, father would come home from his business when it was already dark outside, with his face red from frost and his coat, hat and boots covered with snow. When he greeted us children, his turquoise colored eyes would light up and shine with joy. After dinner, he would smoke a pipe or a cigar, read his newspaper, play solitaire, and sing with us. He adored his children, and enjoyed good food and wine, which he usually made himself in our cellar. He had a beautiful voice and he loved to sing. He sang Yiddish and Hebrew songs. He also loved to sing opera, especially one particular aria from the opera "Tosca". He was at his best singing liturgical songs, called "Chazanut", which he sang with a reverence that came straight from his heart. To me, these songs always expressed the essence of the Jewish soul; the longing for a life free of persecution, and for the return to Zion. They expressed, all at once, blessings, thanksgiving and the celebration of life. The melodies reflected Jewish Middle-Eastern roots and the music of the many countries the Jews had lived in while in the Diaspora. My father sang so beautifully that he was often asked to sing before the congregation in the Synagogue.

Middle Andzia

When Genia and I were children
A lifetime-years ago
Across from golden fields of wheat
Endless fields of snow
Children warm and snug
In Polish winter cold
In soft arms cradled, fairy tales told
Wrapped in lace or woolen shawls
In Yiddish-Slavic minor key
We'd dream and learn to love

*L-R My sister Genia, me and my dog Peecoush,
and Uncle Moshe's daughter, "Black Genia". (1933)*

4

THE HOUSE ON
MAY 3RD STREET

Until I was five, we lived in a charming little rented house with a huge garden that was full of tall sunflowers. The house was on May 3rd Street, across from the Sokol, where all the major social and cultural events in Sambor took place. The street was wide with a center garden lane landscaped with trees and beds of flowers. The house belonged to "Countess" Maniewska. I am not sure whether she was a countess or a baroness; she belonged to Polish nobility and she was titled.

The house my family lived in was divided into three units. My paternal uncle Moshe, his wife Elka, and their two children, Genia and Siuniu, lived in one of them. Between Moshe's place and ours was an exclusive nursery school for Polish officers' children from which Jewish children were excluded.

My crib stood in my parents' bedroom against the wall that adjoined the nursery school. I remember lying in the crib in the morning and listening to the happy songs the children would sing.

"O stawaj mi stawaj sloneczku kochane, bo zionek budzi juz …..Rise, oh rise for me my dear Sun, because dawn already awakens…"

Right in front of our kitchen and dining room windows was the school's playground. It had great equipment. There were metal structures for climbing , slides, sandboxes, swings and seesaws. The playground was not fenced, so I got to play there after the school children and their teachers would leave for the day; on Sundays I could play all day.

All the way in the back of the courtyard was a small red brick house where a fat old lady, Pani Zawadzka lived. (Pani means Mrs.) Her house always smelled of pickles. I heard people say that she had a famous son who lived in Warsaw.

To the left of the driveway and diagonally across from us in the back, was a third house. In the upper apartment lived the Tomszajs (pronounced Tom'shys). They were a childless couple.

Beneath their apartment, in the basement apartment lived a very old lady. She was a reclusive, sick woman who lived in poverty. I don't remember ever seeing her outside her place, although I remember that she was very skinny and wore shabby dark clothes. She had many dogs; her window was close to the ground and her place reeked with foul dog odors. Just past her place were the toilets. The toilets were located in the house in the back and right behind the Tomszaj's apartment.

I never used them, because I was small and was still using the potty exclusively, which the maid would take out to the toilets to be emptied.

Mr. Tomszaj was an electrician. He rode a black motorcycle with an attached caboose in which I sometimes saw his plump, blond wife, riding alongside her husband. He was a tall, slim man with thinning dark hair and long sideburns.

I always loved dogs and horses. My mother told me that when I was very small she gave me a tiny puppy that she named Peecoosh. Apparently I loved that puppy so much that I held it and petted it all the time. I must have squeezed it once too hard because one-day mother found it lying dead near me. Afterwards the maid must have placed it in the garbage bin, which was located near the Tomszaj's windows.

As I found out years later, the puppy was not quite dead. At night the Tomszajs heard it whimpering and rescued it. Nine years later that dog, which the Tomszajs named Niegus, became part of my nightmarish experience with the Tomszajs.

Soon after I lost the puppy my mother got me another dog, a dachshund, which we once again called Peecoosh. Peecoosh and I were inseparable since I was about one year old. He was with me in most of my pictures.

When I was nine months old, my mother told me I was found

by some people walking down the street and around the corner, holding on to the wrought iron fence that fronted our neighbor's large property. That's how she found out that I could walk. Perhaps my dog, Peecoosh, got out and I was trying to follow him.

There were always many Gypsies coming to Sambor. My mother would frequently tell me that if I didn't eat, or if I misbehaved, I would be sold to the Gypsies. At other times she told me that the Gypsies left me on the doorstep when I was little. She would often point out that I was different from the rest of the family because I was mischievous-- not a good little girl like my sister, and because I didn't even look like anyone else in the family. I suppose she was kidding, but sometimes she said that when she was annoyed with me. It was partly true. Although I did have blue eyes like my father, I was blond, and everybody else had black hair.

We children were also often told to watch out, because the Gypsies might kidnap us. One night as I was lying in my crib, I saw a Gypsy woman looking in through the window. I was terrified. I started screaming and calling my mother and father, but no one heard me. We had guests in the living room and everybody was talking very loudly. No one responded to my screams. The last thing I remembered was the crib and the room spinning faster and faster. Then I must have fainted.

On some level I believed my mother when she told me that I was a gypsy child. She said it so often that when I saw their caravans leaving town, I was sad to be left behind and I longed to go away with them. I loved their singing and dancing. They were such dark, handsome and mysterious people, with beautiful glowing black eyes. I loved the long colorful skirts and flowery-fringed shawls their women wore. The women also wore lots of jewelry, especially big golden hoop earrings. The Gypsies often sang and played musical instruments in our courtyard for a hand out, as did other poor, wandering minstrels.

To this day I still love Gypsy music. I love to dance with my granddaughters wearing colorful skirts and lots of dangling jewelry.

An afternoon stroll with Mama (1938), Genia (left) and I

Our street, Ulica Czeciego Maja, was a beautiful tree lined promenade where elegantly dressed ladies strolled on Sundays. One day I saw a big girl, who was about eight years old and had lived near by, throw a night-pot full of feces onto two strolling ladies in their Sunday best, wearing hats with feathers. Although I was very young I understood that the big girl had done a bad thing, but I told no one about it. The girl would have gotten into a lot of trouble. I was embarrassed for her and found the ugliness of her deed very upsetting.

My mother had a small vegetable garden on the left side of the driveway. She even grew strawberries. She later told us that she always fed us fresh vegetables from her garden, especially when we were babies.

Every morning my mother would take me in the stroller for a walk to Linia AB Promenade, which was around the corner from the Sokol. My sister Genia must have been already going to nursery school or kindergarten because I don't remember her coming along on the morning walks.

On the way, we passed a pharmacy and a stationary store.

Further up the street, we would always stop off at Mr. Booksbaum's fruit store, where I would get my daily banana. His store was tiny, and it was squeezed in between two larger ones. Most of the fruit was displayed outside the store in bins.

I loved going to the stationary store; I loved the "new paper" smell in there and getting papers and pencils, because I loved to draw.

When we lived on May 3rd St. we did not much interact with our Gentile neighbors who lived in the back. Nor did we interact with our Jewish neighbors, the Weinerts, who lived on the other side of the fence to the right and around the corner from our street. The Weinerts were more or less assimilated Jews and they lived and acted as if they belonged to Polish aristocracy. Their house was a huge mansion, with columns, terraces and a huge grassy garden. They had uniformed maids and an uniformed chauffeur. We would watch their children, from behind our fence as they drove around in a miniature gasoline powered car. Dr. Weinert was our dentist. His office was across from the Catholic Church.

The Sokol, which was Sambor's cultural center, had a concert hall and a ballroom. Besides other events, once a year a big formal event called "Kinderball" was held there. Men wore tuxedos and ladies wore long gowns. I believe it was a Jewish society and charity event. My sister Genia performed in one of them. She was dancing in a butterfly costume, with yellow wings. At the time I must have been less than three years old. I was told that I was too young to participate, and I was too young to take ballet lessons. Genia's ballet lessons were held upstairs in a house near Dzewinski's store. The children practiced to tunes played on an upright piano by an old man. I still remember the tune, and how the teacher counted the steps. I did get to go to the ball wearing a fancy pink organdy dress and black patent Mary-Jane shoes. I had short hair parted to one side and I wore a big pink ribbon in my hair.

I did not like the way I looked. I hated the ribbon, the short hair and the dresses I wore. Genia had two long pigtails. Her hair was parted in the middle. She was always so beautiful. I remember being ugly. My mother dressed me like a baby. My dresses were gathered high above the waist and they were very short, so that my panties were showing, which was painfully embarrassing to me. I wanted the kind of dress that Genia got to wear; longer, down to the knee, and with a waistline.

Genia was always complimented upon her appearance and her lady-like behavior, but I was told that I was too pale and too skinny, and that I was a cheeky loudmouth; I was wild and bratty like a boy, an "urviszcz". Indeed, Genia was neat and well behaved. I used to climb trees, draw on walls, and my knees were always scuffed. I used to spy on my aunt Laika and once I told her one boyfriend that I saw her kissing another. My mother blamed me for her migraine headaches as long as I can remember. Later she would often talk about my mischievous pranks and cheeky back talk as if it were cute, even though I had been punished for it earlier. But no matter what punishment I'd receive, I assured her that even if she killed me, I would not cry, which in turn made her even angrier. Sometimes I would deliberately get on mother's nerves-- perhaps to get some attention. But I did not want mother's spanking, I wanted her to love me the way she loved Genia, which was of course impossible to achieve, because we were different, both by nature and conditioning.

Genia never got spanked. She was a sweet and beautiful child and would have started crying had mother merely given her a displeased look. She usually sat quietly reading books and would get very upset whenever I disturbed her. I would disturb her as often as I could because I wanted her to play with me in an active way, with a lot of noise, running and climbing. My father enjoyed my lively personality. He would call me his "lechtig leben", (the light of his life). My father was my hero; he was superman, a holy person, and the smartest and wisest of all men.

My grandfather Yanche adored me; in his eyes I could do no wrong. He used to say that he would like to live long enough to see what would become of me, implying that I'd aspire to some extraordinary heights. I often think about that now that I am old and jobless, with no great accomplishments to show for, other then having raised five amazing sons.

I named my first-born son Jon after my grandfather Yanche. His Hebrew first name is Yaacov; his Hebrew middle name is

Hayim after my other grandfather. When he was small we would affectionately call him Yankele.

Sometimes we had two maids. It seemed that Nascia had always been there and she had always been old; like a statue, she never changed. She even wore the same clothes, day in day out. Nascia, who was a small Ukrainian peasant woman, had always lived with us, but she would occasionally go back on foot to her village to visit her nephew Vassyl. But she would soon return. We all loved Nascia, but she was particularly devoted to Genia.

Our other maid was Yanka; she used to play with me. She was young and energetic and willing to dance with the cat on her head, on my command, before I would take a bite of the food she was trying to feed me. It was all in good fun.

Yanka would often take Genia and me for walks. She would dress nicely, and even put on a hat to go out with us. Genia would not go for walks with Nascia because she dressed like a peasant.

I remember one other maid, named Xenia. When I was about four years old, my father and grandmother took me to a resort called "Truskaviec", and Xenia came along to help take care of me while Mother and Genia were vacationing in Morszczyyn (Morshchin) or Krynica. Xenia was pretty, but her large head and face were too big for her short legs.

Once in Truskaviec, when she took me on a walk, she made me walk behind her and a young man, who must have been her lover. Their conversation scared me. He was telling her that if he caught her with another man, he would kill her.

Xenia didn't appear to be scared but I took it very seriously. I was scared of that man. On another occasion (before I was even five), my parents were out one night, and Xenia took Genia and me to visit her lover. Genia and I were huddled in a scary pitch-dark hallway outside the man's apartment for a very long time. We were not supposed to tell on her. I didn't, but perhaps Genia did because Xenia was soon fired.

In our town there were only a few cars and I think that there was only one taxicab. The cab driver was my father's friend. I remember once in the summer when my mother and sister were away on vacation, he took my father and me for a long drive. That was the first time I rode in a car; I was six years old. Usually people would walk everywhere. It was such a beautiful city to walk in, with its tree lined streets and blooming gardens surrounding the small houses. In the spring there were lilacs and jasmine everywhere. Their intoxicating scents would lure people out of their homes to stroll along the promenade AB and in the parks, where lovers huddled among the lilacs and spoke in whispers. Here and there music would be heard coming from an open window. Someone would always be playing Chopin on the piano, or practicing on a cello or a violin. In those days, few people had radios and many children took music lessons. Often at home, Yanka, my mother, aunt Laika, and her friends used to sing romantic Polish love songs. Most of them were in the minor key. My parents planned on buying us a grand piano; they planned for us to take music lessons.

One of the prettiest streets in Sambor was Ulica Zielona. (Green Street). It had many chestnut trees and weeping willows. In the center of town near the city hall, alongside the park we called Planty, horse driven carriages for hire were parked in a row. They were always there, ready to offer pleasant rides on a spring evening, or to be used like cabs to go to the train station or anywhere else in town. The rhythmic sounds of hoofs on the paved roads added to the town's romantic atmosphere.

Every year in the summer my mother would go away on a long vacation, usually to a resort town, Krynica, where her cousin on her mother's side, Benny Heinberg, owned an exclusive and posh nightclub called "Zacisze". There, many famous entertainers would often perform, among them American Jazz musicians. Benny even used to hire male dancers to dance with the lonely and unescorted lady guests. I must have heard mama talking about it to someone.

One of those "elegant" men employed by Benny in his posh establishment was a man by the name of Rakita. He may have been the Maitre-D. Later during the German occupation Rakita showed up in Sambor wearing an SS uniform. For a short time he held a chief SS position in town, before moving on to run the notorious Yanovska concentration camp in Lvov. Apparently he had been a German spy for many years. Early in the German occupation Benny found himself in Sambor where he initially fled. Benny was staying with us. He was a big and jolly man and we children loved him.

As the persecution of Jews escalated, Benny became very concerned about his wife, who had stayed behind in Krynica. He turned to Rakita to obtain a travel permit to go back to Krynica and find her. Rakita personally issued him a permit, but immediately after their meeting, told his SS underlings to intercept Benny at the train station. As soon as Benny boarded the train, he was ordered off and shot right there and then.

Benny, who was my grandmother Tillie's nephew, had a lot of relatives in the US. I met them later in New York. His American sister looked just like him; she was tall and portly with a heavily freckled complexion and reddish hair. Her daughters Beatrice and Isabel were slightly older than I and probably don't even know that Benny ever existed. Why did our American family not inquire about the lot of their European relatives? Benny's (and my mother's) Aunt Jenny lived in the Catskills and she was quite wealthy. I met her while working in her sprawling hotel when I was eighteen, earning ten dollars per week. Although she bore a resemblance to her sister, my grandmother Tilly, she was nothing like my wonderful grandma. I found her to be a cantankerous old woman. Daily, she would ask me to help her put on her earrings and the rest of her gold and diamond jewelry that covered her dry, shriveled hands and neck, but never once did she inquire about her European family, dead or alive. Her children who ran the hotel never spoke to me in a personal manner.

Before the war, when my mother went away for a vacation at Benny's hotel, I remained home in the care of aunt Laika, grandma, my father and a maid. I was told that I was too young to come along with mother. Because of his business, my father rarely got away for long.

Upon mother's return from Krynica, my father would buy a big bouquet of flowers, and he and I would go to the train station in a hired fancy black horse-drawn carriage we called "droszka" to pick up Mother and Genia. Mother would arrive looking very elegant, wearing a hat, high heels and gloves. Her outfits were always well coordinated. Her nose was powdered and she wore lipstick but no other make up. She was a very pretty woman with jet-black hair and an amazingly beautiful white porcelain complexion. My father was very much in love with her till the last day of his life. On his deathbed in 1968, just before he died, he asked to see their wedding picture. He could not speak anymore but Mama understood him and ran home on foot to get it, and brought it to his hospital bed moments before he died.

My parent's wedding picture, March, 1929.

...and with my first-born, Jon (1960)

5

THE MEISELS FAMILY

My father, Yosef Meisels, came from a well-respected Orthodox-Jewish family in Sambor. He was the youngest of five brothers. His four older brothers were Yankiev-Leib, Benjamin, Mendel, and Moshe. Besides the five brothers there was a younger sister, Leah.

My parents met in Sambor at a formal dance, at which father wore a Tuxedo and white gloves. Because he was the youngest of the five brothers he had to wait for all his older brothers to marry before him. That seemed to have been the custom. My parents finally got married in 1929. It was a first love for both of them. My father was twenty-seven, my mother a few years younger.

My father's oldest brother was called Yankiev-Leib. He was a lively and charismatic man with sparkling blue, eagle-like eyes and a prominent eagle like nose. He had a lightening quick mind. He was a sharp businessman, and, like my father, he was also sharp in mathematics.

When Yankiev-Leib was 16 years old, he ran away from Sambor to America. He got on a ship as a stowaway. He landed in New York, where, according to the great stories he used to tell, he subsisted on pretzels that were served free in New York beer halls.

In America, he learned some English, which he later liked to show off. When he was in America, his mother (my grandmother) Gittel missed him very much. She sent her brother to America with a ticket for Yankiev-Leib to come home. At that time, Sambor was part of the Austrian Empire.

Soon after his return to Sambor, during World War One, Yankiev-Leib was drafted into the Austrian Army and was eventually taken as a prisoner-of-war by the Czarist Russian Army and shipped to Russia.

In his youth, my father was a bright and likable kid. He used to hang around Austrian officers, often running errands for them. Soon he learned to speak German fluently. The officers liked him a lot and they would reward him with gold coins. Eventually, collecting rare gold coins became one of his hobbies.

When his beloved oldest brother, Yankiev-Leib, got lost in the war, my father, who was fifteen at the time, set out on foot to find him. Years later he would tell us how he crossed battlefields strewn with dead soldiers. He traveled on foot and sometimes on trains as a stowaway. Wherever he went he would inquire about Yankiev-Leib. When he got to Kiev in Russia, he met some Jewish people who knew Yankiev-Leib. They directed my father to a house where he finally found him. My father found his older brother sitting in the middle of a crowded living room, pouring tea from a big "samovar" and passing around food while wheeling and dealing and doing great business.

My sister Genia recalls father's story: "Both brothers remained in Russia until the end of the war, and returned triumphantly with pockets full of money. They told many colorful stories about their adventures." Soon after my father and Yankiev-Leib returned home, their mother died.

In the twenties, the five brothers Meisels and their father Hayim Zechariah formed a wholesale business exporting grain and importing tropical fruit. Yankiev-Leib took over the fruit section. My father Yosef and his older brother Benjamin headed the grain section.

The third and middle brother was Mendel. My third son Mark Arnon is named after him. My son Mark, like his namesake Mendel, is a free spirit. (Mendel is the Yiddish version of the Hebrew name Menachem which we took to be Mark in English). Eventually Mendel separated from the family business. He was very handsome, with darkly framed hazel-green eyes, jet-black hair, and a Charlie Chaplin mustache and a humorous streak to match. Unlike the rest of his family he was not religious.

Mendel was a gregarious and worldly man. He fell in love and married a pretty blond and green-eyed woman named Regina. By coincidence, the three older brothers, Mendel, Yankiev-Leib, and Benjamin all married women named Regina, although we usually called Yankiev-Leib's Regina "Ryfcia".

Initially, the family did not look upon the match between Mendel and Regina with favor. Regina's father was a butcher, and in those days, the people of Sambor were class conscious. Among Jews, a Talmud learned man or a woman from a traditional and scholarly family ranked first when parents were considering approving a good marriage match for their children. Second in social standing would be perhaps a member of an intellectual family, offspring of a professor, a doctor or a lawyer. Next in the line of status were the well-to-do business people, and only then butchers, tailors, and shoemakers. Towards the bottom came the small time peddlers.

Mendel was a rebel. He married Regina despite all the objections. Separating from the family business, he opened his own store in a prestigious part of town. Although the family was Orthodox, as were most of the Jews in Sambor, Mendel may have even kept his store open on Saturday afternoons, which was very unusual in the thirties in a small town in Poland. He and his vivacious blonde wife smoked, even on the Sabbath. Aunt Regina even served her children ham sandwiches. They had a grand piano, and their children took piano and tennis lessons. Their daughter, "White" Genia, played the piano well. We called her White Genia because she was blond like her mother and had green eyes. Their house was always full of laughter and good fun. I loved visiting there. White Genia had a handsome older brother Motek. I remember seeing him on Saturdays in his white tennis outfits and wearing a tennis cap. Motek was tall and dark-haired, and had a jolly disposition like both his father and mother.

In the early thirties Uncle Moshe, who was the fourth Meisels brother, lived with his wife and two children next door to us on Ulica Czeciego Maja. The two brothers got along fine and they worked well together, but their wives always squabbled. Once, I remember the two sisters-in-law having a big fight over whose bucket was to stand under the gutter pipe to catch the rainwater during a heavy rainstorm. Women liked to use the soft rainwater to wash their hair; it was also was good for doing the laundry.

Elka and my mother were screaming at each other, calling each other bad names. One of them overturned the other's bucket with a powerful swing of her arm and spilled all the water on the ground. The husbands never mixed in, both being men of few words, but the two-sisters-in law were rarely on speaking terms.

In the early twent;ies, while his brothers were doing great business and becoming prosperous, Moshe chose to become a "Haluz", a Zionist pioneer. He left Sambor and went to live in Israel.

The Zionist goal was to return to Zion, restore the barren, sandy, and sparsely populated land that had been neglected for centuries, and create a place for Jews to live safely; a place where they would be free from persecution and humiliation by the anti-Semites of the world.

In Israel, Moshe irrigated the land and planted trees. He built houses, dried swamps, and lived on a Kibbutz (a collective Zionist farm). At one time, he even contracted a bad case of malaria.

In those days, there were few women in Israel. Moshe sent a ticket to a girl he knew back in Sambor, Elka. Elka and Moshe got married in Israel and had a daughter Genia. Life in Israel was very hard in the days of the British mandate. Moshe's wife, Elka, was constantly being urged by her mother to come back to Sambor, to join the "rich" Meisels brothers in business and partake in the good life that the other brothers and their families were enjoying. So Moshe and Elka returned to Sambor with their young child, olive-skinned, black-haired Genia. Back in Sambor, Moshe and Elka had another child a boy named Siuniu. The brothers took Moshe into the business, but he was out of his element in the business world. He couldn't adjust again to the life in Sambor.

In the twenties and thirties, the Meisels brothers continued to prosper, their businesses went well and grew. Eventually, the oldest brother Yankiev-Leib also separated from the family business and started a business importing tropical fruit and had a wholesale distribution. Yankiev- Leib fell in love and married his first cousin Ryfcia Langer and they had three children, Genia, Avram, and Mayer. Ryfcia was a lively, intelligent woman. She was a voracious reader, and rumor had it that she would stand by the stove holding a book in one hand while stirring food with the other, often burning it to a crisp, because she was so engrossed in the book. Their daughter Genia was studying accounting, Avram was delicate and studious and Mayer was a husky and lively kid.

After Yankiev-Leib separated from the business, my father, together with his brothers Benjamin and Moshe, eventually formed a partnership with the three Lindenwald brothers. I think they were distant cousins, and they expanded their grain business. The Lindenwalds were a large and well-respected family in Sambor. As far as I know, no one from that big family survived the Holocaust.

My father, Yosef, who was the youngest of the five Meisels brothers, was extremely handsome and he had a great personality. In the twenties, he was the catch of the town; he was well built, with jet-black hair and turquoise blue eyes. He had a beautiful voice, he loved music, and loved to dance the polka.

There was an air of benevolence about him, and all that knew him loved him. People used to say that when he walked in, he would light up a room. When he looked at people, it was as if he were greeting and welcoming them with joy and a blessing at once.

My father was also a good businessman. He was honest and wise and people respected and trusted him and liked to do business with him. In his grain business, he would deal directly, both with the landed gentry and with independent farmers. He would buy grain from them, which he stored in his warehouses, to be shipped abroad later. He was well liked by his fellow businessmen, the farmers, and the aristocratic estate lords, who were usually quite anti-Semitic. He was also well respected within the Jewish community. He was a religious man with a strict personal code of ethics. He also was involved in many charitable causes, and was an honorary member of the Jewish burial society called Hevra Kedusha, whose members took personal care of the burial preparations of poor people. That was considered to be a great honor and a "Mitzvah" (good deed) among religious Jews.

My father was also a beloved disciple of the great Hassidic Rabbi Pinhas Tversky from Przemysl. My youngest son, Yosef

Pinhas Rosen, is named both after his grandfather Yosef and Rabbi Pinhas Tversky. My father would often travel to Pszemysl to visit his Rebbi, who was also known as "The Stiller Rebbe," and whose wife was the daughter of the famous "Belzer Rebbe."

In the business, Benjamin, the second oldest brother, was in charge of managing the books and office staff and traveled often to Lvov to represent the company at the Stock market there, called the "Bursa". Lvov was a large town, one-hour away from Sambor, by train. Benjamin was a quiet, intellectual man. My second son David Benjamin is named after him.

Benjamin and his wife Regina had two children, Yosiu and Genia, and they owned a large house with a huge garden on Ulica Lvovska. Aunt Regina loved gardening and grew her own vegetables. She was a hardy woman who loved to cook and clean and tend to her family and garden. She also loved to do needlepoint and embroidery. She was not the type one would find showing off the latest fashions while strolling down the corso AB, or sitting at a sidewalk cafe with a bunch of gossipy friends.

Benjamin's Regina came from a well to do family, the Rauchs. Her father a was very tall, slim man. I recall that he had a small head (too small for his large frame), but he was a distinguished looking man and he was one of the richest men in town. He owned a lumber business and a great deal of real estate. He also owned the biggest apartment building in Sambor, on Drohobycka Street, where Mendel's elegant store was located on the ground floor. Benjamin and my father got along well, but their wives were distant. My mother, who, unlike Regina Rauch, came from an impoverished family, thought that the Meisels family preferred Regina because she got married to Benjamin with a big dowry of five thousand dollars. In the twenties, that was a lot of money-- not only in Sambor. Mother thought that Regina looked down on her, which was very unlikely. Regina was such an earthy and good person. But in those days everyone was very sensitive to matters of status. Not until after the war did the two sisters-in-law become good friends.

In the Meisels family, the youngest child was a daughter named Leah. My father's sister, Aunt Leah married Lishe (short for Elijah) Wollman and had two children, a daughter Genia and a younger son Loniu. During the German occupation, Aunt Leah and her daughter were among the first people caught in our town by the Germans and taken to the death camp Belzec, where they were killed. Lishe and Loniu somehow managed to escape. Later I saw them both in the ghetto. Loniu looked forlorn, and I saw Lishe walking around with a new companion who was visibly pregnant. I remember someone in the family saying that Lishe was very embarrassed about his situation, and stayed away from his wife's family. Loniu, Lishe and his pregnant companion were killed during the liquidation of our ghetto.

Grandfather Hayim Zechariah Meisels, my father's father, came from a large family. He was a quiet man, and was known to be very honorable. He was well respected in business and in the Jewish community and he was actively involved in various local charitable causes. He was particularly active in raising and providing "Bridal Funds" for poor couples so that they could marry and set up a home. He was a disciplined man, strictly orthodox, but not scholarly. He was also a sharp businessman and enjoyed wheeling and dealing in the grain business. On market days, he would set up a place in the big farmers market to do business. Like his eldest son Yankiev-Leib, he had beautiful eagle-like eyes, but his were green. He was handsome, lean and in excellent physical condition. Even as an older man, he was known to lift one hundred kilos (200 lb.) sack of grain and toss it over his shoulder.

Grandfather lost his first wife Gitel, to breast cancer around 1918 when my father was sixteen. All his six children later named their daughters after their deceased mother.

Eventually Grandfather remarried. His second wife Fayga was an older spinster. She was a tall, skinny woman with a small wrinkled face. She always wore long, dark clothes and a kerchief on her head. She did not have a close relationship with her husband's family. She was a quiet woman; I never heard her say a word.

Before the war, Grandpa Hyim Zechariah and his wife Fayga lived downstairs in the large duplex, which he shared with his son Benjamin who lived upstairs with his family. On Saturdays, he would attend his "Mizrahi" Synagogue wearing formal orthodox garb. He wore a long black silk coat called a "bekishe" tied at the waist with a silk cord (called a "girtel"), and he wore a round, fur trimmed, black velvet hat called a "streimel." With his outfit and his long, gray beard, he looked very imposing.

Often, on a Saturday afternoon, I, along with his other grandchildren, would come to his house for a visit. All the grandchildren would gather around a large table in the formal dining room and grandfather Hayim would offer us all kinds of treats: nuts, fruits and cakes. The whole time, we would all sit in silence. Throughout the feast, Grandpa would never say a word. He would just look at us with his sharp, green eagle eyes, but he always seemed pleased to have us there. He always looked serious and strict but not mean. His wife, Fayga, who was nicely dressed for the Sabbath and wearing a wig (like other married women who were strictly orthodox), would bring more and more treats to the table. She would quietly walk around the table with a full tray and serve us food, without saying a word, and in turn, we children also did not dare to make a sound. After a brief visit, we would all file towards the door and leave quietly. Grandfather Hayim Zechariah was killed during the second Akcja (a German raid during which Jews were rounded up and either killed locally or shipped to extermination camps). His wife, Fayga, had been taken away previously during the first Akcja and killed in a concentration camp. Everyone from Grandfather's large extended family was killed.

I remember one great uncle, Grandfather Hayim Zacharia's brother, whom everybody called "Szoostak," because he had six fingers on one hand. He was also killed along with his many children and grandchildren. I was particularly fond of his beautiful young daughter, Regina, who used to visit us often and sometimes take me out for walks. Regina was about twenty-four when they took her away to Belzec, where she was killed.

Everyone from the large Solomon family on my Grandmother Gittel's side was also killed. From among the Solomons, I only remember cousins Muniu and Zelig. They were not quite in their thirties and married. No one from the Solomons in Sambor survived the Holocaust.

My father's oldest brother Yankiev-Leib
(est. 1960)

R-L Yankiev-Leib at 88, his wife Ryfcia,
and Moshe in Israel (1979)

My father's sister Leah, in a local folk costume (1920's)

*My father's first cousins, Regina and Malka Meisels
(all three women perished in Belzec)*

6

LAIKA

When I was a child I used to think that my aunt Laika loved me more than anyone else in the world. Losing her when I was 10 was the most painful jolt to my already traumatized young life.

My aunt Laika, my mother's younger sister, lived with us as far back as I can remember, until her wedding day, in 1937, when I was five years old. My mother thought that Laika had a better chance of finding a proper husband while living with us, in a nice house in a good neighborhood, rather than with my grandparents in the poor neighborhood called Blich.

Laika was the town beauty, yet she remained single for a long time because her parents could not give her a big dowry. She was in love with a non-religious worldly young man whose name was Herman, and who probably would have married her without a cent of dowry. But her very religious parents would not allow her to marry him.

Laika was five years younger than my mother. My mother loved her younger sister and took care of her as if she were her daughter. She bought her beautiful clothes, and Laika got to go on summer vacations with us. My mother would brag endlessly to her girlfriends about the many men that pursued Laika and wanted to go out with her. Laika was not only beautiful, though; she was warm and gentle and she spent much time with me. She practically raised me; and I adored her.

When I was about four I caught Herman and Laika kissing, and later I teased them in front of the family; this caused Laika great embarrassment.

Eventually, Laika met and married a very fine and nice looking man who adored her. He had a deep voice, beautiful teeth and high cheekbones; he was a Yul Brynner type. His name was Hayim Koenig. He was an accountant, well educated and from a good family in Lubaczow. When Hayim's parents and sister came to visit, they were well received in our home. I recall mere glimpses of Laika's and Hayim's wedding in 1937 that took place in the Jewish Kehila (Community Center). There was a big crowd of dressed-up, happy people milling around. In the center stood a "Chuppa", a wedding canopy. Someone was holding me up high so that I could see the ceremony. I wore a pink dress and a bow in my hair. My grandma Tilly, Laika's mother, must have worn her pearls, which she usually wore only on the Sabbath. During the war, they were buried and later I inherited them. Genia's daughter, my niece Tamara, had been named after Grandma Tilly. On her wedding day I gave Tamara Grandma Tilly's pearls.

After they got married, Laika followed her husband Hayim to the town of Wolyn, where he had a good position as an accountant with a large lumber company. When their daughter, little Andzia, was born in May, 1939, she was left in my mother's care. My mother hired a full-time nanny to take care of the baby but we all helped. We all loved her, but my mother was absolutely crazy about that child. By that time we already lived in our own house. The guest quarters were a separate small unit and it was kept for Laika and Hayim to stay in, whenever they were in town. It was accessed using our private stairs and was off our hallway. When they were away, the nanny stayed there with the baby.

I remember overhearing my mother when she recounted Laika's difficult labor. Apparently she was in a great deal of pain and in a state of delirium she was calling out, "Herman!", the name of the man she had been in love with but was not allowed to marry. Even at age six I was aware of the drama of this love story. Eventually, Laika got to love Hayim and, I think, they were happy together. Hayim was handsome and of good nature and character; he was loved by all.

Laika and Hayim returned to Sambor for good when the war broke out. Later, in the ghetto, they moved in with Isaac and Dvorka, where the three of them slept in a small bed in the kitchen. There, they were caught during the liquidation of the ghetto and shot by the Germans in the Radlovice forest.

Aunt Laika (1937)

7

OUR NEW HOUSE
ON RYNEK STREET 39

We moved from May 3rd St. to our new house in early 1938, when I was five and a half years old.

Our new house on Rynek 39 was actually a large two-story apartment building. It had a central courtyard, where the janitor's front door faced. I remember that door well, because when the janitor died, a short time after we moved there, they laid him out near the door and for days after, his wife kept the door wide open. I was terrified to cross the yard and pass by that door (even after the dead man's body was taken away for burial). Still, one had to walk past it in order to go out towards the main entrance, which faced a park, which we called Planty. Beyond the park was the city hall we called the Ratusz (rahtush), which was in the center of town.

The apartment house that my parents owned spanned three streets. The side of the house facing the city hall and the park had businesses and a deli restaurant. When mother was away on vacation my father would treat me to hot dogs at the deli. We called them "krzanowki" because they were probably made with horseradish (krzan). They tasted great and I haven't had a hot dog like it since.

Our apartment was at the far end of the courtyard, which was a block long, and our private entrance faced another street, which was actually a small cobble stone plaza, one block over from Rynek Street. The apartment was upstairs. A private, large wooden door and stairs led to it from the plaza.

All the floors in the house were made of wood parquet, and

they were partially covered with large oriental rugs. The balcony in the "salon" faced a hotel and a restaurant across the small cobblestone plaza. The elegant kosher restaurant was owned and run by a woman named Ruchel Langer, who was the mother of our neighbor, Vicia Antman.

Vicia was my mother's close friend and lived upstairs in the house next to ours. Vicia had an abnormal child. The girl, who was perhaps my sister's age, had a small face and a tiny head, which almost looked shrunken. Her legs and arms looked like thin sticks. There were rumors that the child was born that way because Mr. Antman may have had a bad disease at one time. Although I did not understand exactly why this was so, I must have had a sense that it was saying something bad about Mr. Antman, and that it was a secret. I understood that Vicia was not a happy woman. Even as a child I listened to gossip with great interest.

I used to tag along with adults when they went visiting or were running errands. On such occasions my presence was largely ignored, but for an occasional remark by someone that I was too skinny or that my face was green. (A Polish figure of speech meaning that I was too pale.) These casually dropped remarks always made me feel icky and ugly.

Vicia survived the war, but her husband and child did not. At the time she was taken away, the girl was already fourteen but she was small and retarded. People would not allow her into bunkers when they were hiding from the Germans. During one of the raids, Vicia placed her daughter Renia under a bed and told her to be very quiet, while Vicia was hiding near by. When the Germans walked into the room Vicia heard the girl call out to them, "I'm here, come and get me, I'm under the bed" and she was taken away, while Vicia remained hidden.

Years later I saw Vicia in Israel. We did not talk about the war or her child. While I could not stop thinking about her unhappy life and her child, Renia, Vicia talked about how well I looked and asked me questions about life in America.

In the basement apartment of our new house, on the plaza side, lived a shoemaker who worked out of his house. I liked to watch him work. Like all the other shoemakers, he kept the little nails that he used in his mouth, taking them out one at a time and hammering them into a shoe. The place was dingy, dark and had a strong smell of leather and old sweaty shoes.

Below our apartment lived the Zahn family. Mr. Zahn was a pale man with a full black beard. Like so many other orthodox men, he always wore a three-quarters long black coat over his white shirt and black pants, instead of a suit jacket. Mr. Zahn had a small broom factory. The broom factory was just a large room in an otherwise empty house nearby. There Mr. Zahn worked with his father who lived with them. The two of them made all the brooms by hand. Father and son dressed alike, but the old Mr. Zahn had a very long white beard. The Zahns had two daughters, Pepka and Renia, and a son whose name I forgot. The youngest daughter, Renia, was my playmate. The Zahns were not well to do; they did not have a maid to watch the children.

Once, when Mrs. Zahn left the house to run some errands, Renia and I were left alone in the apartment. We played house and decided to do some cooking over a lit candle. Soon something fell on the floor and when I bent down to pick it up I knocked the candle over with my head and my hair caught on fire. I had thick long hair. In panic, with my hair in flames, I started running around the table. But just in the nick of time, Mrs. Zahn walked in and threw a blanket over me, saving me from a horrible death.

Ironically, Mrs. Zahn was unable to save herself and her own children from being reduced to ashes in the death camp crematoria of Belzec where the whole Zahn family was taken and killed by the Nazis.

Around the corner from Rynek 39 ran one of the main streets of Sambor. I think it was Przemyska Street. There, within sight from our balcony, stood Mr. Drzewinski's large store. I liked going there. Drzewinki's store was always suffused with deliciously pungent aromas of exotic imported spices, coffees, and teas. Also sold there were other staples like sugar, rice and flour. Mr. Drzewinki, a nice looking and pleasantly mannered middle-aged Polish Gentile, who sported a big handlebar mustache, usually stood behind the counter in front of the large and shiny brass cash register. Above that store was a spacious apartment where one of my Jewish teachers lived. I used to go there for some kind of private lessons. Her husband must have been a cello player, because from our bedroom and balcony I could hear him daily playing beautiful music on his cello.

In an upstairs apartment in our building, facing the park lived the Raiser family. They had two sons who were students in high school, which we called gymnasium, and which was more on a junior college level than an American high school. The gymnasium students used to wear navy blue school uniforms; these blue uniforms had a connotation of status. Mrs. Raiser was a corsettiere and I used to go there frequently with Mother for her corset fittings. My mother always wore a corset, for as long as I can remember. Every morning she would step into it and lace it very tightly, pulling with all her might on a pair of long laces and then her body under her silk dresses would feel stiff as a board.

As far as I know, one son from the Raiser family survived the Holocaust. I have not met him, but I hear that he lives in Toronto and is a judge.

Our house had two balconies, a large one off of the kitchen, overlooking the courtyard and one off the salon. The one off the salon had flower boxes and pots planted and tended by a gardener. The living room or the salon was huge and was covered with a large Persian rug. There was a green couch and a large table with twelve high-back leather covered chairs. On the left side against one wall stood a huge antique brass or iron safe, where valuables were stored. There was also a large credenza filled with silver ware and crystals. A maid constantly polished the parquet floors, the silver samovar and candelabra and the big brass door handles. She also polished the dark red painted stairs that led from the large main door at the street level to our home upstairs. Maids also did the laundry, the cleaning, and they helped take care of the children. My mother did the shopping and all the cooking.

My mother would also spend countless hours with dressmakers at fittings, pouring over fashion journals with them. All our clothes were custom sewn and fitted and reflected my mother's great taste and sense of elegance.

I liked going with her to shop for fabrics. I especially recall the fabric store near the city hall, across from the park "Planty". I would come home from the dressmakers with fabric remnants to make clothes for my dolls. I loved dolls and dogs and horses. When I was six Mama bought me a beautiful big doll that could open and close her eyes. I insisted that mother treat her like a grandchild. Sometimes on Fridays the doll would come along to have her hair done in the beauty parlor.

One evening, before dinner, our maid, Yanka, was chasing me around the table and accidentally knocked my doll to the ground. When I saw that the doll's eyes had dropped inside her head, I was so distressed that I fainted. When I came to, Dr. Reich, our pediatrician, was sitting by my side and my parents stood around looking very concerned. The next day mother took my doll and me by train to Lvov to a doll "clinic". While we waited for the doll to be fixed, mother took me shopping. Lvov was a big city and there were many elegant stores.

Dr. Reich had always been our doctor. I remember his waiting room and its antiseptic smell. The furniture was metallic and white and there was a Persian rug on the floor. My mother told me that when I was about a year old I had a huge abscess on my neck; it was the size of a large orange. I believe, Dr. Reich was to operate on it. But Mama later told me that while in the waiting room I would not sit still and was playfully hitting the abscess with both hands as if it were a balloon, until the abscess burst and squirted puss all over the precious Persian rug. I still have a big scar on my neck from the torn abscess, which Dr. Reich had to patch up with stitches as best he could.

Once, still on May Third Street, before I was five, when I was sick in bed, Dr. Reich came to our house to examine me. When he was about to use a rectal baby thermometer and a baby enema called a "balonik", I protested and told him: "no, you can do that only to your wife, but not to me". My mother was very embarrassed, and called me "pyskata" which meant loudmouth. Both Dr. Reich and my mother's comments must have offended me. I suppose I remember such isolated incidents from early childhood because of the strong feelings associated with them, and the degree to which adults ignored them. In this case, I was treated in an invasive and disrespectful manner. I did not like being labeled a loudmouth, especially when it was done half jokingly; it embarrassed me, and when I was a child, all embarrassing situations gave me a sinking feeling in the pit of my stomach.

I tagged along with Mama on all her errands, while my sister would usually prefer to stay home doing her homework and reading. She went to public school but also studied Hebrew in the afternoon.

I loved going with Mama to one place where she would shop for yarns, crochet hooks and long knitting needles. It was a general store that even sold hardware and sports items. That's where mother bought me a sled. (Genia got custom-made walnut skis from a different place.) In the general store was a young woman behind the counter by the name of Rechka Pinkus, who had kinky hair and was Mother's friend. Something about that cozy store and about Rechka must have touched me, because not only does her name stick in my memory, but also her face and her warm demeanor. I even remember one particular color and texture of a yarn that mother once bought from her. It was gray, with red bumps, and later when knitted into a sweater the texture was interesting and tweed-like with all those red bumps sticking out.

One day, Rechka Pinkus disappeared from the face of the earth. She was likely taken away and killed early on, because after the first Akcja I never saw her again.

Both Genia and I learned to knit at a very young age and I loved to knit, crochet, and sew. Mother liked to embroider. When we were small she would embroider beautiful little red and blue flowers on our small undershirts, and the head coverings that we would wear after bathing.

Mama loved fine linens, silver flatware, beautiful porcelain, and crystals. Our bed linen and tablecloths were always starched and ironed. On Friday nights and on Sabbath days, the white tablecloths were starched and pressed, and the large silver candelabra and flatware were gleaming. Although she cooked three tasty meals each day, Friday night dinners were like a feast. Mother took great pride in her housekeeping.

Mother also loved beautiful clothes, and she loved dressing up her two daughters. She had several dressmakers. One was near the park on Ulica Lvovska, another on Blich. Once, before

Passover, she went to Lvov to buy us beautiful lilac color spring coats; they were very fancy. On nice afternoons she would stroll with us on the "Corso", or "Linia AB". She would be dressed elegantly wearing a hat, high heels and gloves and a dead silver fox across her chest. Her nose was powdered and she wore lipstick. She wore a hint of perfume called "Evening in Paris". Often she would meet friends on the "Corso"; or she would stop off with us at the elegant local cafe across the park that was owned by her friend Mrs. Frei. There she'd buy us custard filled French pastry, we called "kremoovki" and chat and have coffee with her friends. We would eat the delicious pastry and watch people stroll by.

Among the afternoon elegance on the boulevard stood a "Parisian Pisoir" that exuded a strong urine stench. There was something very "manly" about that little booth, into which men would disappear and then emerge and continue walking while buttoning up. Not far from the "pissoir" stood a round newspaper stand we called a Kiosk which was covered with posters of the latest movies playing at the one theatre in our town.

I loved being taken to see the movies. I loved all the Shirley Temple movies, but "Heidi" was my favorite. I fell in love with the alpine landscape of Switzerland, and daydreamed about living there with Heidi as my friend. Like Heidi, I also had a very loving relationship with my grandfather. I also loved the movies with Deana Durbin. Sometimes, I got to see romantic movies for grown-ups, where very beautiful people would flirt and kiss and sometimes they'd cry because bad things were also happening to them-- like the time when Greta Garbo was coughing and dying of tuberculosis, but it was all happening to the sound of beautiful music.

On the outskirts of town, just a few miles past Blich, were the hills and meadows of Novy Swiat, (The New World). Before the war, on summer Sundays, father would hire a horse drawn carriage to take us there on outings. Past the green hills lay endless fields of wheat and oats and rye. The golden stalks of wheat were sprinkled with deep-red poppies and blue cornflowers, which grew in the fields in rich profusion. While parents lounged around atop blankets spread out on the grass, children ran around freely. Boys played ball and girls picked wild flowers to weave them into garlands for their hair. For that, the little white daisies worked best, because their stalks were soft.

Every time we came to Novy Swiat my parents would take us out to eat in the only restaurant in the area. It was run by a Jewish family and they served only dairy meals. They had the best pota- to "Pirogi". These were made of dough stuffed with mashed potatoes and fried onions that were then boiled. They were served with heavy sour cream and ice-cold buttermilk to drink.

On summer Sundays we would go to bathe in the river Dniester. The Dniester was a wide river that ran fast and deep, and its shores were full of stones and pebbles. I remember stories about people drowning there. Neither Genia nor I were allowed to even try to wade in that river without supervision. Neither one of us could swim. Fortunately, father was an excellent swimmer and he would swim with us sitting on his shoulders.

Winter in our town was magical, when all the roads were packed thick with snow. Instead of horse drawn carriages, fur- coated peasants who came to town from the surrounding villages used horse drawn sleighs. Here and there, a group of cross-coun- try skiers or kids on skis would pass by and sometimes grab on to a fast moving sleigh to hitch a ride.

When it snowed, at dusk one could barely see the outlines of church spires in the gray distance. Dark figures, heavily coated and wrapped in thick woolen shawls, would scurry across the snowy landscape and then quickly disappear behind the white- lace curtains of falling snow.

Sambor, being close to the Carpathian mountain range, had many hilly streets. In winter there were many places where chil- dren could walk to hills that were good for skiing and sledding. I would pull my sled with a long, thick rope and then run up a hill and slide down, over and over again, until dusk. By then, my nose, hands, and feet were frozen stiff. The older kids, like Genia, had skis already; how I envied her! I was told that to get skis I needed to wait until I was as old as Genia. I waited forever to get to be as old as Genia, and never once got to go skiing in Sambor.

In Sambor, there were great rainstorms in the spring, summer, and fall. Before a rainstorm I loved to sit by the window and watch flashes of lightening as they would light up the low and cloud darkened sky. Then the air would become different. The heavy, moisture laden, ozone filled air seemed to heighten one's sense of aliveness, as thunder roared and rumbled. Then the sky would suddenly burst open with a downpour of rain. No wonder American Indians, attuned to nature, do rain dances.

On rainy spring days, Mama often cooked pea soup. Thick and heavily flavored, she served it with thick slices of rye bread, which we covered with yellow spring butter. The butter was so fresh that it still had droplets of water on it. I think that the spring butter was so yellow and so tasty because the cows in the spring pastures liked to eat the newly sprouted dandelion flowers.

Spring brought a special excitement when houses were being thoroughly cleaned in preparation for Passover, when every last crumb of bread had to be found and disposed of. The night before Passover, father walked around, from one end of the house to the other, with a lit candle and a long white feather in one hand , and a wooden spoon in the other. He symbolically scooped up the crumbs of bread, which perhaps he himself sneaked into several places on the floor a short time before. During this ritual the lights were turned off. The crumbs, the spoon, and the feather were later wrapped in a white cloth, tied with a string and burned.

All everyday dishes were packed and stored away, while new dishes, which were used only once a year for eight days during Passover, were taken out of storage, and placed in the freshly paper-lined china closet. Genia and I had special Passover breakfast cups that had girl's faces painted on them. Genia's was blue on white and mine was red on white. Each morning, we would crumble matzo into our cups and then fill them with milk. Both Father and Mama were involved in the preparations for Passover and everyone got new clothes, in which we would parade during the holiday while visiting relatives and taking walks with our parents.

Sometimes I would go to Uncle Isaac and Aunt Dvorka's house a few days before Passover, where women got together in Laizerova's apartment to bake matzos, the unleavened Passover bread. For that occasion, all the furniture in her small apartment was pushed aside and big boards were placed on top of the tables. For several days, a bunch of women would sit around the boards, which were dusted with flour, and roll the round matzos before passing them to a man who stood in the kitchen, in front of the oven, holding a big wooden paddle with a very long handle. Every so often, the crisply baked matzos were retrieved from the oven and replaced by a new batch to be baked. My cousins and I got to help with the rolling, and it was great fun to be included in the matzo baking.

For the Passover Seder, the children had special silver wine cups. They were no bigger than a thimble. The table was beautifully set with special holiday china decorated with little purple flowers. A ceremonial plate, which was set in front of my father, contained an egg, a singed chicken neck, greens, grated horse radish that made us all gag and cry, and "charoset" a delicious mixture of nuts, dates, wine, ginger, apples and cinnamon. Each one of the items on the plate was to symbolize something from the Passover story. Year after year, it was all explained to us at the table. For example, the horseradish was to remind us of the bitter lot of the Jews when they were slaves in Egypt. Also on the table was a white satin pouch, especially embroidered by mother, used to hold the matzos that were passed around during the Seder. Before the ceremonial part of the Seder was over, everyone, including the children, had to finish drinking the four cups of delicious, sweet red wine. In the middle of the table stood a special large silver goblet for a guest of honor who was expected to arrive at every Jewish home during the Seder, the prophet Ellijah. At one point, I, being the youngest in the house, would be told to open the door for him. The whole thing seemed very spooky; I was terrified and barely able to breathe when I opened the door as my father solemnly intoned in Hebrew, "Baruch Ha Baa" (Welcome). Imagining Elijah's invisible spirit floating past me would give me the creeps.

After a few seconds, I was told to close the door and the ceremony continued, going on late into the night. About halfway through the ceremony, a sumptuous feast was served. During the Seder there was much singing, as Father sat at the head of the table recounting the story of the Jewish exodus from Egypt over three thousand years ago.

What a great effort went into preparing for this ceremony to make us commemorate the Exodus and commiserate with the Hebrew slaves in Egypt. But it was only the horseradish that filled our eyes with tears, as we sat there in festive mood, singing and laughing. And then, all too soon, we found ourselves in the midst of a Holocaust and we got to experience and understand slavery, first hand. All too soon we became even less than slaves, because no amount of work or subservience or prayer would redeem us from certain torture and death.

Aunt Laika with my parents (1938)

8

ISAAC AND DVORKA
AND THE BLICH HOUSE

At moments in our life when our heart is touched, we open up and imbibe with all our senses the textures of the world around us. At such moments the colors, smells and sounds that envelop us become interlaced with our feelings, and together, they shape our essence for the rest of our lives. And even years later, we recall the multidimensional backdrops that once framed these meaningful past experiences. We find that often, we are spontaneously drawn to some places, some people, some scents, or some things because they evoke in us not only a sense of nostalgia or excitement or even awe, but because they give us, above all, a feeling, however fleeting, of "coming home".

A heart is fortunate to have known at least once in a lifetime, a beloved place it longs "to come home to". Both the happiest and the saddest memories of my childhood revolve around Isaac and Dvorka's house on Blich. Uncle Isaac Glickman, who was my mother's older brother, and his wife Dvorka and their three children lived in the poor section of Sambor, called Blich. Within two years from the day the Germans entered Sambor, in June 1941, the Blich house was no more and all who had lived there - every person except for the Gentile maid Kasia, was killed.

Unlike his two older brothers Phillip and Benny, who left for America during WWI, Uncle Isaac lived in Sambor. At one time after WWI, when Poland regained its independence, he must have been drafted into the Polish army, because I remember seeing a picture of him in a Polish army uniform, wearing the typical square hat that pointed towards the front, back, and sides.

Isaac married Dvorka Stulberg and they opened a small candy store. Uncle Isaac was a tall, thin man, with a high forehead and thinning blond hair. He was a handsome man and bore an amazingly strong resemblance to his slightly older American brother, Phillip. Later, when I met Phillip, I saw many similarities between these two brothers. Like Uncle Phillip, Isaac was a pleasant and lovable man. Like both Phillip and the older American brother Benny, he was a compulsive gambler and a chain smoker. He was rarely seen without a cigarette in his hand and he loved to play cards.

Isaac and Dvorka made a meager living selling candy and cookies in a small shop on the side of a steep hill walkway, which was terraced with cobblestone steps; it led from the center of town towards Blich.

The street immediately above Dvorka's store, led to Plac Zamkovy (Castle Plaza); the street at the bottom of the cobblestone steps, ran parallel to the Mlynovka River. Nearby stood an old mill and the small wooden bridge that spanned the river. One would cross that bridge to go to Blich. Going down the cobblestone steps, Dvorka's store was on the left side and about ten steps from the top. The store was very small, no more than ten feet wide and ten feet deep. On market days, it was always packed with people, many of whom came from villages and farms outside Sambor. The farmer's market took place in the big field to the right of the small bridge by the Mill. We called that field "Duza Targowica," which meant, "the big marketplace."

Thursdays were market days. Farmers from all around Sambor would come in their horse drawn wagons, and they usually came with their families. They came to sell their farm products and to buy farm supplies, fabrics, tools, buttons, and trinkets. Some local traders had stands there, selling everything the farmers or other locals might want to buy.

The farmer women would often wear distinctive dress or hairstyles according to the customs of their village. I recall that the women from the village of Babin had dark hair, and they all wore bangs cut straight across their foreheads. Usually the women wore big black skirts and shawls, and smaller scarves to cover their hair. I saw the peasant women pee in the middle of the market, right by the side of their wagons, not unlike their horses; they peed standing up by spreading their legs wide. I don't suppose they wore underpants. Their big skirts gave them a measure of privacy.

Aunt Dvorka was a tall slim woman, with an olive complexion and with long brown hair tied in a knot. She was a quiet woman. She had beautiful gray eyes and always looked serene, loving and calm. She worked very hard tending to her family and the small candy store business. At night, she was busy baking cookies, which she would sell at the store the next day.

Usually Dvorka tended her store alone. Isaac would often disappear for hours, gambling away their meager earnings. I loved hanging around the small candy store. Dvorka was always behind the counter calmly dealing with her customers, who, on market days, were mostly peasants.

Isaac and Dvorka had three children. Besides being my beloved and favorite cousins, they were my closest friends. The oldest was Big Andzia. We called her Big Andzia, because in our family in Sambor there were three Andzias. All of us Andzias were named Channa in Hebrew, after the same great-grandmother, who was my grandfather's Yanche's mother. I was the middle Andzia, and little Andzia was Laika's baby. In Polish, Andzia is an affectionate form of the name Anda and Anna.

Big Andzia was a beautiful girl with a peachy complexion, big blue eyes, and thick, long, dark lashes. Her beautiful thick hair was auburn-chestnut color and her two thick braids reached to her waist. Big Andzia also had a beautiful voice and she loved to sing. She was very grown up and mature and whenever she was not in school, she was helping her mother in the store and at home. My granddaughter Sophie Rosen bears a striking resemblance to Big Andzia. So did my American cousin and Phillip's oldest daughter Rhoda Glickman. We, the younger cousins, all looked up to Big Andzia. She was five years older than I was.

Near Isaac's house were some stables for horses that were used exclusively for hauling big carts. Once I saw Big Andzia near her house riding one of the horses bareback. I saw her taking off and galloping fearlessly down the street. She looked wild, radiant and happy.

Big Anda was fifteen when the Germans killed her during the liquidation of our ghetto in June 1943.

Isaac's second child was Bunek. He was four years older than I. I was in love with Bunek; but of course he did not know it. Bunek was very handsome. He had wavy blond hair and was tall like both of his parents. With his tan complexion and gray eyes he resembled his mother. Like other Jewish boys in Sambor, starting with his Bar Mitzvah, Bunek got to wear long pants, and prayed daily like a man alongside his father, putting on "tefilin" (Phylacteries) each morning. Bunek was 14 when the Nazis killed him during the liquidation.

Isaac's youngest child was Zosia, which is a Polish name for Sophie. Zosia was my age and she was my best friend and soul mate. Like twins, we were inseparable. Zosia had long golden braids, blue eyes, and a tan complexion. Zosia was not quite eleven when she was killed together with her family.

My grandmother Tilly, my mother's and Isaac's mother, loved Dvorka very much, and the love between them was mutual. Dvorka did not have much family of her own. She was known for her compassionate heart and good deeds. She was very much in love with Isaac, even though his reckless and compulsive gambling made her life very difficult. But she bore her poverty with great dignity, and always extended herself to help others. She was very wise and I think that the deep peace and contentment that her beautiful gray eyes expressed was there because she and Isaac were so much in love, in spite of their difficult material circumstances. Though I was very young, I must have had a very strong sense of Dvorka's inner beauty because I loved to be around her; she exuded a special aura. She was gentle, calm and yet very strong.

In Sambor, sometimes even poor people had maids, mostly for menial tasks like bringing in water from a well, or for bringing wood and coal from an outside shed or cellar for heating and cooking. The maids of the poor were primitive, like the maid Kasia, who worked for Aunt Dvorka.

Kasia was short and chunky. She had round, red- apple cheeks, and many of her front teeth were missing.

I heard that when Zosia was a baby, Kasia was once caught sitting on the church steps holding little Zosia and begging for money. When Aunt Dvorka found out about it, she was very upset, but she never fired Kasia. Kasia would come and go. Sometimes she looked pregnant. When she went back to her village, it was perhaps to give birth to a baby and leave it there with her family.

The house that Isaac and Dvorka lived in, "the Blich house", was like a long rectangle and it was built low to the ground. The small windows were no higher than three feet off the ground. The house had a long corridor running through its center lengthwise from one end to the other. If there were doors at either end, they were never closed. There were many small, one-bedroom apartments on both sides of the long corridor. Most people who lived in the small apartments had large families and they were poor. Next door to Aunt Dvorka's apartment lived her widowed sister in law with her young son. Dvorka's brother had died of tuberculosis before the war. His widow was a tall quiet woman, who, I remember, was exquisitely beautiful, and looked like the actress Lauren Bacall. The apartment nearest the front entrance, on the right, had one big room which served as a local prayer hall, called "The Stibl", where neighborhood men prayed two times a day, once in the morning before breakfast and once in the evening at dusk. The caretaker of the Stibl was a little old man, Reb Zeesie, who lived with his wife, Tsosieh, in a small room next to the prayer hall. On Thursdays, Tsosieh would go around and knock on the doors of the more prosperous Jewish homes outside of Blich and she would receive food and a few coins so that she and her husband could also have a proper Sabbath celebration and enjoy a good meal. She used to come to our house as well, and my mother would give her chicken giblets, twisted white challah bread and some money. She wasn't quite a beggar, and she was not treated like one. She was addressed respectfully by her name. She never said a word as she stood at the door waiting for the weekly donations, and then she would quickly disappear. She and her husband, though very poor, were decent and pious people. In Sambor, even among the very poor, most Jews were literate in Hebrew prayers and scriptures and most adhered strictly to the orthodox way of life. Among the many Jews of Sambor, few were non-orthodox. Only a few were totally irreligious. Some had traveled and studied abroad, and some were partially assimilated into the secular culture. And there were those who were passionate but irreligious Zionists. A few non-religious Jews were communists.

The poor old "Stibl" caretaker and his wife raised a daughter Zlata, a heavy and not so pretty girl with a big pale face that was framed with short and frizzy black hair. She lived across the street in one room with her shoemaker husband and a small child. In that one room, Zlata and her husband slept, cooked, ate and plied their trades; he as a shoemaker and she as a dressmaker. Sometimes I'd go there with Mama to get some alterations or repairs done. Zlata's customers would change behind a small curtain, while her husband was sitting on a low stool in another corner of the room near the wood-burning stove, wearing a leather apron and hammering small nails into shoes. Just like the shoemaker who lived in the basement of our house, Zlata's husband would keep a bunch of nails in his mouth. With his left hand that was all black from working with tools and leather, he would take out one nail at a time and hammer it into a shoe, draped over an iron stand that was shaped like a foot. No one paid any attention to the baby in the crib. Zlata and her husband were hard working, quiet people.

Across from the "Stibl" in 'the Blich' house lived a man, whose first name was Laizer, with his wife whom we all called Laizerova. Laizer was a red-haired man, who wore thick eyeglasses. I think that he was an accountant but I remember him better for his gambling. Every time I passed by their open door I would see him sitting around the big round table in their kitchen, chain smoking and gambling with a whole bunch of men, my Uncle Isaac usually among them. Neither Laizer nor his wife was orthodox or spiritual in any sense, but on the Sabbath, of course, there was no gambling in their house. Laizer's teenage sons were going to high school and one of them was very artistic. Everybody used to admire his drawings.

One day, before the war, Laizer died of a lung disease. It was either tuberculosis or lung cancer. But the gambling in Laizer's home continued. The house was always full of men and smoke, and there was always a lot of loud talking and laughter. Laizerova was a hearty, jovial and gregarious woman. She was short, with a rosy and crinkled face and twinkling blue eyes. Later, already in the ghetto, I remember visiting Laizerova in a different place, across the street, where the gambling was still going on. At that point, Laizerova was living alone and supporting herself by baking and selling pastry to the card payers, who were hanging out in her one room place. I don't know where her sons were. Maybe they had been communists and had escaped to Russia before the Germans came. They must have perished, because, had they survived, they would have come back to Sambor after liberation to look for their mother. In the ghetto, Laizerova's customers were mostly Kapos. These were the Jewish men who were selected and forced by the Germans to accompany them and help round up people during the raids. Neither Laizerova nor most of the Kapos survived the liquidation of the ghetto. I only knew of two who did. In spite of their bad reputation, the two I knew were decent and gentle people, who had themselves lost their own families.

To the left of Isaac's house, near the back entrance, was a large lot full of finished gravestones and some raw stones not yet carved. Both the bedroom and kitchen window in Dvorka's apartment faced the lot with the gravestones. The grave stone carver and his family lived nearby in a small hut. There was enough space on that lot for us children to play various ball games. In the summer, the girls played a ball game called "trzy ognie" (three flames), but the boys usually played soccer. On the other side of the back door was a large courtyard. A large, unhitched flat horse-cart stood against a tall wooden fence on the right side of the yard. On the Sabbath, the big cart stood idle and the children used to play on it climbing on and jumping off.

Near the back door at the end of the long corridor, against the wall on the left, was a small garbage pile. Across the yard were the outhouses. I did not like to use them and never went there alone. In winter they were dark and cold, and we had to put on a coat and carry a kerosene lamp with us. When it rained the yard was very muddy.

Just in front of the outhouses was a small shanty like wooden house, where a young woman by the name of Hancia lived with her old widowed father. Her father was a "balegule", (from the Hebrew "baal agala,"a horse cart driver.) He owned the big cart in the yard. He had two big horses, which were stabled near the courtyard. He used to hire himself out to haul cargo for businesses and bring loads to and from the train station. He had a long white beard, and he was religious like most of the Jews of his generation in Sambor; he also used to pray daily at the "Stibl".

His daughter Hancia was a warm and gregarious young woman in her late twenties who was friendly with the neighbors, especially with my mother's young sister Laika. Like most people there, the two young women always spoke Yiddish. Hancia was a pretty woman, but unlike Laika she wore a lot of make-up and bright dresses. Often, in the middle of the day, I would see her wearing a colorful silk robe. The robe was black with big red roses and green leaves.

For a long time before the war, a man by the name of Hans Peter used to be seen daily at the "Blich house" where Isaac and Dvorka lived. I saw him gamble, smoke and socialize at Laizerova's place.

Hans Peter was a German, and a convert to Judaism, or a "gher", who spoke fluent Yiddish. In his looks he did not distinguish himself much from the others around him, he was slim, and like Uncle Isaac, had dark blond hair. He was friendly and well liked. Everybody in the neighborhood treated him as if he were one of the regular tenants or guests of the house.

Hans Peter was Hancia's lover. Everybody knew about it, but Hancia was not looked down upon or gossiped about in a disapproving and malicious way. Both she and her lover, Hans Peter, were very much a part of this down-to-earth community. Hans Peter did not appear to have a job; he just hung around. Cigarette in hand, he was always unhurried, strolling between Hancia's shack and Laizerova's place, where there was always an ongoing game of cards. On the way, he would stop in the yard near the backdoor, openly undo his fly and urinate. He paid no attention to the fact that children were playing near by.

When the war broke out, Hans Peter suddenly disappeared. Later it turned out that, all along, he had been a German spy. I heard that he briefly appeared in Sambor as an SS officer. Hancia and her father were taken away during one of the first raids to the death camp, Belzec, and were killed there.

I don't remember anybody locking doors in the "Blich house". Especially in the summer, most of the apartment doors were usually ajar and I liked looking in as the women cooked and tended children. All the apartments were very small and did not have entrance hallways. One would step into the kitchen directly, the entrance door being just a few feet from the stove and the kitchen table. In Dvorka's house the children did not have their own room and there was no "Salon" for entertaining guests. Everybody slept in one bedroom, and guests were received in the kitchen.

The floors were made from coarse wooden boards and the women regularly scrubbed them with a coarse brush and soapy water while kneeling on the floor. The apartments were modest but they were kept clean. The preparations for the Sabbath would start early. Already on Thursdays, the women were busy cleaning their homes. With much hustle and bustle, windows were washed and floors scrubbed. Some were busy doing laundry using round tin tubs and washboards, and some were busy whitening the soot- darkened ovens with brushes dipped in tin buckets that were filled with a thick, chalky goop. On Fridays, everyone cooked and baked, preparing the meals for the Sabbath. No one cooked or cleaned or worked on Saturdays. On Saturday, the Sabbath, everyone looked scrubbed clean and wore their best clothes. Everyone ate the best food of the week, and people socialized and rested. On the Sabbath, no one appeared to be hurried and the children did not go to school, even though the public schools were open and Gentile children and children of the irreligious Jews attended school. Schools were closed only on Sundays and on other Christian holidays. In the neighborhoods where Gentiles lived, Saturday was the big cleaning day of the week.

The people who lived in the "Blich house" were always dropping in on one another and doing things together, like sewing and knitting, baking bread, taking care of a sick neighbor, or having a glass of tea and chatting. The women talked loud, gossiped and sang songs as they worked together and many held nursing infants in their arms. The men often spent their days at work or gambling, or praying in the "Stibl".

Often, aunt Dvorka would send my cousin Zosia and me to the various gambling places in the neighborhood to look for Uncle Isaac, with a message to come home to eat or to go the candy store to help out. Sometimes Zosia and I would go looking for him at the Kupferman family's house. Their young daughter was my age. By now I have forgotten her name, or what she looked like. Although her father survived, she, her mother, Mrs. Kupferman, and their other children were all killed. I later met Mr. Kupferman in Los Angeles in 1965. He was a very sad man.

When I told him that I knew his family and especially his young daughter, he became very quiet and looked away into the distance for a long time. It was a sad yet precious moment of kinship, because not many, if any at all, of the people who knew him now in Los Angeles would have known of his lost family. Out of less than one hundred Jewish survivors of Sambor Mr. Kupferman and I were the only ones living in Los Angeles. His new wife Adella and her sister Henia were from Stary Sambor, (Old Sambor, it was another town nearby.) Although, as a child, I hardly knew Mr. Kupferman, he had known my family in Sambor well, and when we met again in Los Angeles we were like family. He was a decent and sensitive man.

Sometimes Zosia and I would hang around Dvorka's little candy store that was no bigger than a closet. Big Andzia helped out after school, and Zosia and I just wandered around. At Dvorka's, the children were free to come and go, so Zosia and I wandered around the neighborhood free and unsupervised. No one looked for us or worried about us. Usually, I could not have left my home on Rynek 39 at will and wander around town freely. At home, my sister and I would go for walks either with Mama or with the younger maid Yanka.

I especially loved being in Dvorka's house on Saturday afternoons. After morning Synagogue services a big Sabbath lunch was served. Afterwards, my aunt and uncle would retire to take a nap in the only bedroom in the house. The children were sent out to play outside, or to go visit grand parents or cousins. Later, after the adults got up, they would go for a walk, weather permitting, and visit relatives as well. In the evening the men went again to the Synagogue for evening prayers.

Sometimes, on winter Saturdays, after my uncle would get up from his afternoon nap, we children would come in from the outside with cold feet and noses, our cheeks red from playing in the snow, and we would all crawl into bed with Aunt Dvorka. Their two single beds were pushed together. We would lie in the dark awaiting the end of the Sabbath, when we could turn on the lights and put logs into the stove, unless Kasia was there to do it for us. While huddling together, keeping warm in the bed, Big Andzia would sing or tell stories. The sheets had a strong and musky smell; it was warm and cozy and I remember my aunt's smiling eyes - she looked rested and happy.

Whenever Kasia was around, being a Gentile, she would turn on the lights for everyone in the Blich house, even before the Sabbath was over. But when she was not around, we'd stay in bed until Uncle Isaac and Bunek would return from evening prayers at the synagogue, and turn on the lights. Everybody would get up and gather around the table to hear Uncle Isaac recite the "Havdallah" chant. This prayer was always recited by the man of the house at the end of the Sabbath, with a silver cup of wine in hand and two lit candles, which one of the children held up high. Sometimes, whisky was used instead of wine. The Havdallah is a chant about making a distinction between the Sabbath and ordinary working days. At the end of the chant we passed around a special ornamental silver dish. It contained dry and sweet smelling spices, such as cloves and cinnamon. Everyone took turns smelling them. Then the candles were put out by pouring the wine over them and onto a plate. When whisky was used instead of wine, it ignited into a small blue flame. At the end of the ceremony, everyone exchanged good wishes for a healthy new week ahead.

I recall a snowy Saturday afternoon in Aunt Dvorka's kitchen, when a bunch of women, Dvorka's neighbors, sat around on layers of newspapers atop the stove, still warm from the coals and the wood burned the day before, from when the cooking and baking for the Sabbath had been done. All the women sitting in Dvorka's kitchen that afternoon were reading one and the same book at the same time. Dvorka would read a page, tear it out and pass it on to the women sitting next to her. I sat on a stool near Dvorka and I recall reading several pages of this trashy novel along with her and her friends. I was about seven and a half, and barely literate. We could hardly wait to get to the next page to find out what happened next to the irresistible but naughty Aranka.

"Aranka was beautiful, sexy, and evil. Stefan was a rich Hungarian nobleman married to Helena, a sweet young wife who was pregnant and whom he loved very much. But Stefan could not resist the exciting Gypsy Aranka. Aranka was very devious. She arranged to have Stefan's wife kidnapped by bandits, one of whom was her brother. Now she would have a chance to be with Stefan, while pretending to console him. "

"Whatever happened to Aranka? Did Stefan ever find the pregnant and naïve wife, Helena?"

The name of this trashy paperback was "Bol Matki" (A Mother's Pain). The story had many explicit torrid and passionate love scenes described in great detail.

In Dvorka's small kitchen on a snowy winter afternoon, there was a sense of cozy and effortless togetherness and all the children were naturally included in whatever was happening. While the women and girls were busy reading and passing down the pages, the men sat around the kitchen table by the window talking and sipping sweet hot tea, which was served in glasses and with one or two lumps of sugar. Outside the snow was deep, coming up to the low windows, which were covered around the edges with layers of frost crystals.

The kitchen table, we called a "szlaband," also doubled as a bed for the primitive and, perhaps, a bit retarded maid Kasia. Kasia used to sleep on the lower shelf under the tabletop. While all the tea drinking and socializing was going on in the kitchen, Kasia was napping under the tabletop. Oblivious to everyone around, she kept snoring and farting, but nobody paid much attention to Kasia's noises or foul smell. Everyone seemed relaxed and comfortable in each other's company.

When it got dark, the men got up from the table and left to go to the Stibl for evening prayers and the women went home to prepare supper for their families. Dvorka and we children crawled back into the warm bed to await the end of the Sabbath and Isaac and Bunek's return.

L-R, Sarah (Mama) at 18, Tilly, Uncle Issac,
Laika at 13, Grandfather Yanche Glickman

Great-Grandmother Hanna Glickman and Mother at age 14

9

MY GRANDPARENTS: YANCHE AND TILLY GLICKMAN

My grandfather Yanche Glickman, Mama's father, was born around 1870 in Felsztyn, which was a small town west of Sambor. After his father, Pinhas, died when he was fourteen, Yanche took it upon himself to care for and support his widowed mother Hanna and his three younger siblings. (There may have been more siblings, but I only know of four altogether and I only knew three personally). He worked hard to support the family and at the same time he was tending to his Torah studies. In the Synagogue he befriended a nice man, a widower, who used to attend the same prayer services. His name was Moshe. Moshe was a learned man, both in Hebrew and other languages, and he was a scribe by profession. Yanche loved and respected him so much that he decided to bring him home and introduce him to his widowed mother. Within a short time the two of them married. Moshe also had children of his own.

Hanna and Moshe lived happily together for many years. Yanche's Younger brother, Mechel, later married Moshe's daughter Ryfka, with whom he had three children: Sadie, Fannie, and Phillip.

I got to spend a lot of time with Fannie, many years later in America. She often told stories about her beloved grandfather Moshe and his wife Hanna. Inspired and encouraged by her learned grandfather, Fannie acquired a great love for books. Being a scribe, a translator, and a tutor, Moshe would often travel between the different towns near Felsztyn and he would always come home with books for Fannie in Hebrew, Yiddish,

Polish, and German.

At some point, during the battle between Russia and Austria, Moshe was drafted into the Austrian Army. He was not quite the militant type; he was a gentle and scholarly person. One day, on the battlefield, he came face to face with an enemy soldier. The two men stood within a few feet of each other with drawn bayonets facing death, about to be killed or to kill the other, when suddenly and simultaneously they exclaimed in Hebrew: "Shmah Israel, Adonai Eloheinu, Adonai Echad!"- Hear Oh Israel, The Lord is One! – Thus Jews pray in trenches, when they are terrified and when facing their death. They are to utter these words with their last breath.

Upon hearing each other's prayer, both men dropped their weapons and tearfully embraced. That act of comradery may have ended their two military careers, but perhaps being compassionate and saving a life was more important to them. The two men probably never killed before and were glad they stopped before it was too late. They became life-long friends, looking out for one another. As the Austrians began to withdraw Moshe and his new friend returned to Felsztyn.

Soon the town was overrun by hordes of raping and looting Russian Cossacks. Felsztyn also suffered an outbreak of the deadly pestilence cholera. All around there was still much fighting going on. Cousin Fannie, who was a young child at the time, was curious and inquisitive. One day, while the fighting was still raging, she ran out of the house to see for herself what was going on. Her grandfather Moshe feared for her life and went out to search for her. While searching for Fannie, a stray bullet hit him and he lost an eye.

Trying to get away from the fighting and the cholera epidemic, the whole Glickman family fled from Felsztyn to Sambor. Soon after, Mechel and his sister Idle went to America. Mechel and his family settled in Brooklyn, New York.

My Great–Grandmother Hanna lived to be almost one hundred years old. Among her neighbors, she was known for her great wisdom, herbal healing skills, and her interest in the supernatural. Neighboring women used to seek her advice for everything from health to relationships.

Mama had told me that I was named after Hanna (which is my Hebrew name). Her American great granddaughter Anita, who was Mechel's granddaughter, was also named after her and we are good friends. Only recently I got to know Hanna's American great-grandson Art Glickman.

Still in Felsztyn, and before WWI, Hanna's oldest son, my grandfather Yanche, married my grandmother Tilly Heinberg from Pszemysl. They had six children, Benny, Phillip, Isaac, my mother Sara, Laika and Yochevet. I never knew Yochevet. She died of cholera in Felsztyn during the war when she was five years old. Prior to her death my grandparents tried hiding the sick child from the Cossacks who were going from house to house seeking out and taking away cholera-stricken people to a quarantined area. The Cossacks never found Yochevet, but the child never recovered and died at home. Yochevet's death broke Tilly's heart. Mama said that Grandma Tilly mourned the child all her life.

My grandparents had not always been poor. Before World War I, when they lived in Felsztyn they had a furniture store and the family lived well. After losing everything in Felsztyn during the war and resettling in Sambor, my grandparents tried to support themselves by leasing and tending an apple orchard. After harvesting the apples they would sell them to small stores. The apples they could not sell were taken home, sliced, strung up on a laundry line and hung to sun-dry outside their windows.

Their house always smelled of apples. The family was poor, and I'm sure that apples were a large part of their daily food. I think that because they ate so many apples, everybody in that family, especially Grandmother Tilly, Mama and aunt Laika, had the most beautiful complexions. My sister Genia has inherited their love for apples; she eats them daily and she also has a beautiful complexion.

Eventually, my grandparents gave up the apple-orchard business. My father loved them and respected them very much. He wanted, and could well afford, to support them. He even gave them enough money so that they would be able to help others. Grandfather and Grandmother devoted themselves to doing charity work, Torah study and prayer, and they came to visit us almost every day.

Soon after coming to Sambor, Tilly and Yanche's two oldest sons, Benny and Philip, decided to escape the misery of Jewish life in a small town in Poland and go to America. By that time, grandfather's brother, Mechel, was already living with his family in Brooklyn. The departure of her sons, Benny and Philip, added more sadness to Grandma's grief. She missed her sons terribly. She would often talk about them and tell us how loving they had been. Yet, only Benny came to visit his parents, and only once, in 1929, before I was born. Phillip never came back to Sambor. I don't know if they wrote to their parents often, though they did send us pictures.

My grandparents Yanche and Tilly lived in a slightly better section of Blich than Isaac and Dvorka. They lived in a small apartment house next to the old Jewish cemetery and all the windows faced the cemetery.

Grandpa's sister Ethel shared with them thier modest one bedroom apartment, and slept in the kitchen on the daybed under the window. Aunt Ethel was a widow and she was very poor. Although my father had supported Grandpa's household, Aunt Ethel tried earning some extra money selling trinkets at the farmer's market. She had a small stand which she assembled every Thursday. She was a very sad and quiet woman. Like my grandparents she was very religious. She never wore a wig, like Grandma Tilly; instead, she wore a gray kerchief, tied under her chin. Her short stubby hair was all gray and could be seen above her forehead. She had been widowed early and had lost her very learned, eldest son, in a horseback riding accident at a country estate where he was a tutor. Her other two sons, Eli and Mannes, were neither learned or religious. The two brothers were poor and Mannes was a communist. But Eli, who resembled his mother, was the nicer of the two brothers. He seemed to be more sensitive and better mannered. Eli worked out of his small apartment cutting out leather shoe-tops, which he would later sell to shoemakers. I'm not sure what Mannes did for a living. When the Russians came, Mannes, who always seemed like a "ne'er-do-well" hothead, barged into our house, one Friday night during Shabbat dinner. He was accompanied by some Russian policemen. In an angry tirade he suddenly vented all his long held grudges against the rich "bourgeois"(that's how the Russian communists called the rich), which of course, included my parents. He was saying that we, the rich, were still living too well, even though by that time we were all crammed into one room. We had already been forced to share our home with several other families.

I don't know why Mannes did that, but after ruining our Sabbath dinner, he left as abruptly as he came.

In that house where my grandparents lived before the war, there were two other tenants. A photographer and a couple with a son my age whose name was Hesiu.

One day when I was staying at my grandmother's I looked across the hall from Grandma's open kitchen door, and saw that Hesiu's door was also wide open. I saw his mother lying in bed and giving birth to a baby. Her open legs were facing the open doors and she was bleeding a lot but not screaming. My grandmother looked very busy. She was calmly helping the woman deliver the baby. The door remained open and no one bothered about me. I may have been five or six years old and did not understand what was going on until later when the baby was out and crying.

One time when I was on my way from Dvorka's house to my grandma's, I crossed through the old cemetery and I saw the body of a dead newborn baby lying on the ground. Another time, I saw a bunch of discarded photos of beautiful nude people, mostly women, near the photographer's trash. I never told anybody about those things I saw near Grandma's house.

My grandfather Yanche was a very pious man. He was sensitive and delicate, with a handsome, chiseled face. Grandmother, Tilly, whose maiden name was Heinberg, came from a larger town, Przemysl, where she was known for her elegance and beauty. Someone introduced her to my grandfather and they fell in love and married. My grandparents were very religious and in those days it was very rare among the very religious people to marry out of love. Typically, matchmakers would match religious couples. The young people often did not see one another until their wedding day.

They were a handsome couple. I remember them always holding hands when they would come walking to visit us, and I remember my mother's comments about how it was unusual for older and very orthodox people to do so. They were the gentlest people I have ever known. I don't remember either of my grandparents ever raising their voice in anger and I never heard them argue or speak to one another in a harsh manner.

As is customary among the very orthodox Jews, my grandfather wore a long beard and ear locks, grandma wore a wig; her own hair was shaven since the day of her wedding.

Although they themselves were poor, on Friday nights my grandfather would go to the synagogue, and, after prayers, bring home beggars and homeless people for dinner. Mama told us that often, when she was young, she was asked to give up her bed to a homeless person. That used to upset her very much because she had always been fanatical about cleanliness and she knew that the beggars were often dirty and had lice. Yet years later, she would tell us these stories with pride, and she spoke with admiration about her parents' noble character and their lifetime devotion to charity. Mama said that my grandmother Tilly would call the impoverished guests that grandfather brought home from the Synagogue a special gift for her. She would say that they were his gift of pearls for her on the Sabbath.

My grandmother's charity work in our town was legendary. She would help poor families in every direct way, and she even collected money they needed for their daughters' dowries and weddings.

At the end of the main street that ran through the center of Blich stood a large modern hospital. There were always a lot of Polish Catholic nuns wandering around the hospital. People called them "sisters". The nuns were also the nurses. I went there to visit my sister Genia, when she was six or seven and got a needle lodged deep into her hand and required surgery to remove it.

In that hospital that served all of Sambor and the outlying villages, there was no kosher food available for Jewish patients. So Grandmother used to cook daily for the sick poor people and she brought the food to them by herself, walking the several miles from her home. She would bring food for all the poor in the hospital, Jews and non-Jews alike. According to stories told by my mother, whenever the doctors and the nuns in the hospital would see Grandma walk in, they would always bow to her respectfully and refer to her as "the great lady" and they would hold the doors for her. Later, when Grandma Tilly took ill and was stricken with cancer in her leg, the nuns from the hospital would come to visit her. I saw them, in their big black cloaks and white winged head coverings, kneel at her bedside and rosary in hand, pray for her recovery.

This was a strange sight, considering how orthodox my grandmother was and how anti-Semitic most Polish Catholics were at that time. Grandma never recovered. Shortly after she was stricken with her illness she died in early 1940, at start of the Russian occupation. She was sixty-four years old.

My American uncles Benny and Phillip Glickman

10

GOING TO
SCHOOL IN SAMBOR

This will probably be the shortest chapter, because before the war, I never went to school past the first grade. When I was five years old, I went to a Hebrew nursery school a few days a week. I loved it because it was fun to play with other children, to paint, and make play-dough figures. I remember making a horse and carriage and winning "first prize". At school, there was a dark haired little boy, Heniu, whom I was particularly fond of. He was the son of a tailor on Drohobycka Street. My five-year old grand son Yuvali, whom I adore, looks so much like my little friend Heniu. My little friend Heniu and his family were killed later in the Holocaust.

After nursery school, I went to public school. I remember that I loved going to school and learning to read and write. But I also remember feeling bad when the Gentile Polish children were calling me "Parszywa Zydowka" (dirty, or sore covered Jew); I remember them yelling: "Dirty Jew go to Palestine".

I had just started first grade when WWII broke out. Later I was re-enrolled twice again in first grade, but each time in a different language. The second time it was in Russian and the third time in Ukrainian. I never finished first grade and did not attend school again until I was thirteen, when I enrolled in an "ORT" trade school in Munich soon after the war, in 1946.

11

THE START OF
WORLD WAR TWO

The start of WWII created a sharp discontinuity in the placid flow of life in our small town in Poland. It thwarted a future we came to expect while living in a slow paced, peacetime world. Soon, not only did our lifestyles become unpredictable, but also, within a very short time, our survival became uncertain.

The war broke out when I was seven years old. One day, early in the fall of 1939, my mother took me along to shop for rolls of black paper. When we came home everyone helped to cover all the windows with it. There was talk about blackouts and air raids.

Even weeks before September 1939, everybody was talking about Hitler and war. It was the topic of conversation whenever adults got together at home or in the street.

On Friday, September 1, 1939 German bombs started to fall on Poland. In Sambor, air raid sirens were heard at all hours, savagely piercing the cocoon-like serenity of my world. It was a mournful and frightening wail, foreboding death, destruction, and the end of my childhood. Gone were the quiet days and nights in our town; everyone's nerves were shattered. Each time the sirens sounded, I went into total panic, as we all rushed to the cellar under our house, which now served as a bomb shelter. Father used to make wine in that cellar and mother kept a sack of potatoes and a barrel of pickled cabbage there. There, we also stored coal for the winter, and set traps for mice. The mice used to scare Mama and me almost as much as the sirens during the air raids.

Within minutes, the air raid sirens were followed by the roaring sounds of heavy bomber planes. That roar went straight into one's stomach. It gave me cramps and nausea and I would feel stinging, stitch-like pains in my chest. Years later I heard and felt something similar during an earthquake in Los Angeles. During the air raids, my mother would give me Valerian drops to calm me down because she worried that my heart was being affected by fear. Genia took it much better than I did, she would sit calmly and read a book; but I'm sure that she was scared inside.

On Saturday morning, September 2, 1939 one day after the war started, our train station was bombed.

Soon after hearing the explosion, the air filled with smoke and off in the distance I could see a flaming red sky.

A short time after the bombing, an eastbound train from Przemysl was approaching Sambor. The train was full of Jewish refugees. The people aboard were hoping to go further east, because they were fleeing from the rapidly approaching German armies. Large areas of Western Poland had already been overrun by the Germans. The train stopped in Sambor and could go no further because the tracks were destroyed in the air raid. Everybody aboard the train had to disembark and remain in Sambor.

I watched from our balcony as hundreds of Belzer Hassidim (disciples of the famous Rabbi of Belzec), formed a procession towards the train station, to greet and welcome the revered Rabbi Pinhas Tversky, who was aboard the train from Przemsl. They were passing close to our house and there was much excitement in the streets. All the Hassidim were wearing the traditional Sabbath garb, which they put on that morning to go to prayers. They poured out of the synagogues, my father among them, and they were all heading towards the train station. Rabbi Tversky was the son-in-law of the great Belzer Rabbi. He was fleeing with his large family from his home in Przemysl.

Under normal circumstances, orthodox Jews do not travel on the Sabbath by train, car, or any other means because strict Jewish law forbids it. But this was a matter of life and death, and in such cases the Jewish law commands Jewish people to do whatever is necessary to save lives.

When the war started, people were saying that if the Germans come to Poland they would only take the men to labor camps, but they would not harm women and children. So, just before the Germans entered Sambor, my father and his brother Benjamin, along with some of their cousins, got hold of a cart and two horses and fled towards Rumania, hoping that the families they left behind would not be harmed.

After a brief and bloody battle against overwhelming German military forces, Poland surrendered. On September 8, 1939, within one week of the start of war, the German army entered the city of Sambor.

That first evening of occupation a group of German officers knocked at our door and politely asked if they could stay at our house overnight. Father had already fled east, and my mother was alone at home with the maid and us children.

My mother spoke German, and made every effort to be a good hostess, even though she was very nervous. She prepared and served a very elegant supper for the officers, using her best linen tablecloths, china and silverware. At dinner the officers invited her to have wine and dine with them, addressing her as "Gnaedige Frau" (madam, or gracious lady). They left early the next day, politely thanking Mother for her hospitality. My mother, who had always liked Germans for their culture and good manners, felt relieved of some of her fears by the brief and polite encounter with the German officers.

This time, the German occupation of Sambor lasted only twelve days. In mid September 1939, Stalin made a pact with Hitler. As a result of this pact Poland was split and divided between the Russians and the Germans. By September 20, 1939, the German army pulled back behind the river San, which bordered the town of Przemysl on the east. The Russians took over all Polish territories east of the San River. That included Sambor and Lvov. The Soviet Russian occupation of Sambor lasted from September 20, 1939 till June 29, 1941, almost two years.

12

THE
BACHMAN FAMILY

The Bachman family lived on a large estate outside Sambor near the village Krukennice. They had much farmland and raised fine horses. They spoke Polish, and although they were of German descent, they were considered to be Polish. They called themselves "Folk Deutsche" (Ethnic German). My father had many business dealings with the Bachmans, and they became good family friends.

Sometimes we would travel to the Bachman's estate on a Sunday outing and visit, traveling in a horse drawn carriage. The roads to Krukenice were full of deep ruts and my mother was always scared that the carriage might overturn. Once in winter, before I was five, when we still lived on May 3rd St., I remember that the Bachmans sent a driver and large horse drawn sleigh for us. The driver wore a long sheepskin fur coat, and held a long horsewhip in his hand. We traveled in the open sleigh, all wrapped snugly in large brown fur blankets. I loved that trip, but I only remember going and returning home late at night. I remember the crisp and cold air and how beautiful everything was. The snow-covered town was quiet but for the sound of the snorting horses, the cadence of their fast moving hoofs, and bells that were tied to their harness.

The Bachmans used to sell grain to Father's business, harvested from their farmlands. The Bachmans themselves did not work the land; they were very wealthy and traveled extensively. Both Mr. and Mrs. Bachman were educated in Germany. Before her marriage, Mrs. Bachman was sent by her parents to live and work on a farm in Germany in order that she learn good housekeeping and how to run and manage a large estate.

Just before the Germans withdrew from Sambor, in September 1939, the Bachmans suddenly disappeared. They must have left in a hurry, because they left with us for safekeeping many of their personal possessions. Among the things that the Bachmans left with us and had especially valued were many of their albums of photographs. My parents stored them in a drawer in their bedroom and I used to spend hours pouring over them, especially the ones with the large photos of beautiful horses. In one of the albums I saw many pictures of the Bachmans with Hitler. There were also pictures of Hitler in various disguises. In one of them, he was dressed as a woman and standing near a train car. After they left Sambor in 1939, we never heard from the Bachmans again.

13

THE RUSSIANS
ENTER SAMBOR

After the bombings stopped and the Germans left, there was a great sense of relief. The next day, early in the morning, I looked down from our bedroom window onto a sea of gray-pointed, Mongolian Tartar-like hats below and smelled the stinkiest tobacco smoke ever. Russian tobacco was called "machorka"; it was very strong. The soldiers smelled strong too. Apparently they were using some smelly disinfectant powder to keep themselves free of illness and lice. The Russian army had arrived, and it soon became apparent that they had come to stay. Soon they brought their wives and children from Russia, and they also took over part of our house. The Soviet Russian occupation brought on a sudden and dramatic change in my family's life.

My parents, having been well to do before the war, were of course materially inconvenienced by the communist regime, and we were even marked by the NKVD (Soviet secret service) to be sent to Siberia. To escape being caught and deported, we had to be constantly on the run. Little did we know that within a short time, the Germans would return and all hell would break loose for Jews. We would come to envy the people that had the good fortune to be sent to live in Siberian labor camps.

The soldiers in the Russian army sang all the time. They sang whenever they were marching in a group to bathe or exercise. I loved those minor key songs, especially when they could be heard very early in the morning when it was still dark. They sang in a choir of strong manly voices. Usually one man would sing solo and then a choir of voices would join in.

When my father first escaped from the advancing Germans, he kept traveling eastward, hoping to make his way through Turkey to Israel. But when he heard about the truce between the Russians and the Germans, (and wanting to be with his family), he decided to turn around and come back to Sambor, which was already occupied by the Russians.

Father returned together with his brother Benjamin in a wagon pulled by two grayish white horses. He was very happy to see us unharmed by the bombs and the Germans and we, of course, were overjoyed to see him back home. The horses remained stabled in Benjamin's large yard where the shed served as a stable.

14

RABBI PINCHAS TVERSKY

After Rabbi Tversky and his big family arrived in Sambor, they settled down near our Rabbi Yoel's house at the end of Blich. Before the war father would frequently visit "the court" of Rabbi Yoel, who was his rabbi in Sambor. Father would also travel to visit Rabbi Tversky's court in Przemysl. When Rabbi Tversky took up residence in Sambor, I would go with father to see him. Had father had a son, he would have taken him along and I probably would have stayed home. My sister never went along on these visits, but I was a very curious child and wanted to be included everywhere; it was all so interesting and exciting.

There were always a lot of Hassidim (disciples) in the Rabbi's "court". Times spent with Rabbi Tversky and his family were quite memorable. In the evening everyone would gather around a large table to listen to the Rabbi's discourses. The place was filled with religious fervor, wisdom, learning and camaraderie. The rabbi would sit at the head of the table and my father would always sit next to him. In between discourses, questions, and answers, the Rabbi would pass around food to everyone. There was always much singing. I used to sit next to the Rabbi's wife at the women's table near by, and she would smile at me and hold my hand. The Rabbi and his wife had great love for my father.

Once in the Synagogue on "Simhat Torah", the holiday that celebrates the receiving of the Torah from God, I saw the old and frail Rabbi Tversky dance for hours with his eyes closed while holding the heavy Torah Scrolls in his arms. He danced as if he was in a trance. He danced for a long time as the Hassidim stood in awe in a circle around him. Later they all joined in. I sat upstairs on the balcony next to the Rabbi's wife, who looked on proudly and lovingly. Sometimes my father would take me to a private visit with the Rebbi.

Later, in the Ghetto, my father took personal charge to care for the needs of the Rabbi and his family. The revered Rabbi was machine gunned into a mass grave during the liquidation of our ghetto on the holiday of Shavuot in June 1943.

15

THE
SHOENBERGS

One day, shortly after his return to Sambor, my father came home from town, bringing with him a family: Mr. and Mrs. Shoenberg and their sixteen year old son Arthur. The Schoenbergs were refugees from Western Poland after it was overrun by the Germans.

My father found them standing in the street with suitcases in their hands. He approached them and started talking to them, inquiring where they were from, where they were going and if he could be of any help. It turned out that, indeed, the Schoenberg family was desperate; they had no place to go. They had been on that last train from Western Poland, which could go no further than the bombed-out train station in Sambor. When they got off the train, they remembered that they had distant relatives living in Sambor. After they had found them, they stayed with them. But then within a short time, the Russians took over their relatives' house and threw everybody out into the street. The relatives apparently had found some shelter, but the Schoenbergs were left stranded.

Upon hearing their story, my father brought them to our home and my parents invited them to stay with us. I remember that when the Shoenbergs moved in with us we put them up in our "Salon", which was the biggest room in the house. Within a short time, the Russian authorities forced us to give up more space in our house; this time to accommodate members of Russian NKVD, the dreaded police. Our family was crammed into one room and the kitchen was shared by all. Fearing deportation, we soon left the house, which the Russians had by this time all but confiscated anyway.

The Shoenbergs remained in our house until the Russians deported them to Siberia. The Russians did this in a very sneaky way. They distributed forms, asking all refugees from Western Poland to register if they wished to obtain papers and permission to go back home to the German side.

The Shoenbergs registered because in Sambor, they were destitute; they had already left behind most of their family and possessions. They had no idea what was awaiting the Jews in Western Poland under Hitler.

Soon, after handing in the forms, they were picked up in the middle of the night along with other refugees who were tricked by the Russians in the same manner. They were all sent to Siberia. Life in Siberia was difficult, but at least they survived the war.

I met Arthur Schoenberg in Israel, where he is now living with his wife and son. Both he and his son are doctors. His parents died some time ago. When I saw Arthur, he was already eighty years old. Our reunion happened by a strange coincidence. On my last trip to Israel I was visiting a friend of mine, who lives near Tel Aviv. On the last day of my visit, over morning coffee, I told my friend that my trip had been great, but I was disappointed because I was unable to find some people whom I had known as a child and whom I suspected might be living in Israel. I told her that I had searched for the Schoenberg family every time I traveled to Israel. To my amazement she told me that her family doctor is a Dr. Shoenberg, but his name was not Arthur. She called her doctor right away to inquire if perhaps there was some family connection to Arthur; indeed there was.

My friend's Dr. Shoenberg confirmed that Arthur was his father. Within a few hours the Shoenbergs came over with old photographs of their parents, exactly as I remembered them. Arthur told me that all these years he had also searched and inquired about our family. He finally had assumed that we had all perished in the Holocaust. With profound gratitude, he remembered my parents' kindness and generosity.

I was very touched by the way he spoke of my parents and the way he described the scene when his family was approached by my father, offering to help.

Arthur told me that they had a difficult journey to Siberia. The long trip from Sambor in packed primitive trains took many days, and their life in Siberia was extremely difficult.

In addition to the West Polish refugees and political dissidents, the Russians started deporting all former owners of businesses and everybody else they considered to have been even moderately wealthy before the war to Siberia. The young couple who owned the pharmacy across the Sokol was also scheduled to be sent to Siberia. However, just before their departure, they committed suicide. They took poison rather than face deportation to Siberia. By the time the Russian police arrived they had taken the poison already but were still alive. Their baby was already dead and the Russians left them all to die at home. Apparently, a remorseful Russian commissar had come in person to plead with them to reconsider and take some measures against the poison. He was very sympathetic and deeply touched and he mercifully ordered that they should be left alone. I remember everybody talking about this tragedy and going to the funeral. At the time, we also thought that being sent to Siberia would be the worst thing that could happen to anybody during this war. As it turned out, those who were either deported or had committed suicide were in fact spared life in the ghetto, concentration camps, the death camps, and ultimately spared extermination by the Germans.

Our names were on the list as well, and we were scheduled for deportation to Siberia on the same day as the Shoenbergs. At first we escaped capture by the Russian police by sleeping every night in a different house. Often our family was split up for the night among different relatives. Soon we escaped to a small rented hut, away from the center of town.

16

THE SMALL
PEASANT HUT

To escape capture by the Russians, Father rented us an old peasant hut. It was located off a small side street, near Drohobycka Street and the big Catholic cemetery. The small hut was hidden away behind an overgrown big garden. Dwarfed by old trees and shielded from the street by thick bushes of lilacs and jasmine, the little old house seemed to be a safe refuge. It was actually set in the middle of a small farm, which I would estimate to be about ten acres, and was bordered on the far side by a river. To me, our new home was like an enchanted place from fairy tales.

The river, which was deep in places, ran alongside the whole width of the property. Both riverbanks were lined with big old trees. On one of the tall trees on our side, a swing hung from a thick branch. Two thick ropes were tied to the branch at one end and to a thin board, for a seat, at the other. Sitting or standing on the board and holding on tight to the ropes, we used to swing high into the air and over and across the river. No one watched us or warned us to be careful, though neither Genia nor I could swim. I don't think that Mama ever explored the large grounds or walked down to the river.

All kinds of vegetables grew in the large backyard. There was a "little forest" of beanstalks, which were taller than I. Off to the left of the bean patch was the outhouse, and next to it was a small barn for goats and chickens. I would watch our old maid, Nascia, milk a goat and I remember drinking the foaming milk right there, still warm and smelling like the goat, but it was tasty.

The Small Peasant Hut

There were many fruit trees to the right in the back of the hut. I could climb most of them. I remember sitting high up in an apple tree on a quiet Sunday morning listening to my grandfather, Yanche, who sat in a chair nearby, reading Hebrew Scriptures in a singsong. I remember the fruit laden branches and the aroma of the still hard new apples; their pits were still white. This was one of those forever moments, when everything was perfect and in its right place, and one did not long to be somewhere else.

The ancient and primitive hut was nestled among blooming shrubs. The low front door, made of coarse wood, was old and weathered; its big iron hinges were rusty. Inside, past the main door, was a small vestibule. To the left was a small storage shed filled with cobwebs and ancient farm tools. There in the corner lived a big gray porcupine which no one would ever think of disturbing.

From the vestibule, to the right, was a second door that opened to our new one-room dwelling. That room was very large, but its low ceiling made it very cozy. In that one room we slept, ate, baked bread, and cooked. Off the entrance, in the corner to the left, was a big hearth, a wood burning stove and an oven for cooking and for baking bread. Nascia slept in the corner, on top of the hearth. It was a warm and snuggly place.

When we lived in the little hut I thought that it was the perfect home. Being so close together made me feel secure. That's why I used to love being in Isaac and Dvorka's small place where everyone was always together, unlike in our big house on Rynek 39.

My grandparents, Tilly and Yanche, came daily on foot to visit us in the hut, even though we now lived much further from Blich than before. Grandmother would sometimes sleep over. She would sleep with me on the narrow couch by the window. I loved to sleep with her. I would stroke her pink, peachy smooth cheeks. She was gentle, quiet and very loving. There was an aura of nobility about her. I never heard her talk in a loud or angry voice. Even at 64 she was still very beautiful. She died of cancer later that year. I remember walking to the Jewish cemetery holding Genia's hand, and both of us crying. My mother was inconsolable. She mourned and cried for a long time.

Although we children loved living in the peasant hut with the enchanted garden, my mother found living in the small and primitive house very difficult. In addition, my parents lived in constant fear of being found out and deported to Siberia.

One time, in the middle of the night, we heard a loud knock on the door. Later on, during the German occupation, that kind of knocking meant death, and to this day, when someone knocks strongly on my door it sends a chill down my spine and makes my heart pound.

My father put on a robe and went to the front door. It was the NKVD, the Russian secret police. Roused from sleep, we huddled with Mama, thinking that we would never see Father again. The NKVD was known for snatching people in the middle of the night like that and making them disappear without any communication. Fortunately this time, it turned out that the NKVD knocked on the wrong door. They were looking for somebody else.

We knew that it was only a matter of time before the NKVD would be back and next time they would probably come for us, because somewhere on their deportation list to Siberia were our names. Fearing for our safety, my parents decided to leave Sambor immediately.

17

TRUSKAVIEC

We left Sambor and moved to a beautiful small town called Truskaviec. My parents thought we'd be safer there because nobody knew us.

My father assumed a new identity, and he got a job as a food buyer for local hotels, which were all taken over by the Russians. Truskaviec was a health resort. It was well known for its healing, mineral-rich spring water which was called "naftusia". Naftusia smelled and tasted like nafta (Nafta was a petroleum product used in kerosene lamps and found extensively in that region).

At first naftusia tasted very bad, but then I got used to it and I learned to love it and even preferred to drink it instead of plain water.

My parents rented a two-room apartment from a Ukrainian farmer by the name of Habszyi. The farmer, with his wife, four children, and a son-in-law lived across the hall from our apartment. Their youngest child was named Ulana. Ulana was eight, my age, and we soon became friends. Ulana was a beautiful brown-eyed girl with curly brown hair. The oldest daughter, who was big and had a strange little flat nose, got married shortly after we moved in and almost immediately she started to look very pregnant. Ulana of course did not dare to ask her sister how that happened, but she was curious and the subject preoccupied our girl-talks all the time. The second oldest was Darka. Darka was about sixteen years old. She was a pretty auburn-haired, athletic looking girl, who played the mandolin. The son, named Zdenko, was about thirteen.

I loved living on the farm in Truskaviec. There were lots of animals: dogs, horses, cows, pigs, chickens and roosters that crowed early each morning. The horses were used for plowing the fields and for hauling. The farmer Habszyj owned much land. Behind the courtyard and the barns were rolling hills and pastures with grazing cattle. They had a dog, Brishko, who was always tied down with a long rope and had a big wooden doghouse near the barns. He lived outside, even in the winter.

Most of the permanent residents in Truskaviec were Ukrainian. Genia and I were enrolled at the same Ukrainian school that Ulana attended. I had to start first grade all over again, but this time in a different language, Ukrainian. It was quite effortless for me to switch from Polish to Ukrainian. Our maid Nascia had always spoken to us mostly in Ukrainian, while we spoke to her in Polish.

In late fall and winter, we children walked to school in deep snow crossing a thick forest. Dressed warmly, girls wore wool dresses and long warm stockings. We wore hand knitted woolen sweaters, hats, shawls and mittens, and heavy knee-length coats. Our lace-up winter shoes were made of thick leather. On the way to school, early in the morning, the forest was especially beautiful as the rays of the winter sun would break through the pine branches and make the snow sparkle. The frost made our cheeks and noses red and our heavy shoes made squishy sounds on the snow-covered path. That was the only sound to be heard because in the winter the forest was perfectly quiet.

In the early spring, the melting snow ran in gurgling little rivulets. While the snow was still on the ground, we would pick white snowbells and lilies of the valley along the way.

Each morning, when we walked into the classroom, we would all line up to greet the teacher. We would kiss her hand and quietly take our seats. I often thought of the respect European teachers were afforded when I later worked as a substitute teacher in Los Angeles schools where I was treated with little or no respect by students and administration alike.

Using a quill pen and purple ink, I learned to write Ukrainian calligraphy. I loved writing the beautiful letters. Each had to be done perfectly, and I loved my pens and my bottle of purple ink. The wide-lined paper I was given to write on was coarse and grayish yellow. Writing paper was scarce and one did not use it carelessly. Just like the other children in class, I made the quill pens out of big white goose feathers, whittling the ends down to thin points. For other types of writing we used regular fountain pens or pencils.

In good weather, in the afternoon, we would go to a large park in the center of town. A Russian army band played every afternoon in the park pavilion. Most of the recuperating hotel guests were Russian. I used to walk there with Mama and watch the people as they leisurely strolled, sipping naftusia water through glass straws that were a part of special glass mugs. New guests were not used to the strong nafta taste and could sip naftusia only slowly. They had to psyche themselves into drinking it by watching other strolling people do the same. The spa guests would listen to music, socialize and sometimes dance.

Often, I would see a little girl sitting on a bench with her mother in the park. She was the local rabbi's daughter. As soon as the music would start, she would run in front of the band and dance freely and with great joy. She was about five years old. Everybody would stand around her clapping and admiring her. I also wanted to dance like that, because that's what music always made me want to do. But I was too bashful and I held back, and that made me feel terribly unhappy. When it came to dancing, I held back, not wanting Mama or someone else to make an embarrassing comment. Mama never knew how much I loved to dance. From early on, she thought of me as a tomboy, a cute mischief, and a fresh kid. She would associate gracefulness, dancing and all the girly stuff with Genia's ladylike nature, and there was nothing I could do to change that. At school in Truskaviec, Genia got to perform in a dance recital. She was a great success. She wore a beautiful costume and everybody admired her grace.

In winter in Truskaviec, Genia got very ill, she had pneumonia. Just then, our old nanny, Nascia, showed up unexpectedly. She came to be with Genia and take care of her. Maybe she came because she had a premonition that Genia was very ill. It was unlikely that mother could have sent word to her in her remote village. It was the middle of winter and Nascia walked in deep snow for many miles from her village in the bitter cold of a Polish winter.

We were all happy to see her. Nascia did not leave Genia's side for a minute; she did not trust anyone with Genia's care. Every day she washed her and fed her. Every night she would sleep on the floor next to her bed. To ease Genia's breathing, wet sheets were hung all around her, day and night. Within a short time, I also got sick; I had bronchitis, which was less serious. I had a cough and fever. I was confined to the bed in the kitchen where Genia and I usually slept. Genia needed to stay in my parent's bedroom because she required constant care. A doctor came every day, carrying a little black bag, and everybody was serious and talked in hushed voices.

Then, one mid-day, Father came home early with a present for me. When I saw him standing in the door, holding a mandolin, I was so overjoyed that I jumped out of bed and it seemed that I had an instant recovery. The farmer's young daughter, Darka, had played the mandolin and I have always loved mandolin music.

I used to spend a lot of time across the hall with Ulana and her big family. Their house was always very lively. Just before Christmas, the farmer Habszyj slaughtered one of his pigs. In the evening the whole family got involved in preparing it. They made sausages, using the pig's intestines. First they washed them, tied one end and then blew with their mouth into the other end and then also tied that end. The long gut balloons were hung from the kitchen ceiling to dry. Later they were stuffed with ground pork meat from the freshly slaughtered pig.

Ulana and I got to help with everything. The guts smelled stinky, and when I blew into them the taste on my mouth was pretty awful. I knew not to eat unkosher food at the neighbor's home, but it never occurred to me that I should not touch the washed pig's guts to my lips. No one working in the farmers kitchen with the guts, including me, seemed to be in the least concerned about germs. There was a pot of pig's blood standing on the table. Ulana's brother, Zdenko, picked up the big pot with both hands and drank from it. I thought that that must have been why he had such red cheeks. Zdenko was a strong husky youth.

Living in Truskaviec was great. I loved the forests near by. I loved the school and the farm full of animals. Ulana and I could roam the farm, the forest, or the small town, unrestricted and unsupervised. Spring came, and we picked berries and ran wildly up and down the hills where the cattle were grazing.

The lack of luxuries, or the constant fear of being caught by the Russians, may have perhaps affected my parents. But we children did not lack for anything. Food was plentiful, especially since my father was in charge of buying food from the farmers for distribution to the resort hotels. Sometimes he would bring home heavy sour cream and we would make butter in a wooden churning vessel, just like Mrs. Habszyj, across the hall. For me, life there was so very beautiful, though it did not last long.

In June 1941, the German army entered the town and the idyllic life in Truskaviec came to an end.

That day, I was out walking along the main street when I saw the German's entering Truskaviec. There were hundreds upon hundreds of them; a wave of green uniforms roared down the main street on motorcycles. As if riding on parade, they looked crisp in their smart green uniforms. Neither the sound of bombs nor artillery preceded their arrival. The local Ukrainian population received the German army with great enthusiasm; they lined the streets on both sides with flowers in their hands.

Almost immediately, that same day, well-dressed and distinguished looking Jewish people, some with long, gray, beards were seen in the streets with brooms in their hands, being dragged out of their homes and openly humiliated. They were forced to clean the streets while being beaten by some of the local Ukrainians. That first afternoon after the Germans came I saw two men with their hands tied behind their backs being led by soldiers at gunpoint. They walked past our window and towards the forest a few hundred feet away. Somebody said that the two men were Communists and Russian collaborators and they were going to be hung in the forest.

I was not aware of any changes in our relationship with the Hapszyj family, but because of the now open hostilities towards the Jews by the local people in the area, my parents decided to return to Sambor immediately. The next day, my father got hold of two horses and a large open wagon; he loaded it with some of our belongings and we started our journey towards Sambor. Two of his old friends from Sambor, who had also been hiding out from the Russians in Truskaviec, rode along with us. One of them had formerly owned the toy store in Sambor. I remember it well. I think his name was Herschkovitz, but I'm not sure.

I found the trip back to Sambor very exciting. We were like Gypsies, traveling with our family and all our possessions in a horse-drawn wagon. Of course, none of us, especially the children, had any idea what horrors awaited us in Sambor. We stopped several times along the way, camping out. Somehow we got some fresh trout; I think father's friends caught the fish in a river near by. The toy store man prepared the trout over an open campfire and fried it in lots of butter; it tasted incredibly good.

As we neared Sambor we were suddenly stopped by a group of German officers and soldiers. At gunpoint, they ordered my father to get off the wagon. We all got very worried; we were terrified that they might shoot him. One German officer asked him for documents and wanted to know if Father was running away from the Germans because he was a Communist. At that moment my father did something extraordinarily courageous. He decided that if he must die, he would die as a Jew and not as a Communist. My father then proceeded to lift up his shirt and showed the German the "Tzitzit" he was wearing underneath, saying to the German officer that he was a religious Jew and as such he could not possibly be a Communist. (Tzitzit is a white-fringed cloth that orthodox Jewish men wear under their shirts. The number of fringes on this garment is to remind them of the number of God's commandments they are to fulfill daily).

The German Officer looked at my father for a moment and then motioned to him with his hand to move on and he walked away. Everybody in our group was astounded and greatly relieved, as if we had all just witnessed a miracle.

Watching my father living through and surviving the war, we witnessed many more such miracles. His calm dignity and courage were amazing.

My Father

18

HISTORY TAKES
A SHARP TURN

On June 30, 1941 the Germans returned to reoccupy Sambor. The Holocaust that Hitler and his German and Austrian countrymen brought about in my lifetime suddenly cut loose all anchors of civilization. In Europe, WWII destroyed many social structures that were built around generally accepted standards. Suddenly, the political and interpersonal civility which most of the western world seemed to have reinvented at the end of the First World War, was lost.

For the Jews of Europe, WWII was not just another terrible war, whose horrors they would share together and bear with their fellow countrymen. For them it was not just the chaos and random destruction that hostile invasions often thrust upon a conquered people, or the humiliation they are made to endure. For the Jews of Europe, it meant being singled out for total annihilation without any possible recourse. This was done openly while everybody else within Europe and the rest of the world passively watched.

Among those who were watching were all the so called "guardians of civilization": statesmen, the pope, bishops, nuns, priests, Buddhist meditators, the rabbis in free countries, teachers, historians, university professors, doctors, lawyers, scientists, philosophers, poets, conscientious objectors, the whirling Sufis and the mantra chanting holy men on mountaintops.

From the learned and pontificating theologians to the simple churchgoers, didn't anyone see that Jesus was being crucified over and over again? It all was happening with each innocent murder while lectures and sermons and operas and football games went on, on schedule, and newspapers were skimmed over coffee and discarded and radio stations were set on the comedy hour, and a bad day was when one had a runny nose or when one missed a train, or when a baseball game was rained out.

19

THE GERMAN
OCCUPATION IN SAMBOR

We arrived in Sambor a few days after we left Truskaviec. When we got there we found the town's Jewish community in shock. Just two days prior, on July 1, 1941 a massive pogrom against the Jews had taken place in our town. Pogroms were spontaneous bloody raids targeting Jewish communities throughout the Ukraine that took place sporadically for for hundreds of years. They were perpetrated by by mobs of antisemitic locals, armed hordes of Ukrainian nationalists, and paramilitary bandits. The Jews were at their mercy, they had no legal protection from looting, torture and brutal killings.

When the Germans entered Sambor, the local Ukrainian population, many wearing Ukrainian folk costumes, and a few Poles like our former neighbors, the Tomszajs, welcomed the Germans with flowers. While the West Ukrainians around Kiev and Odessa considered themselves Russian and fought the German invasion bravely along with the rest of Russian soldiers, the East Ukrainian nationalists in our region were collaborating with the Germans against Russia, hoping to be rewarded with an independent state of their own.

When the Germans and their Ukrainian collaborators opened the city jail, they found the bodies of local Ukrainian nationalists, who had been imprisoned and tortured by the Russian NKVD. Perhaps as a reward for their collaboration and the warm welcome the Germans received from them, the Germans gave the local Ukrainians one day to do with the Jews as they pleased. The Ukrainians took that opportunity to wage upon the Jewish community in Sambor a bloody massacre, a pogrom.

From thr book Sambor:

> *"During the Soviet occupation many Ukrainian nationalists had*
> *been persecuted, imprisoned and murdered by the Russian*
> *NKVD. Now the Ukrainians expressed their rage at the commu-*
> *nists by killing Jews. The local International Ukrainian*
> *Organization whose members consisted of the local Ukrainian*
> *intelligentsia and Greek Orthodox Church leaders, took a vote*
> *and decided to accept the German offer. The first thirty-two Jews*
> *that were caught were dragged to the Jewish cemetery. Placards,*
> *bearing pictures of Stalin and Lenin were placed into their*
> *hands, and a large procession of Ukrainians carrying picks, and*
> *axes followed them. At the head of the procession was the head*
> *priest of the local Greek Orthodox Church and members of the*
> *local Ukrainian committee. At the cemetery the thirty-two Jews*
> *were hacked to death by the mob, their heads, legs and hands*
> *were torn off and their stomachs ripped open. On the way back*
> *one hundred and seventy more Jews were caught at random,*
> *taken to the jailhouse and murdered in the most savage blood*
> *bath. Jewish properties were looted and there was chaos and*
> *much mourning among the Jews of Sambor".*

The day we arrived in Sambor, my parents rented two rooms
in the home of the Schneider family, who lived on Plac Zamkovy
(Palace Plaza). Mr. Schneider had been a well respected tailor
who catered to a more affluent and fashion conscious clientele.
He used to make coats for our family before the war. (Sometime
in the fifteenth century when people first began to assume last
names; they were often chosen on the basis of one's trade or profession. At that time many Ashkenazi Jews lived in Germany and
spoke Yiddish, which is a mixture of a medieval German dialect
interspersed with Hebrew words. Often family trades, like the
names, were passed on from father to son for many generations.
Schneider means tailor, or cutter in German. The Schneider's
cousins, the Fiedlers, were actually our town musicians and they
were indeed great fiddlers.)

Before the war I used to watch Mr. Schneider sew and even learned from him how to make coat buttonholes. He had passed away before we returned to Sambor and now his widow lived there, with her young son, Willy and an older daughter. They tried to make ends meet by renting part of their place. We rented the two rooms that had been formerly used by Mr. Schneider for his tailoring.

The daughter was a pale and pasty looking young woman, and she wore her straight long hair in a single thick braid. She had very narrow shoulders, thick legs and large buttocks. Everyday her fiancée would visit her, and the two of them would sit at the kitchen table, wordlessly sipping tea. The man was tall, balding, wore glasses and was also very pale.

Although I was only nine years old, I fell in love with Willy at first sight. He was seventeen years old, slightly built, dark skinned, with curly black hair and smiling green eyes.

Across the hall lived an elderly and reclusive spinster. Her apartment had an overpowering smell of mold, and I overheard people say that she was stingy, selfish and unfriendly, because she never invited people in, or shared her food.

Her house was crammed full with things. There was much of everything, from food to linens to clothes. Sometimes she was nice; she once gave my mother some aged blue-berry juice for me to help my upset stomach. It was very alcoholic, strong, and exceptionally tasty.

The day after we moved into the Schneider's house, Willy was caught along with other young men and made to clean up the bloody remains from the pogrom. In the evening Willy returned home smelling horribly of carbolic acid. He sat down, covering his face in his hands and sobbed for a long time. He had just returned from the Novy Swiat meadows where he and other men were made to dig a ditch and bury all the mutilated bodies.

By December 1941, the Germans issued a decree prohibiting Jews from living in most areas of the city and they were also ordered to wear white armbands with a blue Star of David on them. In our town children under twelve were not forced to wear them, as they were in some other cities.

20

THE FIRST AKCJA

Green uniforms, black swastikas, nowhere to run, panic, heavy footsteps, panic, pounding on doors, shouting, children crying, heavy footsteps, black boots, green uniforms, red armbands, black swastikas, horse whips, guns, and the never-ending cries and whimpers, and the children who were too afraid to cry, and the hollow-eyed men who mourned in silence, and the women whose tears became the new river Styx, the one which is not a legend.

It's one o'clock a.m. October 4, 2004, and I am asking myself, how am I to remember it all, the raids, the voices, the fear, and not go completely insane? For the past twenty-five years I have been learning to become meditative, and therefore, be in the moment. Thus, I could dance, play and love with abandon and recapture a state of joyfulness I must have once known when I was a very young child. Through meditation, I was learning to reclaim my birthright to once again live a life that includes joy. But now, to recount how it felt during the difficult times of my childhood, I must give up the security of "the moment" and enter the many dark chambers of my memory that threaten to suck me in, like a black hole.

The first massive raid and deportation, the first "Akcja" in our town took place early in the morning on August 4, 1942.

Around 3 a.m. we were awakened by a frantic commotion outside. We heard people screaming and running up and down the outside stairs of the large apartment houses on all three sides of the Schneider's small house. Wives were calling out to husbands, and mothers were calling out to their children, as they were being separated in the chaos and hauled away.

My parents, Genia and I, ran out the back door following Willy and his family into the small yard, where there already were some other people looking for a place to hide. The German soldiers were out front, knocking on doors and breaking them down, cursing and shouting orders.

In the far corner of the yard was a small, maybe six by eight foot laundry shed. Desperate for a place to hide, everybody rushed into the shed. Someone thought to remove a plank of wood in the ceiling and found a small crawl space between the thin wooden ceiling and the tin roof above it.

One by one, helping one another, the people ahead of me climbed into the crawlspace through the small opening in the ceiling. It must have been Willy who reached for Genia and me and pulled us up through the hole. We barely squeezed in there. Mama and Father could not get in and join us, as there was no room for them.

The board in the shed's ceiling was replaced, and body against body, we lay motionless next to one-another, without making a sound. We were packed like sardines, filling up every bit of space under the roof. It was a miracle that the thin ceiling did not collapse under the weight of the people who managed to get in.

There was no headroom for sitting up and there was only one possible position to be in. We stayed that way throughout the rest of the morning, day and evening, till late at night. Our bodies were sore and our legs were terribly cramped. It was August and during the day, it was impossibly hot beneath the tin roof. We were all totally dehydrated; the thirst was far worse than the hunger. Some people talked about drinking urine. Urine was a problem that we were concerned about, because it could have seeped through the thin planks we were lying on.

All day, we lay in the hot wetness of our sweat and urine, listening to the screams of people being beaten, injured, and hauled away. We heard the Germans shouting: "raus", "los" , "anschliessen" "Verfluchter Jude", "schnel",(get out, hurry, line up... cursed Jew, hurry, quickly...)

A few feet from where we were hiding, close to the ground, was a small opening outside the Schneider's kitchen wall. It must have been an ash clean-out leading from under the woodburning stove to the yard outside. It was a tiny space, where perhaps two chickens could fit in. It had a small wire-mesh door that was less than one and a half feet wide and tall. One man, trying to escape, hid in there, inside that hole in the wall. The space was so small, that one is forced to fathom the desperation of a grown man trying to squeeze into it.

The Germans found him there, crouching behind the small wire mesh door and they dragged him out. We were less than twenty feet from the unfortunate man, and barely breathing. Had any one of us sneezed, they would have found us too.

I don't know where Father hid. Later we found out that Mama managed to hide in the attic in the apartment building across the yard. Later at night we crawled out from our hiding place and joined her there, apparently it was considered safer to stay there till the raid was over. Someone had brought a cup of coffee and we shared it with Mama. The first Akcja lasted two days. Miraculously the four of us survived. Willy and his family also survived the first Akcja.

When we got back to the apartment, it was almost bare. Our neighbors had stripped it of just about everything. They took linens, clothes and even towels. The next day I saw a neighbor's child wearing one of my dresses. It had been my favorite dress in an orange and green plaid pattern. We found most of our Jewish neighbors gone. They had been caught and sent away. The stingy old lady had been taken away and her place stripped-bare as well.

When I came down from hiding above the shed both my legs were infected and I broke out in a rash of boils from having sat in the August heat in human waste. We had been there for eighteen hours, from 3 a.m. till the following night. My legs were covered from top to bottom with puss-filled sores. Mother tried to squeeze out the puss, but that procedure was very painful and I remember screaming in pain. She applied black "Ichtiol" salve, which looked like tar and had a strong medicinal smell. Eventually the sores healed, but I still have the scars.

During the first Akcja, our large extended family sustained heavy losses. Uncle Moshe's wife, Elka and both of their children, black Genia and Siuniu, and father's sister Leah with her twelve year old daughter, Genia Wolman were gone. Also gone were grandfather's Hayim's brother, whom I remember only as Szostak, and his two daughters Regina, and Malka. They were all taken away along with many other cousins, aunts and uncles. All of them were taken to the Belzec extermination camp and killed.

Two days before the Akcja, on the second of August, five empty train cars were initially spotted standing at the train station. Next day, on the third of August "The Judenrat" who were the representatives of the Jewish community, were told that one thousand Jews would be deported to labor camps the next day. But the members of the "Judenrat", not wanting to anger the SS authorities, and that way hoping to save their own skins, chose to remain quiet rather than to look out for the people they represented. And so, they failed to warn the people; instead, they hid their own families. Perhaps they were ordered not to cause a panic. In any case, there would not have been much warning because the raid started that same night at 3 a.m.

Four thousand Jewish people were caught during the first Akcja. This number turned out to be four times the number that the Germans initially warned the "Judenrat" about.

All who were caught in the Akcja were first herded into the local football stadium and then they were taken to death camps and not labor camps. According to witnesses, all four thousand people were crammed into a few train cars and shipped to an extermination camp to be gassed in gas chambers and incinerated in crematoria. Among them were not only Jews from Sambor, but also Jews from the surrounding small towns of Felsztyn, Turka, and Stary Sambor. Stary Sambor alone lost one third of its Jewish population.

From the first Akcja on, the drive to exterminate the Jews in our region proceeded at an accelerated pace. Those who survived the first Akcja lived, from that time on, in constant fear of being caught in the next raid.

On September 12, 1942, on Rosh Hashanah,(the Jewish New Year) there was again an Akcja in Felsztyn. On that day most of the Jews there were in the synagogues, worshipping. The Germans surrounded all the houses of worship and ordered at gunpoint the last remaining one thousand Jews from Felsztyn to get on trains that took them to death camps. By the end of November, all the remaining Jews from all surrounding small towns and villages were brought to Sambor and herded into the Blich area, which was subsequently enclosed with barbed-wire and turned into a ghetto in December.

21

THE DOLL IN THE
BLACK VELVET DRESS

From the day we first moved into the Schneider house, I followed Willy around like a puppy. I was not quite ten years old. I even went along with him on some dates, which consisted of Willy taking a walk with a girl, and holding hands. On such occasions, I followed a few paces behind. He tolerated that and always looked at me with a smile. Our love and friendship was mutual.

Sometimes I used to go with Willy and his friends on hikes to "Novy Swiat", where I would sit on the grass nearby, a few feet away from them. Though the boys ignored me, I could hear their typical boy talk. But then Willy would see me and hush them up. Sometimes Willy took me along to visit his cousins, the Fiedlers. On the mantelpiece in the Fiedler's home was a photograph of an American cousin. Years later I wondered if they were related to Arthur Fiedler from the Boston Pops. The Fiedlers in Sambor were an extraordinarily musical family. The older Fiedlers had a small band and they used to fiddle in our town at weddings and other festive occasions. My parent's anniversary fell on the day after the happy Jewish holiday "Purim". When they celebrated their wedding anniversary with a big party in our house on May Third Street, the Fiedler brothers played music. At the Fiedler home, one of their sons, who was a handsome black-haired boy of twenty, would often play the accordion for us. Sometime he would play at the community house. Once he took his accordion to Novy Swiat, and played it there, while sitting with us on a grassy hill. After the first Akcja, we stopped going to Novy Swiat, because we were forced to stay within a restricted area of town. In the ghetto, the young Fiedler boy's girlfriend had already dyed her hair blond; she planned to escape by passing for a Gentile. I don't know if she made it, but as far as I know the whole Fiedler family of Sambor perished by June 1943.

Immediately after the first Akcja, Willy was taken for forced labor again. His first job was to empty the apartments of the people who were taken away to extermination camps. The Jewish workers, under the supervision of Ukrainian police, were packing everything that had been left behind by the victims. The boxes were then hauled away with trucks and shipped somewhere by train.

One day, when Willy went to work, I followed him to one of those God-forsaken apartments. When I got there I saw that the place was dark. The curtains were still drawn, and the beds undone. The people, who had lived there, must have been roused from sleep in the middle of the night and taken away in their nightclothes. I saw things scattered all over the floor. The place was in shambles.

I watched Willy busily packing everything into boxes. Then I saw him stop to pick up a doll in a black velvet dress from the floor. He stared at it for a while, looking serious and sad, as if he was about to cry. Then he looked over to the open door and when he saw me standing there he handed me the doll and motioned for me to get away.

The horror and sadness of that moment could not have been expressed with either a child's words or tears. Only years later was I able to cry when I allowed myself to recall Willy standing there holding the doll and looking at it. And whenever I did, my chest would feel so tight that I could hardly breathe.

Willy must have understood in that moment that the little girl,who only a few days ago used to live there with her family and her doll, was never coming back and the Germans who took her away would get him and me next.

Even though I was only ten, I must have suddenly fully grasped the horror of our situation; and I was very scared. I quickly ran from the apartment clutching the doll in my arms, never to see another doll with a child's eyes again.

Willy and his family were taken away soon after. They never made it into the ghetto, and they were never seen or heard from again.

Recently, I walked into a store and bought a beautiful doll in a dark dress. It sits on my bedroom dresser. I don't want to avoid thinking about Willy. I also bought another doll for my granddaughters' room. This one is all in pink.

Today's children who live in the security of a peacetime environment and whose basic needs for food and shelter are met, are not aware how good their lives are. Typically they take their good fortune for granted; too often they are dissatisfied and ungrateful, comparing themselves to others who have more of one superfluous thing or another. Often, with a sudden twinge of sadness, I watch carefree children at play with lots of boisterous noise and loud laughter, and I think back, remembering the silenced war children of my generation, knowing at the same time that there are still many children today who are suffering persecution. Thousands of children around the world today, are still being abused, suffering from hunger and diseases and they are frightened. And I am asking myself, what am I doing about it? In the course of many an ordinary day, such thoughts come and go as momentary flashes of conscience; usually they seem out of place and out of context and they remain unexpressed and barren.

22

BENESH
AND THE
HUNCHBACK

Very early on during the German occupation, Jews were asked to hand over valuables under penalty of death. Women had to hand over all jewelry, including their wedding rings and all sterling silver items such as candelabras and good cutlery. Of course, all money had to be handed over as well.

Some people managed to bury some valuables in time, wherever they could, but there was little time to do so.

Periodically, German commandos went from house to house searching for any remaining things of value that they suspected were not handed in yet. They would drop in unexpectedly, creating total fear and panic. Soon there was very little for them to take, but they still used to come around and bully people.

Once, when I was sitting with my grandfather Yanche in the small garden behind the Schneider's house, several young German men in brown "Hitler Yugend" uniforms walked in on us. They wore black swastikas on their red armbands and carried horsewhips in their hands. As usual, my grandfather was sitting and reading the Scriptures. One of them suddenly started to strike my frail grandfather over and over across his back, as he was trying in vain to duck. Then they all left as suddenly as they came.

It was obvious that any evil, sadistic, or crazy person of any age was given a free reign to do with Jews as he pleased. He was free to vent his anger or insanity without any restraint. Each low-life was given an opportunity to wield absolute power over a branded people who were not protected by any law, because they were destined to be slaughtered. The right to abuse Jews as they pleased made all sadistic lowlifes feel that they were now members of the "Master Race," "Die Herren Rasse". The Germans used these barbaric people to the fullest extent to help them in their murderous task of annihilating the Jews.

They also got a lot of help from those local residents who were pointing out Jewish dwellings to them and identifying who was Jewish. The frequency with which the locals were denouncing the Jews trying to flee or hide was mind-boggling. We were even terrified of Gentile children, who not only played "Catch a Jew" games among themselves, but also loved to make themselves useful to the Germans during the raids. Often, when we were hiding we would hear children say in the only two German words they had learned: "hier Jude" (here is a Jew). In addition, towards the end, local people were even offered rewards of five pounds of sugar for exposing a Jewish hiding place. However, most of them did it on their own and did not need much incentive, though it seemed that our Polish and Ukrainian neighbors were very happy to claim their reward. Now, when I see bags of sugar stacked on a shelf in the grocery store or when I'm about to open one to bake something sweet, I sometimes think of the value of sugar compared to a Jewish life during the Holocaust. To think, what price was once paid for it! I shudder to think of the light-hearted manner in which cakes and cookies were baked with the sugar that was bought with human lives, and then used to celebrate weddings, religious holidays, and children's birthdays.

After the raids, either our neighbors or the German search commandos would come around to have first chance at looting the things left behind by the people that were hauled away for slaughter. A few Ukrainian Policemen usually accompanied the search commandos.

In between the major deportation raids, whenever they felt like it, the search commandos would barge into Jewish apartments and take away anything they liked. They were especially looking for hidden money and jewelry.

The "search" commandos in Sambor were ruthless. The name

of the German officer in charge was Benesch. He was about thirty-five years old, blond, tall, and trim. His chief assistant was a
small Ukrainian man who was a hunchback, and who was known
in town as a virulent anti-Semite. Nobody referred to him by a
name. Whenever somebody would sight them they would
scream: "Benesch and the hunchback are coming!" and panic
would erupt. They carried whips in their hands and would strike
people on a whim.

The area where Jews were still permitted to live was becoming progressively smaller. It was as if a noose around us was
tightening more and more with each day. At home there was talk
that soon we may be forced to leave our place at the Schneiders
and move closer to Blich. So, one day my mother took me along
to find a new place for us to move to. We saw one place that she
considered adequate. It was a large empty storage room that
looked like a garage. There was sufficient room for our family;
there was room for a couple beds and a table with chairs. The
kitchen would have to be improvised. We would use a small
kerosene cooker, like a camping stove we called a "prymus".
There was no water or toilet, but the Blich area was becoming so
overcrowded that "the garage" looked pretty good.

On the way back, as mother and I were returning home, we
encountered Benesch and his commandos in the street, the
hunchback with them. Mama, who was holding my hand was
instantly overcome with total panic. She was afraid that they
might search her, or take us to fill a quota, or even shoot us. We
were in a situation where they could have done anything to us.
Mama was worried about being searched because she had sewn
some American dollars in the lining of her corset. That money
was all we had left and was set aside for food or for bribes to save
our lives.

Suddenly Benesh stepped in front of us, blocking our path. He
ordered us to follow him and his band to a small house nearby.
The house seemed abandoned, but it was not empty. The residents of the house must have been taken away to the camps. The
front door of the house led to the kitchen and from the kitchen
there was a door to a dining room. In the dining room there was
a door to a small bedroom. I was told to stay in the kitchen. There

I was left, completely ignored by the commando men who closed the door from the kitchen, after I saw mother forced into the bedroom by one of the Germans. I was terrified of what they might do to her. She looked so frightened, and I was too terrified to do anything other than be perfectly still. After a very long time, perhaps half an hour or an hour, the commandos all came out and left the house through the kitchen door. My mother emerged from the bedroom naked, clutching her corset in one hand as it hung from one shoulder. Her eyes were darting wildly, with the look of an insane woman. She was crazed, and speechless. There was total terror in her eyes and her hair was all disheveled. Seeing that I was not harmed, she quickly retrieved her clothes, got dressed, grabbed me by the hand and we ran out of the house. On the way, people were staring at us. One woman, who knew my mother, tried to stop us and inquire what had happened to her. Clutching my hand firmly and still looking crazed and stunned, all she said was "they searched me," "the Germans searched me," and she kept running towards Blich, where her family lived. After she calmed down, she told her family that Benesch and his men had just searched her, but did not find anything.

Nothing more was said about the incident, at least not in front of the children. I must have buried any thoughts about that incident very deep within me, certainly not daring to talk about it with Mama, knowing that it would have been very painful for her.

Fifty-four years later, as I sat in meditation in my living room with a group of friends, I suddenly broke down. My whole body started to shake and I could not stop sobbing. Memories of that incident suddenly came back with an unbearable intensity. I don't know what brought it on, in the serene and beautiful meditative setting. When I finally talked about it with my sister Genia, she knew nothing about it. At least she was spared seeing Mama in that horrible state. That frightened and crazed look on Mama's face will always haunt me.

23

THE ROLNIK

Before the war, my father's main place of business was a ware-house called the Rolnik. While his brother Benjamin and an accountant mainly worked in the office near Plac Zamkovy, Father was in charge of the warehouses, the purchase of grain from the farmers, its storage in the warehouses, and the shipments abroad.

The Rolnik had once been a cloister. It was built centuries ago, on a hill above Lvovska and Drohobycka Street. The hill was on the corner where Sambor's two main streets formed a "Y." Lvovska Street led to the Railroad station, which was just beyond the city's great English Park. Drohobycka Street led to the big Catholic cemetery. Below the Rolnik, on the street level, directly across the way, stood the courthouse and the prison building. Just off Drohobycka Street, a long and wide road led from the street up the hill to the large and weathered wooden gate that opened to the cloister grounds.

The cloister complex was very large. It consisted of a group of buildings that were at least 200 years old.

Beyond the cloister's tall gate was a big courtyard paved with cobblestones and several buildings that had been built around the circular yard. The main building was furthest from the gate, over-looking the streets below, the court building and the jailhouse.

The main building was enormous. Its big front hall led to several smaller rooms in the rear. The main hall, which was the size of a small church and had perhaps, at one time, served as a chapel, had ceilings that were probably thirty feet high.

After the cloister was converted to a grain business it became known as the Rolnik, which in Polish, meant The Farmer. On any day of the week, the big gate was kept open and the courtyard was filled with horse-drawn wagons laden with the grain that local farmers would bring to sell to my father. Other wagons were loaded to take grain cargo to the railway station to be shipped abroad.

In winter, the farmers came with sleighs, wearing long sheepskin coats and hats with ear-flaps turned down, and in their hands they would carry long whips. The farmers were big, ruddy and hardy looking men, with frost icicles hanging from their long whiskers. They would smoke and spit on the ground, wiping their noses on their sleeves and pissing on the ground behind their wagons. The smell of horse manure, tobacco, urine and grain would fill the air.

All day long, carts and wagons were being loaded and unloaded as workers milled around, carrying the heavy, 200-pound, burlap sacks of grain on their backs in and out of the warehouse. The incoming grain was weighed, sorted and stacked in the various storage buildings. In the main building, the sacks were stacked mostly in one corner; measuring about thirty feet deep on all sides and about 20 feet high. My father, wearing a short winter overcoat with a fur collar, a warm felt hunter's hat, jodhpur-like pants and tall leather boots, would be standing outside, negotiating transactions with the farmers. With his turquoise eyes always twinkling, he looked like a man who loved his life. He was healthy, very strong, and he was always calm and relaxed.

I recall that one of his favorite quotes from the Hebrew book, "The Wisdom of our Fathers" was : "A rich man is one who is satisfied with his share."

Father also loved his work. He liked interacting with people and he treated the farmers and all workers with respect. Among the farmers from the surrounding villages and among the landed gentry, who were also selling their grain to him, my father was well respected for his honesty and fairness. He was also loved by all that knew him because of his jovial and friendly nature. He always saw the good in people; and when they failed him, he would make excuses for them.

When the Russians came, they confiscated the business. Then

the Germans came, and they took it over. Some of the former Ukrainian workers were recruited to be in charge of the Rolnik, but under German supervision. Having been an experienced grain specialist, my father was assigned to work there for the Germans. Together with his brothers and other Jewish men, they worked as slave workers. Soon, my father, who spoke fluent German, was reporting directly to a German officer. This officer did not like interacting directly with the Ukrainian workers who did not speak German and were mostly crude and illiterate peasants. I wish I could remember the German officer's name because my father spoke highly of him and told us that the officer never addressed him in a disrespectful manner. He always called him Mr. Meisels and not Jude (Jew). Later on, as the food situation for us worsened, that same officer used to tell my father to take some food home to the family. On several occasions, when they were unloading shipments of food for the German army at the train station, he gave my father permission to set something aside. Father would take the extra food to his beloved Rebbi, Rabbi Pinhas Tversky, who had a big family to feed. Once he gave the Rabbi a box of spaghetti.

At a different time, on a different job at the train station, my father and his fellow workers were loading a shipment of food under the watchful eyes of some new SS officers, who soon noticed that a box of food was missing. Apparently a young Jewish boy who worked with my father stole the food. My father saw him take it and hide it in the bushes near by. It was tempting to steal food because people were starving. The SS officers were furious. They accused my father of stealing the missing box. When he denied taking it, they asked him if he knew who did it, but my father would not tell on the young boy.

The German officers handed my father over to the local SS authorities in town and they in turn took him to the center of town, near the Ratusz. There they all took turns beating him. They pounded his head with the butts of their rifles and kicked him with the spurs they wore on their boots.

People who saw him lying on the ground while the savage beating was going on, came running to tell us what was happening to my father. They told us to brace ourselves for the worst, that we might not see him alive again. Father later said that during his ordeal he had surrendered to the will of God, but at the same time he knew that he would not give away the name of the boy who stole the food.

Finally, after beating him relentlessly for a long time, the Germans left him for dead. After they left, some people picked him up off the ground and carried him to the Judenrat. Within a short time and to everyone's surprise, he regained consciousness. He immediately stood up and said he was able to walk home. Those that witnessed it, could hardly believe that after such a brutal beating he was still alive and able to get on his feet.

When he walked into the house, he sat down at the table, and told us that he had a headache. I remember that he was very calm. I put cold compresses on top of his head and held my hands on his forehead. I remember how it felt standing by his side and how the skin of his forehead felt on my hands. I remember that seeing him home alive I was no longer worried about anything else past, present or future. His inner strength and his calm demeanor were wordless lessons to last us a lifetime.

People who had witnessed the beating thought it a miracle that he had survived; my father in turn became calmer, and more religious. He was able to have saved a boy's life, and for that he thanked God. I think that from that day on, he became even less concerned about his own life. He rarely went into hiding; instead he would always stand guard, reasoning that when the Germans came they'd find him and perhaps stop searching further.

24

THE SECOND AKCJA

The second major Akcja in Sambor took place on October 17th, 1942, and lasted five days. During the raid, Genia and I and several of our cousins were hiding out at the Rolnik.

Very late at night, the night before the second Akcja, my parents must have heard a rumor that the Germans were planning another raid. Again, someone may have noticed empty box cars at the train station and suspected that another raid was imminent. As with the First Akcja, the Second Akcja happened so suddenly that most people had little time to escape and hide.

Genia and I were suddenly roused from our sleep and my mother hastily helped us put on our winter coats over our pajamas. We put on warm hats, socks, and shoes and were quickly taken out of the house and into the wintery night. The streets were deserted because it was late and the night was very cold.

Not having any other place to hide us, my father and his brothers took their children to the Rolnik warehouse, hoping to find some way to hide us there. The seven children, all first cousins, were taken to the large main building.

Having run his business at the Rolnik for many years, my father knew every nook and cranny of the warehouse, but he had never explored its attics. In the main building, the attic seemed totally inaccessible because the ceiling was so high and there was no staircase leading to it.

In the far right corner of the hall, stood a tall stack of burlap sacks, which were filled with grain. It was probably thirty feet deep and twenty feet high. One person climbed on top of it and another handed him a tall ladder from below. The ladder was then placed on top of the stack and it was steadied against the wall. Then someone climbed the ladder to the top and removed a few boards in the high ceiling, which was made of very old, dark brown wood. One by one, we children were helped to climb to the top of the sacks and up the precariously shaky ladder towards the small opening in the corner of the ceiling. I don't remember whose hands pushed me up and through the dark hole in the ceiling, but after all the children had squeezed through the hole, the wooden ceiling planks were quickly replaced, and my father and his brothers disappeared in a hurry. We children were left alone. There was no time for anyone to check out the attic or to bring us food, water or blankets.

Climbing the shaky ladder so high up was very scary, but even scarier was finding ourselves alone in the huge, cold attic cut off from our parents, and not knowing if we would ever see them again. Within a short time, at dawn, we began hearing screams that came from the streets below. The second Akcja had begun.

The attic was vast and empty and was very dusty. The floor of the attic, which was the wooden ceiling in the main hall, was probably half-rotten and eaten away by termites. It's a wonder we did not fall through it down to the floor below.

It was winter already, there was snow on the roof and it was freezing cold. Afraid to make a sound lest someone would hear us, we huddled together for warmth and because we were scared. All we had was each other. For the next few days we were hearing voices of people being rounded up and led to the trains. Some people were screaming in pain, little children were crying. And we heard adults also crying and begging for mercy. I heard a young woman pleading with her captors, "please let me live, I'm so young". The wailing went on and on for days. The Akcja lasted five days.

In the attic, there were a few small holes in the roof through which we could get some snow to eat. On the second day, we found a handfull of dried up green peas in a sack; they must have been a hundred years old. The peas were like small rocks. They were no longer green but a dusty gray. I held a pea in my mouth and sucked on it, but it never got soft.

On the second night my sister Genia, who was then twelve,

woke me up in the middle of the night and asked me to take off my pajama pants and give them to her. She was sobbing. Genia's pajamas were soaked through with blood. She was terrified; she did not understand what had happened to her. I also was scared that she had been injured and was going to die. All the other children were asleep. Genia cried all night and did not speak to me anymore. I took off my pajama bottoms and gave them to her. Now my legs were exposed and I was very cold. I wrapped myself in some empty sacks that we found under the eves of the attic. Later, to keep warm, we all wrapped our feet in the sacks and tied them with pieces of strings we found. It was so cold, that my cousin Yosiu would not open his coat to scratch a bad itch on his back. He used a rusty nail that was sticking out from a wooden beam and held his itchy back against it, making it pierce his thick winter coat to the flesh. I did the same whenever I needed to scratch; we were all grimy and itchy.

Five days later, my father and uncles came to take us down. They brought us some buttered black bread and some milk. Never before or since, has food tasted so good as that cup of milk with a thick slice of dark buttered bread.

After we got back to our apartment at the Schneider's, Genia crawled into bed and stayed there for days, crying a lot. With her face turned against the wall, she would not speak to anyone. Genia was in shock and my mother was very concerned about her.

Within a day, Genia's old nanny, Nascia, came from her faraway village to be with her. Had word been sent to her to come? I don't know how that would have been possible; no one had telephones, especially in small villages. Nascia came on foot from her village because she may have felt that Genia needed her. Maybe she came to find out if we were still alive after hearing about the latest Akcja.

Nascia stayed by Genia's bedside and watched over her day and night. With her caring and quiet presence, Nascia must have wanted Genia to feel that she was safe and taken care off.

I watched Nascia washing tub-fulls of Genia's blood-soaked clothes. I watched my mother and her friends, whisper about something very mysterious that had happened to Genia and I thought that Genia was deathly ill. No one spoke to me. I sensed that they were all trying to keep a horrible secret from me. I was too scared to ask anybody about what was happening to Genia.

In the course of the second Akcja, two thousand people were transported to the death camp Belzec and many people had been killed locally, my grandfather Hayim Zechariah Meisels, among them. He was shot during the Akcja and was later found dead in his basement. The roll of dollar bills, which, during the war, he always carried in a pouch on a string around his neck, was gone. My father and his brothers took him to the cemetery and buried their father. I saw my father coming home from the cemetery carrying a shovel in his hand and looking very grim.

For seven days after the burial, my father sat every evening after work, on a low stool. He was sitting "Shiva", according to the Jewish ritual of mourning. Every night during the week of "Shiva", people assembled in our place to hold memorial services. The men chanted the prayers for the dead, the "Kadish", the women sat around crying and mourning the dead. Genia stayed in her bed, which was in the same room, her face turned to the wall. I sat quietly in the corner, watching it all.

A day after the Akcja, my second cousin, a young boy of maybe twelve, sat at the table with us at dinner. His father Eli was taken away during the Akcja to the death camp, Belzec, together with his wife and younger son. During the sparse diner there was some bread on the table and a small piece of butter. Butter was a rare item in those days. The boy looked around and then quickly grabbed a big chunk of the butter and put it in his mouth. When my father saw what the boy did, something in him snapped and he slapped the boy's hand. I saw it and I felt terrible because the boy was embarrassed. I was so humiliated for him. He looked startled and ashamed and I'll never forget his face.

Of course, everyone was irritable. We had all been traumatized by the brutality that we witnessed during the past few days. Along with his father, my father lost many other family members in the latest Akcja and he was mourning them. The episode with the butter may now seem like something that was relatively insignificant, but what I perceived and felt at that particular moment at the table stayed with me for a long time. I never knew how to let it go, even though I have long since forgotten the boy's name. I think that the child in me never quite forgave my father. And yet I never spoke about it to anyone. I resented my father for slapping the boy's hand, and I felt bad for resenting my father, whom I always thought of as the best and kindest human being in the world.

25

BREAD

After the first few akcjas, the hunger among the Jewish people was becoming desperate and pervasive. Everything we had that could have been sold or bartered for food had been confiscated or plundered by the Germans and locals. There were many forlorn looking people, young and old, walking around listlessly, hungry, cold, unwashed and unshaven. They had lost their homes and their families; many of them were sick. Hunted like animals, they went hungry and were searching for a place to keep warm and stay the night. The small synagogue in Uncle Isaac's house, "The Stibl", was converted into a hospice where some of the homeless people would find a corner to stay. From one end of the small prayer hall to the other, the place was packed with people and with what bedding they had. Mama's friend Mrs. Goldfischer, found refuge there with her little son and daughter, Basia, who, before the war, used to be Genia's friend. Mr. Goldfischer was not with them. He must have been caught and taken away some time before. I stopped by to see them there one evening, when Basia tried to help bathe her little brother in a washbasin that her mother had filled with boiling water from a teakettle. Before her mother managed to cool the water down, Basia sat the child down in the basin. He was scalded badly and he was pitifully screaming in pain, and Mrs. Golfischer was beside herself with grief.

Before the war Mrs. Goldfischer was often seen strolling on Linia AB with Mama; both were always elegantly dressed. She was a pretty and vivacious woman, and was occasionally subject to some gossip when she would be seen strolling with Father's accountant, Bobo Lindenwald, who was unmarried. Bobo was tall with a round pudgy face and thick red lips. Mr. Goldfischer was a diminutive thin man who, I think, was more religious than his wife; he always wore a big black hat that made his small face appear even smaller. We used to visit the Goldfischers often. The cellar where we later hid was not far from their apartment. Mrs. Goldfisher and her children were killed during the third Akcja.

My father and uncles continued working at the Rolnik, and at the warehouse on Przemyska Street. To help ease the hunger in the community, these men risked their lives daily, bringing some grain from work. Usually, my father and uncles would wear two pairs of trousers to work and they would tie the inner pant legs at the ankles and fill them with wheat kernels before returning home. At night after coming home, they would empty the trousers on a sheet spread on the floor. The wheat was then ground in coffee grinders and the women would bake bread. Our old nanny, Nascia, who had come to take care of Genia, helped my mother bake bread; daily, they would hand it out to the many hungry people. Sometimes there was a line of people standing outside our door. I remember how they looked and how they smelled. I remember their hollow eyes, as they stood quietly in front of our door, waiting for a piece of bread. One time, someone pointed to a boy of about fourteen, who was also standing in line. He was all wrapped up in rags and he was unable to hold his urine. They said that the boy was the son of a formerly wealthy and prominent family, whom he must have lost. The boy looked confused and listless. I wish I could remember his name, because I don't think that anyone else does.

My father and uncles continued bringing grain in their double trousers each night, and with increasing urgency, when two months later everyone was forced to move to the ghetto where the food shortage was even greater and the hunger worse. In the ghetto, Aunt Dvorka baked the bread daily and she would distribute it among the hungry.

26

THE KITCHEN
CUPBOARD

In November 1942, about four hundred old and sick Jewish people were rounded up and taken away to be killed. I don't remember where they took them. Soon after, the Germans issued a decree that all the Jews of Sambor were to live in a ghetto. In panic, people scrambled to find hiding places outside the designated ghetto borders. Some tried to obtain "Aryan" documents and move to other cities, where they would be less likely to be recognized as Jews. Of course, the Jews who had Semitic features would have never been able to pass as "Aryan" and many members of our family had black hair and eyes and dark complexions.

Within each country throughout Europe, Jews usually were the only minority group among the otherwise racially and religiously homogenous people. Having lived in the Diaspora for almost two thousand years, over time many Jews appeared to be racially indistinguishable from their fellow countrymen. After all, Jewish women were raped during pogroms, and other intermingling must have taken place during the long time they had lived in Europe. According to Hebrew religious precepts, if the mother was Jewish, her offspring was born Jewish as well. Therefore, all children born to Jewish women were included in the Jewish community no matter whether they were blond or dark-haired, light skinned or olive skinned, blue eyed or black eyed. But official intermarriages or conversions to Judaism were very rare. Jews do not proselytize.

To varying degrees, there were also cultural differences between Jews and non-Jews; but no matter how subtle the racial or other differences were, our Polish and Ukrainian neighbors were very good at recognizing them and all too happy to point them out to the Germans.

A few people managed to find a compassionate Gentile family who was willing to take in a Jewish child and either hide him or her or pass them as their own. Some Gentile people did it for money. "Aryan" looking children stood a better chance of being placed with Gentile families. Male Jewish children were difficult to place, no matter how they looked, because the Gentile population did not circumcise their boys.

Those who could not escape into hiding or otherwise, were forced to move to the ghetto. It was not easy to find a place within its borders. The area of Blich, which was designated to become the ghetto, was already very crowded, because all the Jews from the surrounding areas that had escaped deportation to camps had also been forced to move to Sambor's restricted areas in and near Blich.

Anticipating that the persecution would escalate, my father started searching for a hiding place outside of the Blich area.

Soon, together with some of his coworkers, he found a cellar that could serve as a refuge for us, away from the ghetto. In the meantime, while the cellar was being readied to become a safe and viable bunker, my parents searched for a better way to keep Genia and me outside the ghetto. I was ten and Genia was twelve and a half.

When we lived on Ulica Czeciego Maja, my parents were on very friendly terms with our Polish landlady, Madam Maniewska. She was a spinster, and before the war, she lived with her older bachelor brother on a large estate near Sambor. They were quiet, gentle, and quite wonderful people. They belonged to the Polish aristocracy. When the Russians first came in 1939, they must have confiscated their estate in the country, because Maniewska now lived in a modest place near the railway station. My parents always spoke very highly of her. She was a truly noble human being, unlike the many other Polish titled and landed gentry who were mostly known to be very anti-Semitic.

My parents got in touch with Maniewska and asked her for help to save Genia and me. They were hoping that we could survive by passing as Gentile children and that perhaps Maniewska could find a way to place us with someone and help with the arrangements.

Maniewska promised to do everything possible and immediately started to make inquiries about convents that might accept us. But her efforts to place Genia in a convent failed because even though Genia had green eyes and a peachy white complexion, she had jet-black hair and would have stood out among the mostly light haired Polish girls.

My parents hoped that perhaps I could pass for a Gentile child in a convent because my hair was light brown and my eyes blue. But that too failed because I was too young to be accepted in a convent. Maniewska continued with her efforts to help us. She looked up her former tenants and our former neighbors the Tomszajs.

The Tomszajs did not have children of their own and they were open to the idea of taking me in. They wanted money. For the right price they said that they would be willing to pass me as their child. They assured Maniewska that I would be safe and well-taken care of; and she apparently believed them.

There were not too many options left, and the ghetto was being closed shortly, so my parents decided that I would live with the Tomszajs while Genia would go into hiding with Mama. Maniewska would remain the intermediary between the Tomszajs and my parents. I don't know how much money my father paid them initially.

I don't think that Maniewska knew them too well. She obviously did not realize the degree to which the Tomszajs hated Jews and how happy they were living under the German occupation. Mr. Tomszaj was even proud that his name sounded somewhat Germanic. I found out later that even though neither of them could speak German, they began to represent themselves to be "Folk Deutsche" (ethnic German). Later Mrs. Tomszaj bragged about it and she would tell me that they were among the people of Sambor who welcomed the German army with cheers and flowers. In the same breath she would say that soon all the Jews would be killed, including my family. It was strange that she would tell me these things; after all I was only a child of ten, and a very frightened one at that.

Although I was aware that my parents were looking for ways to place us with Gentiles, I was told about going to live with the Tomszajs only the day before I was to leave. I understood that while living with the Tomszajs, I should act as if I was their own child. My mother assured me that I was lucky to have this opportunity because I'd be safer and better off than my sister Genia living in the cellar that Father was preparing. She also remembered that Mrs.Tomszaj liked me a lot when I was a baby.

When Mama told me that I was to leave everybody and go live with the Tomszajs, I accepted it.

I neither protested nor did I cry; although I would have preferred to stay together with Mama and Genia, even if that would have meant living in the ghetto or in a cellar. I was not given a choice. I did not think that I could ask for or expect anything other than what I was getting. Even the children knew that as Jews, we had no options and no rights and that we had no way of doing anything about it. The children of the Holocaust were amazingly mature and brave. They fully understood the gravity of their situation. Not only did they experienced the fear of being caught by the Germans, but they also suffered, together with the adults, hunger and the loss of family. They also learned to mistrust their Gentile neighbors. To survive, they had to grow up fast, be sharp and alert and pay attention to everything that was happening around them. They learned to keep secrets about their identity or where the bunkers were. In bunkers they understood that if they cried, they'd be discovered and killed. They learned that in order to survive they had to bear their lot quietly. And indeed, in difficult situations, they often adjusted better than adults. It was only after coming to America, to a good and normal life, did I encounter cranky, whiny, disrespectful or destructive children.

The imminent, forced move to an enclosed ghetto cast upon our Jewish community, once again, a dark cloud of desperation and helplessness. Being forced to abandon their already meager dwellings, the people were packing what little they had left and were getting ready to move. A tall barbed wire fence had already been erected around the Blich area.

The night before I was to leave to go live with the Tomszajs, my mother wanted me to sleep with her. That night she cried a lot. She made me repeat Hebrew prayers over and over again, so that I would never forget them. She told me to say the prayers only silently, to say them every day and to never forget that I was Jewish. After the war, I was to find a Jewish community or any Jewish people and tell them that I had two uncles in America, Phillip and Benny Glickman, who lived in New York, and ask them to help me find my uncles. Then I was to go to America and live with my American family and they would take care of me.

My mother tried to describe her brothers to me. She said that they were very good people, they were handsome and well-to-do. Above all, she said, no matter where I find myself, I should always remember my heritage. I must have fallen asleep repeating: " Shma Israel Adonai Elohenu Adonai Ehad", "Hear oh Israel The Lord our God is One".

The next day, as evening approached, it started snowing. Later that night, my mother dressed me warmly and told me it was time for Father to take me to meet Mr. Tomszaj and go home with him. Mama said goodbye to me at the door, she was crying. My father took my hand and we walked out into the dark street. By then there was a snow blizzard outside; it was very windy.

It was a short walk from the Schneider's house to the big Catholic Church on Drohobycka Street. In the distance, I saw a very tall man in a long trench coat and a hat, standing in the snow under a tree near the church. The church grounds were slightly up hill from the street. When we approached closer, Tomszaj grabbed my hand and pulled me away from Father. No words were exchanged. My father quickly disappeared before I had a chance to say goodbye to him.

Tomszaj and I turned right on Drohobycka Street, passing the pharmacy near the church. We walked at a fast pace toward the center of town but we did not have to go far. We crossed Pszemyska Street and walked past our old house on Rynek 39, then past Mrs. Frei's cafe and turned left onto the Corso, the promenade where, before the war, elegant people used to stroll.

Tomszaj, who all this time never said a word to me, was taking me home to his apartment, which he shared with his wife and his dog, Niegus. The two-story apartment house where he lived was to the right of another pharmacy, which used to belong to father's distant cousin, Dr. Linhart, who was a pharmacist.

It was late at night, all the stores were closed and the streets and all the houses were dark. Before the war, the Corso and the streets around the center of town used to be lit up brightly with lamps atop tall wrought iron posts.

Entering a street level doorway, we walked into a dark hallway and up an unlit stairwell. Before the war there used to be a ballroom or a dance studio upstairs, with its windows fronting the park and the Corso. Tomszaj's apartment was also on the second floor. When we got upstairs, Tomszaj opened a door and we walked in directly into their small kitchen (it must have been a back door).

The kitchen smelled of cabbage and pork sausage. To the left of the entrance was a stove, and to the right, in front of the window, stood a table with a couple of chairs. Past the table, along the wall, stood a tall and narrow kitchen cabinet, with upper and lower cupboard shelves and doors. In the far-left corner stood a bed, which was pushed against the wall. Between the bed and the cabinet was a second door. That door led to a second room which was cluttered and dirty. Except for a little light coming through a small window, the room was dark.

The room was used for storing firewood and coal. It was unheated and full of junk. In one corner stood a bucket, which I was told to use for a toilet, when needed. I was also told to never go near the window, and to never make a sound. No one must ever find out that I was there, or we would all be killed.

Actually the Tomszajs lived in their kitchen. That first night I was to sleep with them in their one bed. Terrified of Tomszaj, who always seemed angry, I crawled into the space against the wall near Mrs. Tomszaj and lay motionless and afraid to breathe.

The next morning, after I was hastily given some food, Tomszaj ordered me to crawl into the bottom part of the small kitchen cabinet, the one standing across from their bed. I did as I was told.

Tomszaj, who was an electrician, left for work and Mrs. Tomszaj left for the Market. I was to remain in the cabinet at all times. The cupboard was less than four feet wide, two feet high and eighteen inches deep. To fit inside, my legs had to be bent at the knees and my head and neck bent forward with my chin on my chest. I could neither sit up nor lay down. On the outside, the dog Niegus lay down near the cabinet doors, blocking them.

I have loved dogs all my life, and was never afraid of them. But Niegus did not like me and growled at me all the time. He was a mean dog. One day, Mrs. Tomszaj told me how they got him. Nine years earlier when they lived on May Third Street, at night they heard him whimpering outside their window. It was the same puppy that I accidentally hugged to death when I was a baby. Assuming that it was dead, our maid must have taken it outside. The Tomszajs found him in the trash bin and took him in and named him Niegus.

Tomszaj did not seem to have a steady job and he was home often. He was morose and did not talk much. In the evening, I would hear him play his small trumpet. During the day, they let me out for a few minutes to urinate or to eat. At all other times the cabinet doors remained closed; it was dark inside.

I don't remember crying in the cabinet. It would have made Tomszaj more furious. (How strange it seems to me now, when I hear children fuss and cry when they don't get their perfect spot at the table, in a car or on a couch.) All I could do in the cabinet was repeat the prayers Mama had taught me.

Every day Tomszaj told me in a very strict manner that when they were out of the house, however long that might be, I was to stay in the closed cabinet. Otherwise, he said, somebody might see me through a window and report me to the German police, who would kill me.

Initially, Tomszaj was paid and he promised Maniewska he would take good care of me. He was told that more money would be given to him as soon as possible; in any case, he would eventually be greatly rewarded for saving me. But already after a week or so he tried to extort more money. He became very angry when the additional money was not immediately forthcoming. Had Maniewska promised him that he'd also be further rewarded, even if my parents did not survive? Could she have done that without arousing suspicion that she was sympathetic to Jews?

She had to be careful because she too was secretly hiding Jews in her apartment.

Each time Tomszaj looked at me, he seemed angrier; each time I saw him he was scarier. He frequently talked about killing me. He said he'd choke me if I didn't hurry up with eating my food and quickly crawl back into the cabinet. I was so terrified of him that I was hardly able to swallow the small amount of food I was given. Not a day passed when he was not angry and mean. He would curse and call me a damned Jewish bastard and at the same time he'd curse all Jews.

Every time the Tomszajs left the house they put the dog near the cabinet to guard me, to make sure that I would not get out. One night, long after they had left, I needed to use the bucket, but I was scared to leave the cupboard because Tomszaj told me that he'd kill me if I did. On the outside, Niegus was blocking the cabinet door and growling. The dog seemed to hate me as much as Tomszaj did. I was scared of him, but even more of Tomszaj.

When I could finally stand it no longer, I got out and tiptoed to the dark room where the bucket usually was. The growling dog followed me. The dark, unheated room was freezing cold and I could not find the bucket. They must have taken it out to be emptied on their way out.

There were two other doors in the dark junk room. One was locked and must have been the front door to the apartment. Still searching for a bucket to pee in I tried opening the second door; it was not locked. I opened it and found myself in a huge empty room that must have been the former dance hall. The half-open broken windows were swinging in and out and rattling in the wind. It was cold and very dark and there was no bucket to be found anywhere. I was terrified of the growling dog behind me and of Tomszaj catching me but I was also scarred because it was so spooky that night in the big hall. Beyond this point something in my brain turned off and I can't remember what happened. That night, something must have happened there that must have frightened me terribly. In my anxious state of mind I felt exposed and vulnerable; maybe I imagined seeing an apparition. Maybe the Tomszajs, had found me there and found the floor soiled and had punished me severely. But my memory stops right there. I only remember sheer terror.

I lived in the cabinet for at least two weeks. I had no way to keep track of time; all the days and nights were the same. I know that I got there some time before the enclosing of the ghetto, which was on December 1, 1942 and left on the last night of Hanukkah, which according to the lunar calendar for that year fell on December 10, 1942.

By December first, the whole area of Blich was surrounded with barbed-wire walls, and was being patrolled twenty-four hours a day by armed guards. Anybody attempting to escape the ghetto would have been shot on the spot. Only workers were permitted to leave to go to work and return. They would usually be marched in and out escorted by guards. Anyone who was not under guard had to have a special permit and even then one was not safe from being stopped and being detained or even shot on a whim.

Mrs. Tomszaj may have shared her husband's hatred for Jews and his love for Hitler, but she had known me since I was a baby and she never spoke to me in a harsh manner. She may have even felt some pity for me. She was afraid of her husband, and she was afraid that he would actually kill me, one day, because he would not know how to get rid of me otherwise, without taking a chance that someone would find out that he was harboring a Jew.

She turned to Maniewska and the first few times, demanded more money to calm her husband's rage; but there was no more money. The last time she went to see Maniewska was to tell her that it was not safe for me to stay with them any longer. She confided to Maniewska her own fears. She spoke of her husband's threats. She told Maniewska that she wanted to get me out of the house that same evening, before her husband got back home. She said that she intended to leave me near the entrance to the ghetto as soon as it got dark.

Unbeknown to Mrs. Tomszaj, Zelig Salomon, my father's fist cousin, was in the next room listening to what was being said between Maniewska and Mrs. Tomszaj. Maniewska was secretly hiding him. He had overheard before, conversations between Maniewska and the Tomszajs about my stay at their house and he was aware of their attempts to extort more money. This time, he must have known that my life was in serious danger and that something needed to be done immediately to save me. He knew that a Jewish child left alone in the cold at night outside the ghetto would not have been able to knock on any door and ask for help. And if the guards had spotted me, a Jew outside the ghetto, they would have shot me.

Zelig got Maniewska's attention and told her to advise Mrs. Tomszaj to bring me to the bridge across the Mlynowka River, which led to Blich. She needed to get me there around the same time the Jewish workers were being escorted back into the ghetto. Concerned about my safety, Zelig left Maniewska's home immediately and, risking his life, he sneaked into the Rolnik where Father was working, to let him know about me and to look for me by the bridge when crossing it that evening. Zelig was forced to remain at the Rolnik till the workers were escorted back to the ghetto later that evening. It would have been too risky for Zelig to walk back to Maniewska and he would have endangered Maniewska as well.

That same evening, Mrs. Tomszaj, who had been busy decorating for Christmas, got me out of her apartment before her husband got home, and we walked to the bridge. It was snowing heavily and the streets were empty. When we got to the bridge we waited off to the side, near some bushes so as not to be seen by anyone. Soon the workers were approaching the bridge and as they came close to us, Mrs. Tomszaj quickly shoved me into the group of men. The guards who escorted the workers did not spot us. The workers walked fast and I had to keep up with their fast pace. Zelig and my father were somewhere among them. Immediately, as soon as I found myself among the workers, a whisper in Yiddish passed among the group from one end to the other, " Yosef Meisels' kind is du." (Yosef Meisels' child is here) and the words soon reached my father. The men guided me along towards Father and soon we found each other. Seeing me walking beside him, alive and well, and me holding on to his hand, he got all choked up. Only his beautiful turquoise eyes, glowing with emotion expressed his feelings; a nervous smile betrayed his concern for my safety. I was still in danger of being spotted by the escorting guards. About a hundred yards beyond the bridge, hiding between the legs of the workers, I sneaked into the ghetto through the guarded gate.

It is now over sixty years later. When I think about the people who helped me survive, I know that I should say more about Zelig, but other than having seen him occasionally during festive family get-togethers, I did not know him too well. But I do know that I'm the only one left who remembers him and I know that I want my children to know about him. Cousin Zelig, a very handsome, tall young man, not even thirty years old, was not able to escape from the ghetto again, to save himself. He was soon caught and taken to the Janowska death camp in Lvov where he was killed.

After we passed through the guarded gate, and came into the ghetto, Father took me to Isaac's home in the Blich house where he had been living since the establishment of the ghetto. My mother and Genia were staying in a cellar outside the ghetto, where they went into hiding right after I left to stay at the Tomszajs.

Isaac's place at the Blich house was a small one-bedroom apartment. Isaac, his wife and three children, my sick old grandfather, Yanche, and my father, slept in the one small bedroom. My three cousins slept in their parent's beds, my father slept on a little couch pushed against the window and grandfather slept in a small child's bed, near the door; it looked like my brass crib. My Aunt Laika, her husband Hayim, and their child, little Andzia, had a small bed, in the corner of the kitchen to the left of the kitchen table. I was to sleep with them.

That night as they did each night, after coming from work, my father and uncles emptied their double trousers in which they carried stolen grain. It was the last night of Hanukkah. My father and Uncle Isaac lit eight Hanukkah candles and chanted the blessings. Then my father gave all the children a few coins, as is the custom on that holiday, and the other children and I played cards. I won quite a few coins. After a meager supper, my father took me to see his old Rebbi Tversky. The frail old Rabbi looked at me lovingly. He placed his pale and thin hands on my head when he blessed me. Father told him that I was a very frightened child and the Rabbi seemed to be very concerned about me.

On the way out, I put all the coins I had won that night in the small bowl near the door, on top of what Father had placed there first.

Later that night, after everyone went to sleep, aunt Laika stood me up in a small wash tub filled with warm water that she had heated on the stove. As she washed me, she pulled dozens of lice off my body, and head. During the time that I stayed at the Tomszaj's I had not bathed or even once washed my hands or face.

As I stood there naked, being washed by Laika, she kissed me and lovingly smiled because she found on my body a few pubic hairs. I was not embarrassed because I loved Laika and I wanted to grow up to be a woman just like her. I was always sure that Laika, who had lived with us since I was born and had practically raised me, loved me more than anybody in this world, even her own child.

That night I slept peacefully, happily snuggled up to my beloved Laika. Uncle Isaac's small apartment, Laika's bed in the kitchen corner was now my home.

27

EGGS FOR BREAKFAST

Often an echo from the past cuts through the thin veneer of everyday trivia, and casts its hue on a present scene. Our perspective shifts and the values we ascribe to things get reassessed accordingly. Thus for those who were once hungry, it is sometimes easier to eat stale bread than to throw it out.

To me, a slice of bread, a glass of milk and an egg are still a feast. And often, I find myself extraordinarily excited and grateful to live an ordinary and uneventful day.

The morning after I came into the ghetto, it felt good to be out of the cupboard, to be able to stand up, walk around and to be, once again, among people who loved me. While at the Tomszaj's, I did not know if I'd ever see my family alive again. That morning, to find myself in aunt Dvorka's kitchen, among my cousins, was sweeter than anything I had experienced for some time, or ever. It was the middle of December. Outside it was very cold, the snow kept falling and almost came up to the kitchen window. But inside it was warm. The men had already gone off to work. Grandfather Yanche was sick in bed; he had been moaning all night. He had severe pains in his groin area, and medication for him was probably unavailable. Dvorka, Laika, and five hungry children (my four cousins and I) hung around the small kitchen. I watched as Aunt Dvorka was trying to feed us breakfast. There was nowhere to go and nothing to do, and yet this was one of the happiest mornings in my life.

There was some bread and only one egg in the cupboard. Aunt

Dvorka must have felt sorry for me because I had been so traumatized by the Tomszajs. Dvorka decided that I should be the one to eat the egg and she fried it up for me. I was only ten, and I was very hungry. I ate that one egg while my cousins, Dvorka's three children and four-year old cousin, little Andzia, looked on. I alone ate that one egg. Thinking about it still makes me cry sixty years later.

Eggs scrambled, sunny side up, devilled, in omelets, at home, in restaurants, served at champagne breakfasts; I get to eat them now almost every day.

I serve eggs to my guests who never heard of Dvorka. In fact, nobody I now know has ever heard of Dvorka, nobody ever will, as if she never existed. I loved Aunt Dvorka; she was one of the noblest people I have ever known.

It would appear that life goes on as if Dvorka, Isaac and their children never existed. But when I am complemented on my charming European accent, I do not smile and say thank you, as if their European killers never existed.

28

LIVING IN THE
SAMBOR GHETTO

The German effort to reduce the Jewish population in Sambor was going on continuously. In the brief intervals between the Akcjas, quotas to extermination camps were being filled by taking old and sick people. In September 1942, 188 old people were taken away. In November 1942, some 488 more of the old and the sick were seized*.

We lacked a medical facility and medicines. At first, a large Synagogue was converted into a makeshift hospital. One day a group of German SS men burst in and shot all the sick people lying in their beds and the doctor who was taking care of them was taken away**.

Many people in the ghetto had typhoid. One of them was my first cousin Avram, who was Uncle Yankiev-Leib's eighteen-year old son. The high typhoid fever seemed to have affected his brain and although he recovered from typhoid, his brain was damaged and he was never normal again. Being the only surviving triplet, he was, from birth, always very delicate.

In addition to suffering from ill health and the lack of medicines, the people in the ghetto were starving. Sometimes peasants would come up to the barbed wire fence, towards the rear of the ghetto, and trade food for our old clothes or the few other items we still had. The guards did not spot them because the guard booth was at the other end of the ghetto. I saw a woman holding

---

*The exact dates and numbers were recorded by my family members and other survivors, in the book "Sambor".
**Eye witness account in the book: "Sambor"

up her bra, trying to exchange it for some food. I heard her lamenting in Yiddish that she no longer needed it because her breasts had shriveled from hunger.

For a few months, after I came to the ghetto, things were relatively calm. I was happy to be with my family in Dvorka's and Isaac's house. Isaac's youngest child, Zosia, was my closest, my very best friend and we were inseparable. We ran around together within the confines of the ghetto. We found some other children and an old wrecked and abandoned place and we pretended that it was a theatre. We put on shows among ourselves. We sang Polish, Yiddish and Ukrainian songs. We watched adults pick up cigarette butts in the street and we also rolled the bits of tobacco from the butts we found, in pieces of newspaper and smoked it. We watched young couples stroll and kiss in doorways and at the cemetery.

From the first days of occupation, the German authorities in charge of our town ordered the Judenrat to recruit a group of young men from among the Jewish community to help the Germans keep order while they were rounding up the Jews. They too were slave workers. These young men, called kapos, were hoping that they would be able to warn their families of impending raids and and help them hide. They were also trying to delay their own deportation to death camps and execution.

Across from Dvorka's kitchen door, behind a hanging sheet in the neighbor's kitchen, lived Lusiek Bones. He was a handsome, eighteen year old Kapo. With his robust physique, blond hair, blue eyes and the smiling face I remember, he looked more like the young men we would see outside the ghetto. The kitchen doors were always open and everybody would know when Lusiek was making out with a girl behind the hanging sheet that separated his bed from the rest of the kitchen. Outside in the front of the "Blich House", young people would hang out in the evening, they would flirt and smoke and sometimes drink. Most of these young men were Kapos. I remember when one of those young Kapos contracted typhoid. I went along with someone to visit him when he was sick in bed. His young companion was very beautiful and probably around sixteen years old. She was olive skinned, with long dark hair and she was delicately built, like a child. I remember her fainting near the cemetery gate, at her lover's funeral. She was so overcome with grief.

I remember one beautiful seventeen year old blue eyed girl in a blue knit dress, that always used to hang out with the Kapos. She had very curly reddish blond hair and was always surrounded by a swarm of young men. I remember that she ended up with Escia Freiman's brother-in-law, whose wife, I overheard, was lying in the morgue near the cemetery. The young woman had also died of typhoid. I clearly recall the day when I was passing by the morgue, knowing who the woman lying in there was. It was a beautiful day; it was almost spring. As I walked by the small, white, square structure where the woman's body was, suddenly the chief SS commandant in charge of the ghetto appeared on a big white horse, galloping past me towards the cemetery. I recall, how seeing him, I got frightened. Not till now, did it occur to me that he must have gone there to survey the cemetery with a plan on his mind, because shortly after that day, twelve hundred Jews from our ghetto were executed there.

My cousin Zosia and I talked about boys all the time; she was my age. Some of the children in our gang of friends were a year or two older; one of the bigger girls was already well developed and talked about boys in a way I could not yet relate to. But I was in love with a sixteen-year-old boy by the name of Yosiu (whose last name was Held or Feld). Of course, neither he nor anybody else knew about it. He was Aunt Ryfcia's nephew and lived in a small place near the cemetery. He had some sort of serious illness and stayed in bed. I would visit him often and bring cards to play. He seemed pleased to see me when I came, even though I was only a child of ten.

Zosia was in love with Manny, a dark skinned and dark blond boy whose hair on top was sun bleached. Big Andzia was secretly in love with Manny's older brother, who may have been a year older than she, about sixteen.

Manny also had a little brother named Aaron, whom we all called Aronciu. Of all the children in the ghetto that I remember, somehow Aronciu touched my heart the most and he stands out in my memory. Aronciu was about three years old. Both Zosia and I loved that child and we took care of him, because no one else did. I never saw the mother. I think Manny and his brothers came from some village nearby when all the Jews from the surrounding areas were herded into the Sambor ghetto. There were many orphans in the ghetto who somehow escaped being taken away with their parents; they were separated and left behind. Wrapped in rags they roamed the ghetto streets and begged for food.

Near our place in the ghetto, I often saw a little barefoot girl wandering in the streets, unsupervised. No one seemed to pay any attention to her. She was very small, probably less than three years old. She had curly golden hair and blue eyes, and though she was dirty and unkempt, to me she looked like a little angel. Whenever I would see her I would spend time with her and carry her around with me. I never knew her name.

Manny's little brother, Aronciu, had big brown eyes and his hair was sun-bleached like his brother's. He was always barefoot. I used to carry him around, and keep him by my side whenever I would play near Isaac's house. I loved holding his dusty little brown feet in my hands.

How strange it was that we children were able to feel love with such intensity in spite of the unspeakable hatred that was directed at us from the outside. With a heart wide open, a child knows how to love totally, but for the same reason it is also vulnerable and fragile and feels deeply the loss of beloved people.

By the time the war was over, I also felt anger and hatred towards an indifferent world with an intensity equal to the love I had for the family and the little friends that were murdered.

Manny, his older brother and his little brother, Aronciu, and the little golden-haired girl, were taken away and murdered during the third Akcja in mid April, 1943.

Now, in my lifetime, in Israel, within that ancient womb of the Jewish people, the miracle of new life is springing forth. I lived to see new generations of Jewish babies being finally born at home, where their fathers and mothers can fight, if need be, to protect them.

Aronciu and the little golden haired girl are still with me when I hold my grandchildren in my arms, dance with them and hear their laughter.

I don't know why I felt so much love for little Aronciu. Later when I was a woman, I would remember that kind of feeling and feel its echo within me, when showering my children and my grandchildren with love. Sometimes, naively, I would even bestow and squander it on strangers who, for whatever reason, did not understand it. And some would even ask me: " Anda, why do you love me so much?"

29

THE ORPHANAGE

In the early spring in 1943, in the ghetto, we were hearing encouraging rumors about the Russian front. People became hopeful that the war might have taken a new course. After the Jews were confined to the ghetto, the big raids had stopped for a few months and we thought that we might soon be liberated because the Russians were fighting back fiercely.

The conditions in the cellar where Mama and Genia were hiding were very difficult, and Mama wanted to be with father, me, and the rest of the family. Soon Mama, Genia, Uncle Moshe and Yosiu left the cellar and crept back into the ghetto one evening, returning with the workers from the grain warehouse.

My parents found a room in a small apartment, which they shared with Mr. and Mrs. Lasser and Mrs. Lasser's brother. The Lasser family lived in the kitchen, and our family lived in the one bedroom. Soon after we moved in, Mrs. Lasser's brother became sick with typhoid. His high fever made him delirious much of the time and, at times, he would lie on his bed in our shared kitchen and expose his naked body.

Cramped as we were, the four of us living in one small room, we also took in an eighteen-year-old girl, Dina, to live with us. She was from a small village. She had the healthy physique of a Polish peasant girl but she spoke only Yiddish. Dina had lost her entire family, and she had no place to stay. Our apartment was located between the Jewish cemetery, on the left, and the ghetto's edge in back and on the right. The cemetery became the "Ghetto Park", where Genia used to take little Andzia for walks, and young couples went on "dates". I did not like to walk there. I was afraid of dead bodies, tombs and ghosts.

Two houses down from us and almost up against the barbed wire fence was a small and dilapidated empty house whose occupants must have been taken away. My mother and uncle Moshe took it upon themselves to turn that small house into an orphanage. Uncle Moshe fixed it up, while my mother and the young girl, Dina, cleaned it. Mama brought food, and together, the three of them gathered up eleven orphaned children and made a home for them. Uncle Moshe put together some bunk beds for the older children, and Dina slept with the little ones. Dina was a big help, keeping the kids clean and the place scrubbed. I spent a lot of time there. I helped with the babies, who needed to be held and fed. A few of the children were as young as one year old and they were malnourished and sick. There was one little girl who cried pitifully every time she had a bowel movement because her rectum protruded way out.

The children had been separated from their parents during raids. Their parents were either killed during the raid or sent to concentration camps. One day, a Gentile nanny brought one little girl back to the ghetto. The woman must have heard about our orphanage; she pushed the child under the barbed-wire fence and then she must have called out to someone to pick her up and bring her into the orphanage.

30

NASCIA

Our old Nanny Nascia

Our nanny Nascia wore a peasant shawl
It could have been a regal mantle
She was noble of heart and rich with love
And her rough callused hands were gentle
Her back was stooped, her shoulders round
Her old face was furrowed and weary
Many a child she had rocked to sleep
And pails full of coal she would carry

She never went to school, she never married
She cleaned, and she served and she children carried
We were her borrowed children
We were her world

When Nascia saw us behind ghetto walls
She reached to touch us, crying
But tears alone were not enough
To give us hope, to save the dying

And as she left she kept looking back
Would she stop and turn around ?
With head low she looked frail and small
Pure love like Nascia's not again to be found

Much has changed since I saw Nascia last
The war has ended and years have passed
If she only knew that Genia and I
Lived to tell our story

I never did go back to my hometown.
Too many are still there, whose hatred I blame
That none were left alive to go home to again
But Genia just told me that she still cries
Whenever she thinks of Nascia

As far back as I can remember, our old nanny Nascia had always been a part of our family. Her formal name was Anastazja Balicka, but no one ever called her by that name; to us she was Nascia.

I remember she was always old; like a statue, she never changed. She even wore the same clothes day in and day out. She wore a big, long black skirt down to her ankles, and a black button-down blouse, and on her head she always wore a black scarf. In winter, she wore a thick woolen-plaid peasant shawl over her shoulders instead of a coat or jacket. Nascia's hair was always pulled back in a tight knot, and she had a big black mole on her face.

Although her life had been difficult, she had a sweet and soft face and her eyes twinkled with a smile. She was like a beloved old family member; she was quiet, intelligent and gentle.

Nascia was a Ukrainian peasant woman. She was illiterate but smart. She never married, and she was totally devoted to our family. She loved my sister Genia more than anything in the world; she lived for her.

Mama used to tell stories about how, sometimes, Nascia would refuse to serve cookies to guests if she thought that Genia would like to eat them. To my mother's embarrassment, she would count the number of guests and serve only one cookie per guest, and then hide the rest for Genia.

She was amazingly intuitive. Throughout the war, when she could no longer stay with us, she would walk from her village on foot and somehow find us by asking around, and she would show up when she felt that Genia was ill and needed her. Here and there she'd still stay with us for a few days, until we were confined to the ghetto and after that we lost all contact with her.

Sometime in the first weeks of April, just before the third Akcja, Nascia made an attempt to find us. She may have gone first to the Rolnik where she knew father would be working, if he were still alive.

I assume she found him at work, and he must have told her that Mama, Genia, and I were still alive and living in the ghetto. He must have also told her where we lived. That same day, we saw Nascia standing near the barb-wire fence of the ghetto. We lived right by the fence, and Mama, Genia and I went out to talk to her. It was a dangerous thing for Nascia to do, to be standing by the fence talking to us. She could have been shot on the spot, but she wanted to see us for herself, still alive.

When she saw us children, especially Genia, she was overcome with emotion. She couldn't stop crying, and I remember that she was literally ringing her hands in despair. Seeing us behind the barbed wire fence, she realized the hopelessness of our situation. She also must have bemoaned her own helplessness to come to our aid.

Genia, who is writing her own memoirs, remembered how Nascia tried to reach through the fence to touch her.

Mama, who, in her desperation, was clinging to "straws," begged her to find a way to save Genia and me, hoping that perhaps Nascia, who was living in her native village with her nephew, Vassyl, would talk to him and then come back to take us children back to her village.

It was out of the question, though, because Nascia knew that Vassyl hated Jews. Nascia was very smart; she knew the mentality of the people she now lived with. The vast majority of the West-Ukrainians living in and around Sambor were rabid anti-Semites from way back. Hitler's propaganda and policies only validated for them and reinforced the centuries old superstitious slander of Jews, who were referred to among our Gentile neighbors as the "Christ killers". To them, the Jews were as evil as the devil himself.

Of course Nascia was different. She could think for herself, and although she was religious and, when she lived with us, she attended the Greek-Orthodox mass daily, she did not harbor even a shred of bad feeling towards anyone. It was dangerous for her to linger around too long near the ghetto. Mama told her to leave. That was the last time I saw Nascia.

Even before she disappeared from the ghetto fence, it felt like an even more impenetrable wall was separating us from our beloved Nascia and her from us. Though we were both still the same, in flesh and blood, in feelings, still trusted friends, we were now being classified under different labels; she was Aryan and we were Jewish. It did not take more than that to divide us into different categories of the human species.

Too often, all it takes are mere labels, mere words from a few evil men who know how to exploit mob mentality to instgate hatred and create walls between people. Anti-Semitic words were exploited for centuries by opportunnists without conscience and allowed slander to take root and fester in the crevices of simplistic, ignorant minds, until they spread like a pestilence. What started as mere words, words of slander, was enough to brand for slaughter a people on the ghetto side of the fences.

Throughout history there were many lies spread and often false social and economic rationalizations given to gullible and dissatisfied people and presented in a manner that in many people's minds justified the persecussion of Jews. This was done against a background of religion-based slander of Jews, as spouted by Christian clerics in Europe for centuries. But why do people so easily believe this slander? What predisposes the human mind to believe viscious lies about a peaceful community? Perhaps people who feel inferior and lack self-respect tend to enlarge themselves by the villanization of others? Creative, productive and self-respecting people take responsibility for their own lives and do not need to make themselves feel more poweful by putting down others.

A few days after Nascia had come to see us, the third Akcja, the Passover Akcja, took place in our ghetto. So many got killed that poor old Nascia must have assumed that she had lost us forever. I'm sure she had no one to share her grief with. She must have died not knowing that her beloved Genia had survived.

31

THE GERMAN ARMY
IN SAMBOR

For the German war effort, Sambor became a central connecting point for the trains that carried troops to and from the Russian front. Because of that, our town was always full of German soldiers and officers. While waiting their turn to go to the front, the soldiers were made available by their commanders to help the local SS town commanders in their murderous task to make Sambor "Judenrein" (cleansed of Jews). During the raids, their military skills were used to surround the ghetto and prevent anyone from escaping. They also helped with rounding up the people, and leading them to the executions or to the trains that took them away to death-camps.

How many still remember Hitler's heroic army? How precisely they goose-stepped on parades. How elegant they were, these sharp looking soldiers and officers with their polished high boots, pressed uniforms and their upward curving visored hats. How arrogant they were, these proud descendants of Wagnerian warriors, when shooting at starving, sickly and helpless old men, women and children. I remember the way they looked then, and the way they looked later on the Russian front at the outskirts of Stalingrad, when I saw them in war documentaries. There, in the Russian winter, they must have shed some of their arrogance, when facing soldiers who had a better cause to fight for. The Nazi armies had fought for a license to kill, but the Russian and the allied soldiers fought to defend their own right to live.

In the documentaries, I saw them in their stiff and tattered green uniforms, as they lay frozen dead in the Russian winter. They too must have had parents who wept for them. Their mothers, wives and children shed for them tears that were not unlike ours. How could one not be touched by human suffering? Surely among them, there must have been many innocent young men whom their nation had sacrificed at the altar of the worst evil in human history.

32

Between
Love and Hate

I'm only vaguely familiar with what Jesus is said to have spoken in his sermons. I think that he was teaching about love and compassion. Yet, there I was, at age ten, drowning in a sea of European Christianity.

While I often point out the many people that actively perpetrated the Holocaust, the many who nodded their heads in approval of Hitler's racial hatred and killings, and the many who acquiesced passively, I know that there were many who were truly sickened by what they saw happening around them. They must have been deeply ashamed that their fellow countrymen were committing acts of racial hatred and violence. I feel sorry for them, because while most forgot and are forgetting, these people did not and do not forget. They carry all the guilt and shame for the Holocaust on their shoulders, although they themselves would have never committed such acts. I have met and befriended Germans who have expressed to me directly and indirectly their inability to reconcile their recent history, with who, they themselves are, at the core of their being. We have shared together tears and hope for healing and enlightenment.

Grzegorz, and his wife Aniela were a humble Ukrainian janitor couple who risked their lives to save my father. They, Madam Maniewska, and our old nanny Nascia were such people. Some of these people were deeply religious Christians. Others were perhaps agnostics or atheists; they were just good people, without sectarian labels. Pope John Paul II was one of these noble people. His conscience spanned the width of the globe, and the depth of its bloody history. Before he died, he took upon his frail shoulders the whole history of Christian anti-Semitism, wanting to heal the scars it left behind. I cried, when I saw pictures of him standing at the Western Wall in Jerusalem, and perhaps even more so because he was a Pole of my generation. He was in Poland during the war.

Even though I consider myself an agnostic, I nevertheless think that we need more spirituality in our lives. If God represents love, compassion and justice, I think that rather than trying to be saved through God, we should make it our task to save God within our own hearts. Good people of faith, or no faith, love equally; they have compassion for their fellow humans and for all living things. Therefore, they can all be united in moral action, even when differing from one another in personal preferences when celebrating holidays and expressing their spirituality. But why are the good people so impotent? Evil allows passion to convert itself, hastily, into destructive action. Does evil inspire more passion and a greater drive to express it than love? Why is it easier to incite people to join and follow those who murder and destroy, rather than to follow, join and support wise, moral and spiritual leaders who want to help create a better society? Good people are slow to act and react. Unfortunately, it often takes only a few to destroy, within seconds, what took many to create over generations.

In all of us there are traces of darkness and confusion, but there are also sparks of goodness, creativity, clarity and intelligence. If only we would each make it our own personal mission to reward, empower, and expand the good within ourselves and within others.

33

THE THIRD AKCJA:
THE PASSOVER MASSACRE

Eleven Orphans

It was April - it was Spring
But I only remember the darkness
And the wailing mothers and children
From the merciless, begging for mercy

Everyone was running losing one another
God in heaven, someone screamed
The children, someone save the children

That early morning in April
Eleven orphans had been left alone
Without fathers to hide and protect them
Without their mothers, so far from home

Where were the neighbors?
Where the loving nannies?
Who once sang to them, rocked them
Kept them clean and fed?
They forgot about the little orphans
Now eleven orphans lay dead

The Christ killers' lives need not be spared
The once loving nannies must have been told
Across the barbed wires they now silently stared
At eleven little bodies so cold

One nanny crawled under the barbed wire wall
And then she ran towards the cemetery gate
And she covered one child with bitter tears
Though she came to her one day too late

One more time she came back
To the child she once loved
She dressed her and a ribbon bright
She tied around the injured head
But nothing could ease this baby's chill
All eleven orphans were dead
"Sweet little Jesus" she whispered
"I could have saved you"

Early, on a Saturday morning, around Passover time, on April 14, 1943, we awoke to gunshots and a sudden commotion. People in the ghetto were calling out to one another in Yiddish: "Jews wake up, everybody get up! We are surrounded. The whole ghetto is surrounded by German soldiers."

We jumped out of bed and looked out the window. Hundreds of German soldiers stood on both sides of the barbed wire fence, inside and outside the ghetto. We lived less than one hundred feet away from that fence and about 100 yards from the cemetery. Right outside our window, which was facing the front, we saw SS officers, with handguns drawn, pacing back and forth in front of our house and shouting orders. Several of them stood under our window, and groups of soldiers were posted at every door to every house, including ours.

There were houses on both sides of us and several houses stood across the yard. All around us, everywhere we looked, there was tumult and panic. We had no time to get away, and in the bedroom where we were, there was no place to hide.

In the nick of time, my father pushed Mama, Genia, me and the Lassers out the kitchen door and through a door in the hallway that led to the attic. We later found out, that after closing the attic door behind us, Father returned to the kitchen and sat down at the table with a cup of tea in one hand and a newspaper in the other. He figured that if the Germans saw him sitting at the table, relaxed and not running away, they would take him and perhaps not look further.

Within minutes, German soldiers pushed the doors to the kitchen open and when they saw Father sitting calmly at the table, they simply told him to get up and immediately join all the others at the cemetery where they were being assembled. Maybe, because he was not running away, nor resisting capture, the Germans did not grab him and take him away at gunpoint. Apparently they confronted him as if they were just passing along their orders to him, one human to another. My father showed neither panic, nor was he pleading for his life. He got up and calmly told the German, "Javol, Herr Officer" and walked out the back and then he hid somewhere outside, under the house.

His strategy to divert attention from us worked for a short time only, but it gave us enough time and a chance to look around the attic and make an attempt to hide. We had not lived there very long and never had any need to go there. I was there once, smoking with my friends. After we ran up the stairs we found an attic that was completely empty. How does one hide in an empty attic?

Someone among us quickly noticed that off to the left there was a small and separate space that jutted out from the main attic. It was the space that was above the front porch and under its small roof. The little attic above our front porch was about six by six feet. The slope of its roof was less inclined than the main roof, and therefore its eves were a bit lower. That space was still totally exposed and it was plainly visible to anyone looking around the attic, especially when standing in front of it or walking past it.

As quickly as was humanly possible, all six of us lay down flat under the eves and remained motionless. We heard a lot of commotion coming from the outside. People were being dragged away amidst curses and angry orders shouted in German, telling people to get out, and to move fast. The shouting voices of the Germans mixed with the cries of children, and the frantic voices of their mothers.

At any moment we could have been discovered, as one German after another came up the stairs to search the attic. We lay there frozen with fear, totally exposed and barely breathing. The fact that they did not find us bordered on the miraculous. They kept facing us, and passing by us, coming and going, shining their flashlights right into our faces; still, they did not see us. At times, they were only a couple feet away from us; had they bent down to look, they would have seen us immediately.

The fact that the attic was empty worked to our advantage. Over and over again, when new search parties came up the stairs with their flashlights, they were shouting to others below, "Da ist Niemand da." (There is no one here). Had there been clutter, like boxes or old furniture to hide behind, they would have had cause to search the attic more thoroughly. But seeing that the attic was empty they did not bother to hang around for long.

Suddenly an urgent problem came up for us. Mr. Lasser, who had been suffering from a bladder problem, had to pee and could hardly control himself any longer. We were afraid that his urine might seep through the few thin boards we were lying on, which made up the ceiling above the entrance porch. We could hear several Germans who were standing on the porch and talking. They were guarding the entrance to the house.

In between the frequent search parties that came up to the attic, I was the one given the task to make a quick run and find an empty bottle, somewhere in the big attic. I was the smallest and I was quick on my feet. There was no time to think, or be scared and hesitate. I was ten and a half and I no longer thought of myself a child. Finding an empty bottle had become a matter of life and death. I can only imagine how anxious and worried Mama must have been that I might be caught while searching the attic for a bottle. In the course of the day, I had to do the search several times, each time returning with a new bottle that I was fortunate to find.

When we ran up to the attic to hide, our neighbors, who had lived in an identical house to the left of us, apparently had the same last minute idea. They also ended up hiding above their porch; there we few options to choose from. They too were lying on top of the thin ceiling to their porch, which was about thirty feet from ours, but their attic was separate, with separate stairs leading to it, and on top did not connect to ours.

Suddenly, we heard a shot; it came from below. One German,

who was standing on the neighboring porch, shot his gun in the air just for the hell of it. The bullet passed right through the thin ceiling and hit one neighbor in the shoulder.

Our neighbor took the bullet in total silence. He did not cry out, in fact, he did not even make a sound. Neither did anyone else who was with him. Somehow they managed to control the bleeding so that the blood would not seep through the gaps in the boards and drip onto the porch below where the German soldiers were standing.

The raid lasted for many hours. Later we found out that during the time we were hiding in the attic, twelve hundred people were caught. At first they were herded together at the cemetery, near our house. Then all that could walk were marched to the prison in town, under the guard of the SS, the soldiers, and the many police dogs they used during the raids.

After the Germans had led their victims out, and all the soldiers had left, an eerie silence befell the ghetto. Then, slowly and cautiously, people started to emerge from their hiding places, walking about dazed and frantically looking for their missing loved ones. They searched for them at the cemetery, among those who were shot during the raid. Some people found each other still alive.

Father came up to the attic, looking for us. We crawled out from under the eves, went downstairs and stepped outside. The courtyard, which was usually full of people and children, was deserted and deathly quiet. We ran down to the orphanage and saw that it was empty. All the children, and Dina, were gone. The poor children had been roused from sleep only to be plunged into a nightmare, from which they would never awaken.

People returning from the cemetery had told us that they saw our eleven orphans there. They had each been shot and left lying on the cemetery grounds. My cousin Yosiu, who was almost fourteen at the time, also went to the cemetery immediately after the Akcja and saw them lying there. The scene was gruesome, the children's small heads were perforated by bullets, ear to ear. I heard someone say that the children had been used for target practice.

Only a few days earlier, a Polish woman had left a little girl at our orphanage. The barbed wire fence was about five feet from the small orphanage house. The woman had been the child's former nanny and was hiding the two-year-old girl. One day, she decided to bring the child back into to the ghetto. The child's parents had already been taken away in a previous raid. Perhaps the woman thought that no one would be there to reward her for hiding the child, as she may have been promised.

She must have heard about the raid and may have been concerned about the child. In the evening, after the raid, she came up to the barbed wire fence, talked to someone and found out what had happened to the orphanage and the child that she had once cared for. Later that night she returned once more and this time she crawled under the fence and came into the ghetto. She found the child in the cemetery lying on the ground with the others.

She washed the child, combed her hair, dressed her up and cried bitterly. People who saw her at the cemetery came to tell us about it, as the Lassers listened anxiously and with concerned interest. The Lassers must have found that story particularly distressing, because a Gentile woman outside the ghetto was also entrusted with hiding their infant daughter.

Although, after the earlier raids people were shipped to concentration camps; in the two most recent raids they were shot and buried locally. The people that were caught in the Saturday raid were held over in the local prison without food or water- to weaken them, until their execution which took place the following Wednesday, five days later. The prison guards were mostly Ukrainian police. On Monday, two days after the raid, we saw a truckload of Ukrainians with shovels arriving at the cemetery. They started to dig a pit and then they came back on Tuesday to finish the job. By the time they had finished, the pit was huge. Coming and going, the men riding in the truck were singing.

It became obvious that the mass grave that had been dug was being readied for the people who had been caught during the Akcja.

Who among us, living in our homes, in relative safety, somewhere in the free western world, could ever comprehend the impotence and the helplessness of the fathers, mothers, husbands, and wives of the twelve-hundred people trapped in that jail, marked and destined to fill that pit in the ghetto cemetery? In the ghetto, we were isolated and without any communication with the outside world; not that anyone in the world would have necessarily been jumping to their feet to help us. The men in the ghetto, my father and uncles among them, would have given anything to be able to get hold of some weapons to defend their families with. Other than through our Gentile neighbors outside the ghetto, there was no way. But it seemed that they too wanted to get rid of us. At best, they ignored that part of town, the fenced-in Blich-ghetto area, and acted as if we were no more than rats in a cage.

At Isaac's place at the Blich house there was a hiding place built for the people who lived there. The underground bunker had been built just several weeks earlier, just in time for them to hide during the latest Akcja. The residents of the house had gotten together and hired an engineer to advise them on its construction, so that it would not collapse on top of them. The men who lived there did the work. It took some ingenuity to accomplish it, because the people in the ghetto did not have access to tools and building materials and they had to improvise. The construction of the bunker had to be done in secret and at night. The hiding place had to be kept secret because there were too many desperate people who had no place to escape to and hide and they would have forced their way in, at the last minute. Desperate to survive, they surely would have either overcrowded or displaced the people who built the bunker and ultimately, all would have perished.

From within the cellar of the Blich house, to the right of the wooden cellar steps, the men dug a bunker under the yard where the idle horse wagon stood. The space they created was only about three feet high. One could only crawl there or sit on the damp ground. The ground above the bunker was held up with wooden boards and some short make-shift posts. After digging under the front yard, the earth needed to be disposed of and that too had to be done in secret. The access to the bunker was a small opening that was about two and a half feet wide, one and a half feet high, and it was close to the ground. That opening could be shut from the inside in such a way that its cover would look like the rest of the earthen cellar wall. It had to fit exactly and seamlessly. When replaced, it concealed the opening completely.

On Wednesday morning, the day of the execution, it appeared that another raid might follow immediately and more people would be rounded up. Since we did not have a hiding place, and were living close to the cemetery and the ghetto fence, we were easy prey. We decided to run to Isaac's house and hide together with them. We got there just in time to crawl into the bunker with the others, before the shooting in the cemetery started. The cemetery was less than a mile away from Isaac's house.

The executions had begun around noon and went on, without stopping, until sunset. By evening, twelve hundred people, men, women and children had been murdered. Before they were shot, the people were made to strip naked. Their clothes were later collected and removed in truckloads by the Ukrainian helpers. We stayed in the bunker till night, having sat in the same position the whole day.

Among those killed during the Passover raid was Rabbi Tversky's whole family, including his wife. The Rebbi himself had not been caught this time; he must have been hiding in a separate place. He was caught and killed two months later.

Among the victims were my mother's close friend, Mrs. Zenft and her ten-year-old son, Tolek. Before the war, the Zenfts were among the richest people in our town. They owned factories and had an estate-like home on Ulica Lvovska, near the English Park.

Among the victims must have also been the little, golden-haired girl, and little Aronciu with his two older brothers, because after the third Akcja and the execution in the cemetery, they were gone and I never saw them again.

Shortly after that execution, Mr. Zenft, who had lost his young wife and his only son, came to us to share his grief. Tearfully, he told my parents, that the night before he had a dream about his wife in which she asked him to go to the cemetery and cover her blood with earth. In the morning, when he got to the cemetery, he found a puddle of blood where she had told him to look for it.

On several occasions, my mother tried to find out from the Lassers where their child was being hidden. She told them that, in case she were the only one to survive the war, she would make sure that the child would be cared for. Nevertheless, the Lassers would not tell anyone; they kept it a secret.

The Lassers had once told us that during an earlier raid, as the Germans barged in on them early in the morning, they had barely managed to slip under their bed and hide, while their infant was still in her crib a few feet away. They overheard one SS man telling another, in German, to leave that child alone because it was too beautiful to be killed. Both Mr. and Mrs. Lasser were light blond and blue-eyed people, and the child must have also been fair. This one time, I suppose, the German saw a child he could relate to. Apparently he saw only an Aryan looking baby as human, and worthy of life.

The Lassers were killed two months later, soon after I had left the ghetto to go into hiding. No one knows what happened to their baby.

After the war, some Jewish organizations were active in bringing these Jewish orphans that had been hidden by Gentiles back into the Jewish community. It was a difficult task, as many of the children were very young when they were separated from their parents and did not remember them. Often, the adoptive parents did not want to come forward and give the children up or tell them the truth about their Jewish identity. I knew of three such cases. In early 1946, a woman and her eight-year old niece were staying overnight at our place in Munich. After liberation from the Nazis, while looking for surviving relatives, her search led her to her little niece. The woman found that the child was living on a remote farm with a Polish peasant family. She had a hard time reclaiming her.

I listened in, as the child's aunt was telling my mother the story. The child had great problems readjusting to living away from the peasant family, which was the only family she remembered. First she was torn away from her family to go live on the farm, and then, after being with the peasants for four out of her eight years, an aunt she did not remember came to take her away. She did not want to go with her aunt, even though the primitive and Jew-hating peasants beat her often and made her work like a slave, even though she was still a child.

At night in my room, I watched the girl kneeling by the bedside and crossing herself in prayer. She continued to do so, even though she had been away from the Gentile family for some time already and had been told about her real parents. Her aunt was patient and loving, but the girl kept angrily denying everything that her aunt had told her.

The fact that she had been raised to believe in Jesus was not the harmful issue. Rather, it was that she had did not have guidance and care from good people. It was the poison of blatant "Jew hating" that she was imbued with, at such an early age and that was deplorable. She was perhaps too young to understand the irony, that the poison she learned from the peasants had also murdered her very own parents. The child had been thoroughly indoctrinated to hate everything Jewish. Considering the primitive nature of the stepparents, to say "infected" might be more accurate. The girl spoke to me about her bitter hatred towards all Jews and especially towards her aunt. She left with her aunt the next morning and I did not hear from them again. Then in 1976 I heard that she was happily married, orthodox and was living in Toronto.

In some cases, a Gentile family did not even know that they were adopting a Jewish child. Sometimes the child was placed by a well meaning intermediary. I personally know of a Ukrainian priest, who was a good man and saved the life of one of my girlfriends in this manner. In this case too, the adoptive parents frequently voiced their Jew-hating views. After the liberation, the girl heard them say that it was too bad that so many Jewish bastards had survived. Eventually my friend escaped from them.

34

ESCAPING
FROM THE GHETTO

Lilacs Make Me Cry

When my favorite flower you asked to know
I remembered spring and melting snow
And the birds flying north
And the wonder in a child's heart
When in gardens of purple lilacs
I heard lovers whisper in the night

Now, spring has come this year
Rekindling childlike wonder
In a heart scarred by fear
Before me a barren landscape awakens
And your breath upon my cheek
Speaks to me of purple lilacs

Some day soon when we'll embrace
Unto my arms perhaps you'll place
A bouquet of my favorite flowers

Wait, dear friend, wait
Don't bring me lilacs yet
The night is late and we've just met

How can I tell you why
Each spring lilacs make me cry
Though I can't wait to see them

When I find them in the florist's tubs
Lilacs fill my vases, my garden shrubs
I press them against my face
Still, I see them from afar
A child in cellar dark
Longing for sunlit gardens!

Dear friend, don't bring me lilacs yet
Let's you and I run in magic meadows
Where spring suns shine
But cast no shadows

On a bright spring day in April 1943, I escaped from the ghetto and went into hiding in the cellar that my father and his brother Moshe prepared for us outside the ghetto walls. It was the same cellar where Mama and Genia were hiding when I went to live with the Tomszajs.

Leaving the ghetto, I left behind my beloved family, grandfather, aunts, uncles and cousins at the Blich house, and all the other people, who were desperately trapped behind a barbed wire fence. I also left behind spring, trees, and the sky, and entered a dark, musty and rat infested dungeon. A trap door closed behind me, shutting the world out of my life for the next sixteen months. Outside, lilacs and jasmine were in full bloom, and the radiant beauty of that spring day somehow underscored the reality of our death sentence. On such a day, the ugly brutality of our executioners seemed out of place. Once outside the ghetto, on the way to the cellar, I saw carefree Gentile children, Polish and Ukrainian boys and girls my age, playing outside under a bright blue spring sky.

At a time when the earth was awakening and sprouting new life, the people trapped in the ghetto knew that their life was coming to an end. After the third Akcja, the Germans were stepping up the raids and in between, they were catching people in the streets and in their homes to fill their quotas for extermination. Those who had a place to go outside the barbed-wire fences took steps to escape. Few had that option, and many who got out were caught and shot.

Though we considered ourselves fortunate and grateful for having a hiding place like the cellar, the sharp contrast between the beauty of the blooming gardens and balmy air and the moldy dampness in our dark underground burrows was hard to bear.

I escaped right after the third Akcja. Shlomek Freiman, a young man who worked with my father and knew him from before the war, came for me one day to take me out of the ghetto. He had special work papers for himself, that allowed him to leave the ghetto to go to work. I don't know what papers or bribes he needed to give the guards at the gate to make them let me out. He may have had a note that I needed to see a doctor.

On the way to the gate, I asked him if we could stop off at Isaac's house so that I could say goodbye to my family. He told me that I was not supposed to say goodbye and let anyone know that I was leaving the ghetto, or where I was going. Hiding places were kept very secret. Later it turned out that several people entered our cellar during the liquidation of the ghetto, risking getting us all killed.

Little did I know that that would be the last time I would see my family at the Blich house. Shlomek let me see family and then as I was walking away, little Andzia ran after me. She grabbed my hand and would not let go. She begged me to let her come along with me, saying: "take me with you, please take me with you".

I adored that child; she was my youngest cousin, and had lived with us since the day she was born. I have since spent all these years agonizing over that scene and reproaching myself for letting go of her hand. Why did I not take her with me? Knowing that at the time I was only ten years old and could not have made such a serious decision does not help. She and her mother, aunt Laika, were scheduled to join me a few weeks later, but on that day the final Akcja took place in the ghetto and I never saw them again.

After getting past the guard gate, it felt strange to be on the other side of the ghetto fence. I was nervous and terrified like small prey about to be devoured by wild beasts. Shlomek wore a white armband with a blue Star of David; I did not, because in our ghetto children under twelve were not required to. I walked a few paces behind Shlomek. I, a small girl with two long pigtails, looked no different from the girls my age outside the ghetto, and I tried not to draw attention.

We crossed the small bridge near the mill, walked up the cobble stone steps where Dvorka's candy store used to be, and headed towards Przemyska Street. Finally we got to a large building in the middle of town; it was a warehouse. The warehouse workers had already left for the day. Shlomek opened the door to the attic, knocked three times on the third step from the bottom and said in Polish "twenty-five-six", which was our password. The third step was removed, and I followed Shlomek into the dark tunnel ahead, sliding down on my backside. Soon I found myself in our cellar, the mysterious catacomb that was to become my new home.

I think that I felt relief to have gotten there safely, the same kind of relief I felt during each raid when I would reach a place I could hide in. But this time it felt like I was crawling into a safe cocoon, where I could put my anxiety on hold and rest and hibernate for a while. Everything outside the cellar was no longer my world. The outside world had excluded me from its life.

When I got to the cellar, most of the crucial work to make the cellar somewhat habitable had been already accomplished. Several people who did most of the work were already there: uncle Moshe, cousin Yosiu, Luzer Weizengreen, and Arco Velker. Arco's sister, Mrs. Dachinger and four people from the Teicher family were also there. My sister Genia was to join me a few days later.

A few days after I escaped from the ghetto, Uncle Mendel was seized in the street outside his house. The Germans needed a few more Jews to complete a quota for the transport to concentration camps and they came into the ghetto and grabbed who ever they could. Watching through the window his son Motek saw one of the Germans strike his father and ran outside to defend him and so he was also taken away, while his mother and sister helplessly watched through the window.

Just then, cousin Zelig and his brother, Cousin Muniu Salomon, happened to be passing by. When Zelig and Muniu saw the Germans grab Mendel and Motek, they panicked and ran to Uncle Benjamin's place, which was across from Mendel's house.

The Germans followed them, and in addition to Mendel and Motek, they took Zelig, Muniu, Uncle Benjamin, as well as several other people they found in Benjamin's house. All caught were taken to the Janowska concentration camp in Lvov, where they were killed*.

In the ghetto, I used to sometimes see Motek huddling in the long dark hallway in uncle Isaac's house, with a beautiful girl with long red hair and freckles. The girl must have died together with Motek's mother Regina during the liquidation of the ghetto. Motek's sister, White Genia, the only one out of the family of four to have survived, was hiding in the cellar where I was.

---

*Read the book Janovska Road, written by Leon Weliczker Wells, one of the few inmates who survived the camp. In the book, he described the atrocities that took place in that extermination camp.

35

THE FOURTH AKCJA

On May 22, 1943, the fourth Akcja took place. In the fourth Akcja over one thousand people were caught and taken to the Belzec Extermination camp. Among them was Uncle Benjamin's eleven-year-old daughter, also named Genia. She was the youngest Genia in the family. She too was supposed to join me in the cellar. Heartbroken, her mother Aunt Regina came into the cellar by herself to join her son Yosiu. Her husband, Uncle Benjamin, had been sent to the Janovska death camp only a short time before this latest raid. During the fourth Akcja Uncle Yankiev-Leib and his wife Ryfcia lost all three of their children, nineteen year old Aaron, fourteen year old son Mayer, and their twenty-two year old daughter Genia. Thus, the youngest and oldest Genia in the family were taken away together.

In the ghetto, Benjamin and Yankiev–Leib's families lived together in the apartment house across from their brother Mendel. The residents of the apartment house got together and created two bunkers that they could hide in during raids. The one deemed better and safer was designated for all the children of the apartment house, the more vulnerable one was for their parents and grandparents. Among the tenants of the house was a couple who had two sons. I can't recall their names. The younger one, whose face I remember clearly, was about fourteen. The older son, who may have been eighteen, was a Kapo.

In the last minute before the fourth Akcja began, wanting to improve their children's chances of survival, the residents of the house decided to putt the Kapo's parents in the children's bunker. They were hoping that their young son, the Kapo, would watch over them and try to deflect the German's attention from their bunker. During the raid, when the Germans entered the apartment house and found it deserted, they proceeded to search extensively for the hidden residents.

The young Kapo panicked and made a tragic mistake. Apparently he was not aware of the last minute switch. Assuming that his parents were hidden together with all the adults of the house, and desperately wanting to save them, he panicked and deflected the Germans' attention from the adults' bunker, making the one full of children more vulnerable. And so, the Germans found the "wrong bunker", the one in which his family and all the children were hiding. Satisfied that people were found, they did not search any further. The adult residents of the apartment house were saved, but they all lost their children. The children and the Kapo's parents were shipped to Belzec, where they were killed. The young Kapo himself did not survive. I wonder if he had joined his family by choice.

In normal times, unfortunate things happen; a family sometimes loses a child in an accident, through illness, on the battlefield or through homicide. Usually the neighbors gather around them to console them and offer their support. In that community, all the parents lost all their children at the same time. There can be no greater pain than the pain of surviving one's own children. That day, the tragedy that befell that apartment house reverberated between its residents to an unbearable crescendo of pain.

To my knowledge, most of the parents of these children perished less than one month later, during the final liquidation of the ghetto. Only Aunt Regina and Uncle Yankiev-Leib and his wife Ryfcia survived. They survived the war to live on for many years in perpetual mourning for their children until the day they died. Ryfcia spent her days caring for wounded Israeli soldiers in hospitals, saying, often, that these were her children now. Aunt Regina also moved to Israel in 1948. There, like many of her fellow survivors, she mysteriously transformed much of her pain into an amazing capacity to love. She showered that love on all that knew her, but especially on her grandchildren Benny and Michal and her niece Yaffa and White Genia's daughter, Renia. When I visited her in 1954, she prepared for me special dishes and in the morning, I caught her washing my clothes by hand. When

I protested, she said to me, "Child, I'd bring down the moon for you, if I could" and I believed her.

Immediately after the fourth Akcja, Mama, Aunt Regina, and a few other people fled the ghetto and joined us in the cellar.

Aunt Regina and her grandson,
Yosiu's son Benny, in Israel (1970)

36

THE END OF
THE SAMBOR GHETTO

The final Akcja took place on June 5, 1943. Four days later, the last three thousand Jews were executed in the Radlovice forest.

After Mama, Genia, and I had left the ghetto, Father moved back to Isaac's small place. He did not plan on joining us in our cellar. He would not abandon the family that was still in the ghetto and for whom there was not enough room in our cellar, and he would not abandon his beloved old Rabbi Tversky.

The liquidation of the Sambor ghetto started early morning on Saturday, June 5, 1943.

The day before, on the fourth of June 1943, the head of the "Judenrat", Dr. Schneitcher, had some, supposedly good news to report to the Jews in the ghetto. He told them that several of their representatives had traveled to the town of Drohobycz and they had just returned. The SS at the headquarters in Drohobycz had apparently made a deal with them.

In return for bringing gold jewelry and other valuables to hand over to the SS commandant at the headquarters, the Judenrat was given guarantees that no new quotas of people for deportation would need to be met and the ghetto would remain safe. In his talk to the people in the ghetto, Dr. Schneitcher expressed optimism; so much, that for the first time in many months, people undressed to go to sleep. Having been reassured by the Judenrat leader, they felt some relief from the constant state of anxiety in which they were living all the time. They wanted to believe him. Encouraging rumors about the Russian and

Allied front gave people hope that the nightmare would soon be over.

Apparently the Germans had also told the Judenrat members to get their families out of the ghetto immediately and bring them to a place where they would be transported to a labor camp in Drohobycz, where they would be safe and would receive favorable treatment. Late Friday night, after everyone went to sleep, the Judenrat leaders secretly snuck their families out of the ghetto, expecting to be transported to Drohobycz.

On the way to Drohobycz all the Judenrat members and their families were shot. Ironically, the betrayers had themselves been betrayed. They were the first to perish in the liquidation of the ghetto.

That same night, at 3 a.m., the German army suddenly surrounded the ghetto on the outside of the barbed-wire fences. Hundreds of soldiers then entered the ghetto and surrounded each house to make hiding or escaping impossible. The operation was based not only on a cunning deception, but it was planned so well, that within a short time, the whole ghetto was flooded with German soldiers, SS commandos, and their Ukrainian helpers. In the past, there were usually some warning signs before such raids. Someone would spot empty railroad cars at the train station or see some unusual activity and some information would leak through from the outside; but this raid was so unexpected that no one had time to go into hiding. Within minutes, total chaos erupted in the ghetto. Witnesses described the smiles on the faces of the German soldiers who apparently enjoyed watching the panic among the trapped and desperate people*.

Although there was a well-constructed bunker in Uncle Isaac's cellar, and even though the entrance to the cellar was less than ten steps from Isaac's kitchen door, there was not enough time to get to it before the Germans appeared at everyone's door. Everyone in the Blich house was caught immediately.

In the sudden commotion that ensued, when the German soldiers entered the house, rousing everyone from sleep, Isaac's fourteen-year old son, Bunek slipped under the bed, trying to hide. Father later told us that, while being led away with the oth-

---

*From the book: "Sambor"

ers, he heard Bunek, crying and pleading for his life, when a German soldier found him hiding under the bed and was forcibly pulling him out.

In one fell swoop, they took my whole family in the Blich house: Isaac, Dvorka, Big Andzia, Bunek, Zosia, Chaim, Laika, little Andzia, my ailing grandfather Yanche. My father was taken too.

Escorted under heavy army guard, the people taken from all the houses were first herded into the Jewish cemetery. By evening, when the SS commando thought that they had gotten every last Jew, the people were taken on foot from the cemetery out through the ghetto gate and across the bridge over the Mlynowka River on the march to the jail on Drohobycka Street.

Just as the group of captured people was crossing the bridge, my father suddenly broke away and jumped into the Mlynowka River. The German guards heard him hit the water and started shooting at him with a barrage of dum-dum bullets. Those were the kind of bullets that were used on the Jewish victims. After impact, these bullets explode violently into many fragments within the victim's body.

Miraculously the bullets missed him, as he remained submerged; breathing through a reed, he hid among the tall reeds in the river. After some time, the Germans assumed that they had shot him dead and the group moved on. The river was not very deep so my father lay motionless at the bottom of the murky water, breathing through a reed. He stayed that way until late at night. I don't know how many other people tried to escape by jumping into the river and how many were hit and died there. Later, it turned out that Uncle Isaac and another man had also managed to escape in the same manner, when their turn came to cross the bridge.

After lying still in the river for hours, my father got out of the river in the middle of the night. By that time, it had already been twenty-four grueling hours since the start of the raid. He got out on the side that bordered the big field of the market place and crawled through the muddy and manure-strewn field on all fours, where the farmers had held their market, just two days ago. While crawling in the field, Father found Uncle Isaac and the other man with him, also crawling on all fours. The three men had to hurry and get off the empty and highly visible marker area and reach a hiding place before dawn.

Father decided against joining us in our cellar. He would not risk the lives of his wife and children and the many other people who were hiding with us there. He remembered that his oldest brother, Yankiev Leib, was hiding out at the home of Grzegorz, the pharmacy janitor, and he chose to go there.

Isaac and the other man decided to head towards the forest, where they were hoping to find Polish partisans and join them in their fight against the Nazis. It was still dark and the two men made it to the forest. Just before dawn, they came across the partisans.

What followed was the result of such deep-rooted hatred which the Poles bore towards their Jewish fellow citizens that it boggles the mind. The Polish partisans shot and killed Uncle Isaac. They said that they did not want a Jew in their midst.

In his youth, Uncle Isaac had served in the Polish army. He would have gladly fought with partisans against a common enemy.

The man who had escaped with Isaac did not look Semitic. He passed himself off as a Gentile Pole. Having to watch himself at all times, he survived and fought along side the partisans. He had known our family well from before the war. After we were liberated, he found us and told us how Isaac was killed.

The partisans could have saved hundreds, if not thousands of young Jewish men and women who had wanted desperately to defend themselves and fight along side them for their country of birth.

In January 1943, attempts were made in the ghetto to acquire weapons and organize an underground resistance movement. The Jews desperately wanted to defend themselves, even if that would have been a fight to the death.

According to the personal accounts documented in the book, "Sambor", they were betrayed by a Polish man. The ammunition was found and taken away and the people who were hiding it were executed.

Here and there, I hear that the Polish people in Warsaw were different, that they helped the Jews during the Warsaw ghetto uprising by selling them guns. This still begs the simple question, why would the Poles living on the outside sell and not give the guns to the destitute ghetto people?

I'm sure, many were helpful somewhere in Poland or the Ukraine. I'm sure that there are still many Polish, Ukrainian, and German unsung heroes, people with a heart, a conscience and the courage to live and act accordingly.

My parents and I knew only of a few such people in our town of over thirty thousand. In the book, "Sambor," some people mentioned a few other local people that risked their lives to help them. I knew of two cases in which two Ukrainian policemen, who were collaborators, rescued two very desperate women who happened to be young and very pretty. They were rescued without their families. I knew the two women personally. After the liberation, the women ran away from the Ukrainian men because they had been abused by them and were scared of them. All the collaborating Ukrainian policemen were brutal murderers. In our town, they actively participated in all the raids and the brutal treatment of the victims while they were being held over in the fields and the jail, and they participated in the executions.

I knew of a case in Sambor, where the Gentile maid who had worked for a Jewish family had also been the husband's lover, even before the war. Being Gentile, she was able to save the man together with his wife and their two children. These people had been relatives of the Schneiders, and I knew one of the children, a boy, who was about my age. When I saw them soon after liberation I knew that they all still continued living together; the maid was visibly pregnant. The man did not abandon his family to save himself, nor did he abandon the pregnant woman who saved him and his family. I don't think that among the few survivors in our town, they were judged. In that union, a wife's jealousy must have given way to gratitude and acceptance, and the other woman's love for a man went beyond her own interests and expanded into compassion for his wife and his children. Even at the young age of twelve, after liberation, I understood life from a more mature perspective. To me there was something very touching about that family unit; it seemed extraordinarily humane.

37

RADLOVICE

New York, June 9, 1943
The show, "Oklahoma" opened on Broadway with the song, "Oh What a Beautiful Morning".

Radlovice, Poland ----June 9, Shavuot 1943

Did you ever hear of Radlovice?
But how could you?
Not even God knew of it

Radlovice is a forest near Sambor
Each spring, the few who know its story
Pity the trees and the flowers that grow there

Radlovice is a forest and a grave
It's a memory, a stifled pain, a tale not told
It's a silent scream, it's a smoldering fire
That could a conscience forge

Its history not yet understood
Is tainted already by ignorance
Political platitudes, words irrelevant
And truth-distorting, words profane

On this bright day of spring and budding trees
Filled with song and calls of mating birds
On this day, I will talk to you my children

Radlovice

About Radlovice when I was a child
When I heard the sounds of three thousand bullets
And engraved upon my heart so young the fate
Of three thousand people- some families still whole
People old, children young and babies small
Cradled in their parent's trembling arms
As they all stood there on that day in the forest

And I engraved upon my heart the terror
They must have felt as they stood there naked
At the edge of a pit in Radlovice
Forsaken and forgotten by God
And all the good people far and near

Injured, starved, emaciated
Facing uniforms, guns and curses
Did they try to fight?
Did they run or call for help?
Their neighbors locked their hearts and doors
And called them Christ killers

By evening of next day
The shooting stopped, time stopped
Thinking stopped and somewhere beyond
The pain of violated love and helpless hate
Our hearts and tears would turn to stone

In voices hushed and hollow
Peasants must have talked about their earth
That heaved and groaned for days
And about the screams in the forest
That still cling to its silence

Radlovice is a forest, a black hole
It swallowed my family, three thousand people
It swallowed their sun, their stars, their sky
And perhaps their God and mine

Middle Andzia

Its black rays are like a widow's veil
They make me shun all those
Who mix ignorance with anger
And those who speak lightly of hatred

Talk to me about a God of love and mercy
And I will tell you how it felt to live that day

For those who have not been there
How can I translate pain into words?
That they may feel and understand?
That day was Shavuot - it was a day
When God gave Israel the light of the Torah
To bring forth dignity to mankind
Through justice, mercy, and love

Once, the bright sounds of church bells
Used to mark off the hours of my childhood
But were they meant to do and say more?

One day they turned empty, shrill and ugly
Louder than church bells and pious sermons
Louder were our cries for help
But our Gentile neighbors missed
Their Prophet's message of love
And even turned it into hate

"Damn you all, forever, damn you!"
My scream joined the cries of the dying
On that last day of my childhood
And I was also stripped naked
Of faith, illusions, aspirations and hope
Who is created in the image of God?
Who? The killer, or his victim?
Or is it the one who idly stands by?

Radlovice

On that day on Shavuot in 1943
Did my beloved God man the guns?
Or did he die three thousand times?

A dark chapter in the history of mankind
Lies on the path from our noble heritage
Towards a destiny it may yet define

Once upon a time in Christian Europe's shadows
Were rich green forests and clover –covered meadows
And old medieval towns I used to love
Now they are stained with Europe's shame
And yes, sanctified at once, with innocent blood

To you my children I pass on this history
So that in your hearts and in those you teach
You may transform it not into bitterness
But into love and wisdom

Value life
Your own and other's
But don't ignore evil
And know your history

This spring when you are free
Free to hike and laugh in forests
Be grateful
Be proud to be a good human
Be aware

38

THE ROAD
TO RADLOVICE

On Saturday evening, June 4, 1943, all the people who were caught during the liquidation of the Sambor ghetto that had begun at three a.m. that morning were led by German guards over the bridge across the Mlynovka River and to the prison on Drohobycka Street. The Germans shoved all three thousand people into the few cells that were there and kept them there for four more days without food, water, or toilet facilities. Later, a Gentile witness who had worked there (as recounted in the book: Sambor) recounted the horror stories about the sub-human conditions at the jail and the groans and wailing coming from the jam-packed cells. The guards told the caged people that pits were being dug for them in the forest of Radlovice. Was it to taunt them, or to assure them that their suffering would soon be over?

Weakened and dehumanized, the people were loaded onto trucks with armed guards positioned on each corner of each truck. It was the morning of June ninth, 1943, the first day of Shavuot. The trucks headed to the forest in Radlovice. There, the people were made to strip naked and one, by one, they were machine-gunned into the two mass graves, some dead and some injured and still alive.

The same witness, a Pole, later told that the German SS Officer in charge of the mass execution in Radlovice, upon his return to Sambor went insane.

For one week after the executions, the local farmers of Radlovice stopped bringing their wares to the markets in Sambor, they would not cross the forest for the sounds of moans coming from the earth. Years later, the local peasants told of the earth above the two mass graves that was still moving for days after the executions. No one came to help the tortured people to live or die.

During the massacre every person living in Sambor was close enough to Radlovice to hear every shot of the never-ending staccato of machine guns.

I, a child of ten, frozen with fear, also heard all the shots. Thick cellar walls and walls of German soldiers and hostile local people separated me from Radlovice. I did not pierce them and run to Radlovice to claw the earth with my hands and nails. And no amount of logic can change the fact that to this day that makes me cry and feel that I should have done something other than crouch in the corner of a cellar and cry.

I felt like I betrayed my slaughtered family. I not only felt guilty that I got away and did not stay with them to share their lot, but I also felt that surviving without them would be too painful to be worth while. Why struggle to survive, to live in a world that allowed such a Holocaust to happen?

Utterly overcome by grief we sat in the cellar crying together for weeks, until our eyes and faces were swollen. We were prisoners in a forsaken dungeon, helplessly witnessing the slaughter of our loved ones and bitterly feeling our impotence to do anything about it.

Then, as it is with all people in mourning, after a while our grief turned into numbness. In that state of numbness not only could we not think about a future without our loved ones, but also, it mattered little how we lived.

Six days after the liquidation, the ghetto was still surrounded by the German army day and night, and at night it was lit up with searchlights and reflectors. Soldiers were also guarding exits from sewers that led from the ghetto to the outside. Many who tried that exit returned back into the ghetto. Some tried to hide crawling up the chimneys of baking ovens, some in the pits under outhouses.

Some tried to hide inside graves in the cemetery. On June 23, 1943, one hundred Jews were found hiding inside tombs in the Jewish cemetery; they were shot right there on the same day. On July 6, 1943, forty more were found and executed. On July 22 another twenty five were found and executed.

Out of eight to nine thousand Jews who had once lived in Sambor only a few hundred escaped, but ultimately less than one hundred survived the German occupation.

Survivors find the mass grave at Radlovice

39

GRZEGORZ
AND ANIELA

"Abaye said: In each generation the world must contain at least thirty six righteous people who see the divine presence clearly. For it is written, " Blessed are all they that wait for Him (in Hebrew Lo); the numerical value of Lo is thirty-six...."

Talmud-Mas. Sanhedrin 97b

Hours past midnight, on the night he emerged from the river and crawled across the market place, Father got to the shack where Grzegorz and Aniela lived. Uncle Yankiev-Leib and his wife, Ryfcia were already hiding there.

When he heard the neighborhood dogs barking, he threw himself over the fence. Grzegorz and his wife Aniela opened the door and without saying a word or a moment's hesitation, they took him in. He was wet and covered with mud and horse manure. I can only imagine his state of mind, after having lived through the brutal liquidation raid and having watched his family, his revered Rebbi, his friends, and all the remaining Jews of his town, young and old, being led to slaughter.

Grzegorz (Gregory) and Aniela (Angela) were a Ukrainian couple who worked as janitors and caretakers at the pharmacy near the big Catholic Church. They lived in an adjoining one-room shack. Their place was small and primitive. They were poor and simple people; they never had children, and they were devout Christians. After their children were taken away, Uncle Yankiev–Leib and Ryfcia turned to them, and Grzegorz and Aniela offered to take them in and save them. They were still hoping that their children, being young, strong, and able to work, would stand a chance to survive the camps where they were taken.

Yankiev–Leib and Ryfcia had known Grzegorz and Aniela from before the war. Aniela used to help with the cleaning in their house. Grzegorz was a poor man; he swept floors and sidewalks for a living. Their means were very limited. Their tiny shack was highly visible because it was attached to the busy pharmacy on one side, and bordered the church courtyard on the other. On Sundays and during funerals the church and its courtyard were always full of people. The pharmacy was in the middle of Drohobycka Street.

By offering to save Yankiev-Leib and Ryfcia, Grzegorz and Aniela put their lives at risk. Harboring Jews was punishable by death. Living in one room, they were also personally inconvenienced. Above all, they had to take great care that the owners of the pharmacy or their other employees did not find out that Jews were being harbored next door. Grzegorz and Aniela had a small fenced garden in which there was a small, narrow, tool shed-maybe big enough for three people to sit close to each other.

After the fourth Akcja, having nothing more to lose, Yankiev –Leib and Ryfcia snuck out of the ghetto and managed to get to Grzegorz' place without being seen. Grzegorz and Aniela hid them as best they could. Most of the time, they lived in the garden shed, even in winter, when it was bitter cold. As often as it was possible, when no one was around, they would let them sneak into their one room home.

My father stayed there together with his brother Yankiev-Leib and sister-in-law, for thirteen months, until liberation. For the rest of his life, he would talk about these two noble beings, Grzegrz and Aniela. Not only was he grateful to them for having saved his life, but also for giving him cause to be hopeful that there were still good people in this world. At a time when there was so little hope to hang on to, they affirmed his own innate desire to believe that the good in people would ultimately triumph over evil.

Whenever my father talked about them, he would say that they were truly two of the very few, the "thirty six" righteous people, who, according to Jewish legend, were holding up this world. My father, a truly religious, orthodox Jew developed a deep friendship with Grzegorz.

Grzegorz was a simple man who probably never went to school; the Bible was probably the only book he had ever read. At night, the two of them would talk about scriptures, God, life, right and wrong; they both must have sensed that in their hearts they stood on common ground. The common ground was kindness, compassion, and a spirituality that transcended a fleeting material world with its greed, its hatreds, politics and divisions.

Grzegorz and Aniela took great care when buying and preparing food for the three people they were hiding. Mainly, they made sure to avoid buying non-kosher food.

Both before and after liberation, they emphatically refused any monetary compensation for saving three human lives, under extraordinarily difficult conditions.

It would seem that a man like Grzegorz would have no reason to run away in the weeks before liberation. Only the German collaborators were leaving town as the Germans began their retreat from our region. Grzegorz should have had have nothing to fear, in way of reprisals. Not only was he not a collaborator, but he had risked his life to save people who otherwise would have been killed by the Germans. Being a man with a clear conscience, he remained in Sambor.

Ironically, the Russians, who were very angry with all the local Ukrainians, seized Grzegorz soon after they liberated Sambor, and sent him to a labor camp in Russia. This happened right after we left Sambor to go west, and therefore, unfortunately, we were unable to help him. Both father and Yankiev–Leib would have done everything possible to help free him, but once we went West, all contact with us would have endangered him even further. Eventually Grzegorz returned to Sambor and was reunited with Aniela. Their economic situation was very bad. While Grzegorz was gone, my parents and uncle Yankiev–Leib sent packages to Aniela. They continued sending them whatever they could for the rest of their lives. Because of the cold war, packages and letters could only be sent via Israel (so that the Russians would not penalize Grzegorz for being in contact with Americans).

40

THE
CELLAR

When, in the fall of 1942, word got around that the Germans were planning to round up all the remaining Jews in Sambor and herd them into a ghetto on Blich, people started looking for ways to escape. Some who did not look especially ethnic Jewish bought false "Aryan" papers; many dyed their hair blond and moved to other cities.

In those days, there was not too much mobility among residents of small towns; people stayed in their apartments for a long time and everybody knew who their neighbors were. Strangers were always subject to suspicion. Many people who tried to pass as Gentiles were denounced and caught right away. Some tried to join the partisans. They were local Polish men who armed themselves and went to live in the forest. The partisans did not want Jewish fighters in their midst. Another option would have been to find some compassionate Gentiles, perhaps former friends and neighbors who would have been willing to hide them, often at substantial risk to their own lives. There were a few of these good people, but there were never enough. Some Gentiles were willing to take a risk out of greed, hoping to get paid handsomely for hiding Jews. More often than not, a Gentile neighbor would betray his Jewish neighbors and point out their hiding places to the German authorities.

Always on the lookout for a potential hiding place, my father and his brothers and coworkers discovered an old, long-forgotten cellar under one of the warehouses where they often worked, located in the middle of town on Przemyska Street. This grain warehouse was one of several that my father and his brothers had owned before the war.

When the Germans came, they confiscated all the grain warehouses. All the grain was to be used exclusively for the needs of the German army throughout the region. A coarse Ukrainian peasant became the new manager of this particular warehouse on Przemyska Street. My father and several of his brothers, along with other men from the ghetto, became slave workers there as well as at the Rolnik. The Ukrainian manager reported directly to the SS.

The warehouse building was very old. It took up a large lot that extended from Przemyska Street in the front, to another street in the rear, adjoining a small cobble stone plaza. Once or twice a week, the plaza, which we called "Mala Targowica," (Small Market place) turned into a flea market and a small farmer's market. The main entrance to the warehouse was off Przemyska Street. Przemyska Street was one of the three main streets in Sambor. It was the main road leading west to the city of Przemysl and the rest of western Poland. (Later on, the retreating German army and the caravans of fleeing collaborators moved west via Przemyska street and we could watch them through small holes in the roof and doors of the warehouse.)

From Pszemyska Street, one would enter the warehouse from a huge gate, which opened to a large courtyard. All the way in the back of the courtyard, was a large storage building with its many chambers and the manager's office.

Near the entrance to the building, along the wall to the right of the door, and close to the ground, was a small rusty door that was about two by two feet square.

My father, uncle Moshe, and a couple of their Jewish coworkers had noticed the small rusty door before, but now, being on the lookout for possible hiding places, decided to find out where it was leading to. Obviously, they had to explore in secrecy. They could check it out only after the other workers and the manager had left for the day, and after it got dark, so the guard there would not see them. A couple of them stayed at the warehouse overnight.

That night, they pried open the small door. Using a flashlight, they ventured inside, cautiously lowering themselves to the ground level of the cellar, which was about four to five feet below the level of the courtyard. It soon became obvious that the place they had discovered was a huge dark cellar that had not been used for a very long time. Cautiously walking around and exploring the place, the men found out that this extraordinary, and perhaps centuries-old cellar, had many chambers. Its brick walls were two feet thick and the rounded brick ceilings were over eight feet tall.

The men were awed by what they had discovered. They realized that the place had great potential for being converted into a hiding place for their families and they immediately got to work. Even though everyone hoped that the war would not last much longer, the hiding place had to be made at least minimally habitable, to be fit, if need be, for a lengthy stay.

To get it fixed in time so that it would be ready to be occupied before the enclosing of the ghetto, the men worked on the cellar every night, for weeks.

Each step of the project was difficult and fraught with danger. Every day after work some of the men secretly stayed behind. Using the small opening, they would enter the cellar after all the workers had left for the day and they would continue to work on the cellar. First they had to clean it. All work had to be done quietly and in total secrecy. An armed guard patrolled the facility at all times. Work was done mostly in the dark and with limited tools and materials. Being under a grain warehouse, the cellar was teaming with huge rats.

Getting the cellar ready was a monumental task. There was a great urgency to get it prepared for our families so they could come and hide because everyday the noose around our necks was tightening; everyday people were being caught and murdered.

Some major practical problems had to be solved immediately. At first, after walking in and out of the cellar through the small rusty door, they would push a large garbage bin to cover it from sight. The men had to find a less obvious way to access the cellar so that they could hide the small door up front, because it was easily seen from the courtyard. Sooner or later, it would arouse curiosity and suspicion. The new entrance had to be secret and the old one covered without a trace, as if it had never existed. The men made that project as their first priority.

Cousin Yosiu, who was 14 at the time, stayed in the cellar from early on, helping out and watching the project unfold. The first group of men to stay in the cellar overnight were Arco Velker, Luzer Weisengreen, Yosiu and uncle Moshe.

Having worked in construction when he lived in Israel before the war, Uncle Moshe thought of an ingenious way to access the cellar in a secret and inconspicuous way. Across from the Ukrainian manager's office door was another door that led to the attic. From inside the cellar the men dug a tunnel that reached to a place just behind the attic stairs. Then they loosened the third step from the bottom of the stairs, so that it could be easily removed and replaced from inside the tunnel. That step could slide in and out like a drawer. As soon as that was accomplished, the small door from the courtyard to the cellar was covered with bricks and a thick layer of cement. Garbage was piled up in front of it to make the fresh cement inconspicuous. From then, one could enter the cellar only by sliding out the third step and then crawling through the freshly dug tunnel.

The tunnel had been dug mostly by Arco Velker, who was a young man of about twenty-five, and Luzer Weizengreen. Weizengreen was a very strong man. He was well over six feet tall and a powerfully built. Before the war, he used to be a farmer. He had sand-colored hair, a big face and head, big teeth and childlike pale blue eyes; he was not a bad looking man. Although we never spoke, I liked him. He was a quiet and gentle giant. Arco was skinny and muscular. He had a full head of auburn hair, blue eyes, and the hollow cheeks of a heavy smoker.

The tunnel the men had dug from the new entrance off the attic stairs, was at a more or less, 30 degree slant upward and it was about twenty feet long. It was narrow, and low. One could only crawl up, slide down or sit in it. The cellar was, dark, cool, damp, and musty. There was very little fresh air and no ventilation. The men worked by the light of a kerosene lamp.

It was crucial to bring electricity into the cellar. That task fell on Uncle Moshe. When connecting electricity to the cellar, it was important to bypass the electric meter in the warehouse, so that we could have unlimited use of electricity without leaving a trace. A dramatic increase in the electric energy used would have been recorded in the meter and would have aroused suspicion. To bypass the electric meter in the warehouse, Moshe had to start with the electrical work outside the building. He needed to connect directly to the transformer atop the electric pole outside. That was the hardest and most dangerous part of the project. Moshe had to time his work, so as not to alert the armed guard who was circling the building.

At a propitious moment, when the guard was walking on the opposite side of the building, Moshe climbed up the electric power pole. He did that without the aid of special foot braces, the kind that electric workers usually wear to climb power poles. Working fast, he connected two wires directly to the appropriate transformer terminals. Moshe then climbed down, bringing the wires down alongside the roof and through the attic and the tunnel, and finally into the cellar.

This maneuver took tremendous skill, courage and great timing. The electric wires Moshe worked with were always "hot". He could have easily gotten an electric shock and fallen to the ground. The guard could have spotted him on top, holding on to the pole. Had he sneezed or slipped or dropped a tool, the guard would have heard him. He worked at night without so much as a flashlight to help him see the wires, the tools and the transformer terminals.

When I think of Moshe up on that pole at night, working under such stressful and dangerous conditions, I can't help remembering that as a young man in the twenties he labored with equal courage to rebuild a Jewish homeland in Israel. While living and working there, he also had to help defend his fellow pioneers from Arab marauders. He used to tell us stories and describe how he had to keep a gun on him, even while working in the field or when working in construction.

The many stories about his life in Israel and his incredible work in the cellar gave me a glimpse into the character of the people who laid the foundation for the rebirth of Israel. They must have been like Uncle Moshe: courageous, selfless and determined to survive.

Except for Yosiu, none of the men who prepared the cellar for us to hide in are alive today; I wish I could hear them now, describing in person the details of this operation. I knew from father's conversations, at that time and after liberation, how hard and ingeniously they had to work to accomplish it all. My cousin Yosiu, who now lives in Israel knows more about the cellar project than anyone else still alive. He also was one of the first people there, helping and watching the others put it all together. Sadly, he refuses to talk about the Holocaust and our time in the cellar; it depresses him too much. He wants to focus now, his mind and energy, on his present life and on his family. Lately he took ill and he even has difficulty speaking.

I know that they all worked under very stressful conditions. Even a small misstep would have aborted the whole project and cut our chances of survival to zero. Had the workers been caught staying at the warehouse at night, let alone fixing up a hiding place for Jews within the German army's domain, they would have been shot immediately.

Getting electric power was a major accomplishment. It gave us light, and we became less dependent on our limited supply of kerosene both for light and the preparation of food. The fumes of burning kerosene would have been very harmful because we had almost no ventilation. Now, with unlimited use of electricity, we had the possibility of cooking and baking on electric hot plates.

Before the place could become viable for a lengthy stay, we had to make a toilet and figure out how to get water. The toilet part was easy. It was a matter of digging a pit in one of the two furthest chambers of the cellar.

There were several separate areas. Crawling out through the narrow tunnel from the attic stairs, one entered a central chamber which we called the hallway. Then there were two large (about 20x20 feet square) chambers, one to the left, and one to the right. These were designated to serve as dormitories. Because the soil from digging the tunnel had to be disposed of somehow, the men used it to build up a platform all around the first room on the left. On top of these raised earthen platforms they used wooden planks to make a place for us to sleep on.

Even before the electric power was installed in the cellar, my father had started to think of ways to bring in all the things we would need to hold us over for the duration of the war. We never imagined that we would be there for two years. (Moshe, Yosiu, Arco, and Weizengreen were there the longest; Mother, Genia others were there for twenty months. I was there for sixteen months)

Every day, farmers delivered grain from their farms to the warehouse. They came in horse-drawn wagons, filled with two hundred-pound burlap sacks of grain. These were the same farmers who used to be my father's former suppliers, and he knew many of them well. Whenever it was possible, and for a fee, my father would borrow a cart from a farmer he could trust. Of course, my father did not trust the farmers enough to tell them the real reason for borrowing a horse driven wagon. He would usually say that it was needed in connection with work at the warehouse. The conditions had to be just right for transporting things to the cellar.

This is how Father brought the things needed to make the cellar habitable. He brought in bedding, dishes, books, towels, sheets, first aid items, and kerosene. He also brought lumber to build platforms for sleeping, and tools, light bulbs, electrical wires, and hot plates for cooking. In case, at some point, the electricity was not available, we had small kerosene camping stoves. Then he brought food supplies: sacks of potatoes, onions, oil, salt and sugar. All those items were loaded onto the cart first and then covered with sacks of grain. Obtaining many of the items and the loading of the cart had to be done very carefully, so as not to arouse suspicion. The unloading of the cart was done in the dark, after the workers had left for the day and the big gates were closed. The courtyard was big enough for the carts and the horses to drive in. The guards were patrolling on the outside. Only unusual noises would have aroused their suspicions.

The people who stayed at the warehouse overnight brought the supplies down to the cellar through the opening in the stairs and the long dark tunnel. In addition to the supplies they brought from the outside, the men stole, over time, twenty sacks of wheat from the warehouse, and gradually brought them down to the cellar through the tunnel. Now the rats did not even have to bother going up for their food, it was brought to them. Among us lived the fattest rats ever.

The two rooms furthest from the main living area, were chosen for a toilet pit and a place for washing up. One was across from the other. The earth dug up from the toilet pit was placed in the washroom across the way, raising its floor by at least a foot.

Depending on how much water was available to us on a particular day, we washed up in a small hand basin and most of the time, only with a mere wet cloth. For privacy, we hung a sheet for a curtain.

In the span of the sixteen-months that I lived in the cellar, altogether three pits had been dug for toilets. Each pit that had filled up was covered with the dirt dug up for the next one. The first one was dug in the rear of the chamber, the second one close to the front and the third one across the way. A board across the open toilet pit gave us something to stand on, while crouching. The pits were very deep and I was always terrified of falling in. My mother or my sister would come with me and hold my hand. Miraculously no one fell in, but perhaps some rats did.

The stench of those pits was awful. They were close to our sleeping areas and the place where food was being prepared. After a while we got used to it, and it became the least troubling thing we learned to live and cope with.

Next we had to find a source of water. The warehouse did not have running water. Our men decided to search for water by digging in the dirt floor in one of the rooms. Arco Velker, Luzer Weisengreen and Shlomek Freiman started digging in the center of the first chamber, the one on the right. They began to dig a hole that was about four feet square.

I was not there at the time they were digging the well, but Yosiu later told me that every half a meter (1.6-ft.) they made holes in the dirt walls of the well so that they could have a foothold while digging on deeper. Since the pit was small to maneuver in, they had to use a small hand shovel. The dug up earth was brought up to the surface, one bucket at a time, and used for bed platforms in the same room. Soon the hole got very deep. Still, after digging as much as twelve meters, (39.4 feet), they had not yet found water. Finally after digging one and a half meters (4.9 ft), more, they finally found water. The completed well was thirteen and a half meters or 44.3 feet deep.

To get water from the well we would lower a bucket, tied to the end of a rope, dip the bucket in the well and bring it up. The well was usually covered with heavy planks of wood. I had nightmares about falling in. After all, it would have been like falling from the roof of a four-story building.

In the summer we had many water problems; the well was drying out fast and there was very little water in it. At times ,the water level dropped so low that there was a mere puddle at the bottom of the well. What little water we would find was yellow, and full of sand. Sometimes there was so little of it that someone would have to go down and scrape it up from the bottom, one cup at a time, and we had to ration it. At such times my mother, Genia and I would share a total of one cup of water per day between us. By the second summer, after we were already using the third toilet pit, waste from the pits started seeping in underground and into the well. The water smelled and tasted badly, but the well was our only source of water. Fortunately, that began to happen only towards the last few months of our stay there. Several times, we found a dead rat on the bottom of the well. It was a mystery how they got there because the well was always covered. I suppose the rats were thirsty too, and maybe they were also digging tunnels.

When water was scarce we tried drinking rainwater, but it tasted awful because the sparse rain in the summer would contain all the soot and dust that would wash off the dirty roof. Still, we used what little rainwater we could safely catch to wash ourselves with, and to wash our hair and sometimes to hand wash our clothes. We could catch the rainwater in the courtyard on Sundays, but during the week we could do it only after the workers had gone home.

From the hallway of the cellar, immediately past the toilet pit, was a second long tunnel. Its walls and rounded ceiling were made of brick. That tunnel was about 3.5 feet tall and maybe thirty feet long. It had a small window at the end, near the top, so that the bottom of the opening was on the ground level outside. One could crouch beneath it without being seen by someone near the fence. The window did not have glass, it was just an opening with vertical iron bars. On the other side of the opening was a six-foot iron picket fence that went around the warehouse on that side of the building. That fence was just a few feet away from the opening in the tunnel. The little window faced a large cobblestone plaza. On market days, on Mondays and Thursdays, the small plaza was filled with farmers and locals selling and buying various flea market-type items.

After I came into the cellar, new people kept coming in, almost daily, until there were twenty-six of us living down there.

Each family group had a designated spot for sleeping. We slept on the boards that were placed on top of the earth dug up from the tunnels.

In the room on the left, there was one big L shaped bed. In the room on the right, the one bed was made all along the left wall. In the burrows under our beds lived the rats. All night they'd chew and gnaw on something or other, or on each other. One tried to bite Genia's toe. It scurried away when she lifted the cover screaming.

When rainwater was available to us, we would sneak up to the attic on a Sunday and wash our hair. After hair washing, my mother would pour kerosene on my hair and rub it in; then she would comb it with a fine-tooth comb to remove hundreds of lice. My waist long thick hair was full of them, and there were lice in our clothes, on our bodies, and on our bedding. I'd see them crawling on people all the time. My mother spent hours delousing me, rather than cut my long wavy hair which she loved so much.

In the first chamber on the right where the well was, the men made a long makeshift bench that stood against the wall on the right side. We would sit there when grinding wheat kernels with a meat grinder or a coffee grinder. The women took turns grinding the wheat and preparing food. All the cooking was done in the large hallway, in the left side corner. This corner was only a few feet from the open toilet pit. Several hot plates were placed on top of a box with two long carbon-composite cooking plates placed on top of the boxes, to form something like a grill.

After the wheat was ground, the finer portion was mixed with water to form a dough, which was then baked on the grill. That was our "daily bread", we called them "placki" (platzki). They looked like tortillas. The coarser wheat parts were used to cook porridge. At first, we had some jam. That went well with the porridge. That was actually the first meal I had in the cellar; it tasted so good, and I could have my fill.

41

HADZEMAN

The name of the Ukrainian manager of the warehouse above us was Hadzeman. Hadzeman was a rabid anti-Semite. He hated Jews and greatly admired the Germans. He was often heard bragging that a "Hitler spirit" lived within him.

According to one of his farm neighbors, who happened to be with us in the cellar, he shot and killed his Jewish neighbor, who had also been a farmer, and he even shot the neighbor's dog and placed him under the dead man's head, as he buried them together on the farm. Hadzeman then took over the neighbor's farm.

His son-in-law, a vicious man by the name of Holovey, was one of the most dreaded Ukrainian policemen in our town. Once, in the ghetto, on the way to Isaac's house, I came upon a group of people in the street standing near a large puddle of blood. The victim was a young orthodox man whom I vaguely remember; he was very short and was slightly deformed with a hunchback. The people were saying that Holovey had come into the ghetto the night before, and killed him by cutting his head off on this very spot, leaving him lying there in a puddle of blood.

Hadzeman had an apartment in town, but often commuted from his farm, where his large family lived. He had at least six children and some were married and had children of their own.

At first, all work in the cellar was done secretly at night and Hadzeman did not know anything about it. Everybody knew how anti-Semitic he was and that he would report us to the Germans if he had ever found out about us. But within a few months the senior people in our group realized how difficult it would be to keep this secret from him for any length of time. Hadzeman would have eventually become suspicious and certainly not kept quiet. Knowing how shrewd and greedy he was, a decision was made to let him in on our secret and to keep him quiet with money. Soon he named his price.

Just for keeping quiet, Hadzeman demanded two hundred American dollars per month and a young, pretty, Jewish girl from among us, to be available at his beck and call. I find it hard to write about it. My stomach is cramping into a knot when I recall the "chosen" girl, how injured she was, often returning to the cellar in tears after being with him.

She was our "Queen Esther", the legendary biblical figure whose heroism and sacrifice the Jewish people celebrate each year during the holiday "Purim". Some three thousand years ago, the biblical Queen Esther went before the Persian king to plead for the life of her people. The king fell in love with Esther. The Hitler of those times was the king's minister and henchman, Haman. Because of Esther's influence over the king, Haman was deposed and executed thus saving the Jews who had lived in the Persian kingdom.

Besides being crude and vicious, Hadzeman was an ugly old man. He was big, heavy around the waist and bald with a few gray hairs on the sides of his head. He had a large mustache and big black warts on his pudgy cheeks. His small, pale blue eyes were sly and cruel. He must have been at least fifty-five years old. The girl he selected from among us was about eighteen. For the sake of this writing I will call her Luba.

Hadzeman knew Luba from before, she grew up on a neighboring farm, and indeed she was beautiful. There was something angelic about her. Luba had wavy reddish blond hair, a peachy complexion and beautiful hazel-green eyes. She was naïve and sweet, and came from a very good and traditional Jewish family.

In the cellar, there was a man among us who I strongly disliked, whom I will call Max. I think that everyone else disliked him as well. Max was a nasty young man, with beady black eyes and a narrow band of black hair, fringing a large bald head. Max had befriended Luba in the ghetto, knowing that she and her family had a place to hide, leading her to believe that he would marry her after the liberation. In the cellar, Max was always mean to her, making her feel dirty and unworthy of him. He was also a snob, because both he and his family were well educated. Luba by contrast was a simple farm girl.

Immediately after liberation, a marriage ceremony between them was performed. I found out later, that Luba spent her wedding night at a girlfriend's house, crying all night. He refused to sleep with her.

Thirty years later, I saw Luba again. She was still with him and they had had children. By that time, she was a very wise middle-aged housewife, well read and quite intelligent. She was still beautiful. She served me tea and some cheesecake she had baked. She seemed at peace, but we did not talk about the past. Having been made to feel dirty by the man with the beady eyes and, perhaps by her own standards of chastity, marrying him was not a reward but a due punishment, which perhaps she thought would somehow cleanse her. She became a very religious orthodox Jew.

In New York, in the Museum of Modern Art, there is a mural by Pablo Picasso called "Guerenica". In it, the horrors of the Spanish civil war are poignantly depicted. It shows a cow with a quivering tongue that appears to be bellowing in pain and crying out to the heavens. Years later I found out that our "Queen Esther", Luba, had died of cancer of the tongue. Whenever I thought about her I also thought about that painting.

She cried often, but only to herself. She never complained about her lot. She had repressed her screams until her tongue erupted in a silent rage that killed her. At night, sitting on top of the sacks in the hallway, I used to watch her coming out of the tunnel, wiping her tears, shamed and humiliated.

Hadzeman was a sadistic man and often he amused himself by playing cruel jokes on us.

Once, out of the blue he sent a message for us with Luba, saying that we would have to leave the cellar within twenty-four hours. We took that message very seriously and were overcome with gloom and desperation. For us, this was not just a matter of having to relocate. For us, it was a death sentence. Here we were, in the middle of town, and in daylight, anyone would have spotted us leaving the cellar. We were all pale, skinny and sickly looking, wearing old tattered clothes. German SS and soldiers, their collaborators, or Jew-hating locals were everywhere. We would have been shot on the spot. Even if we had tried to leave at night, the armed guard who was circling the warehouse around the clock would have seen us. Besides, there was nowhere to go. The local population would hardly risk their lives to help us. Among them we had become like lepers, and most likely, they would have reported us to the Germans, as they had done in the past.

The next day, while we were in the middle of discussing what to do next, trying to figure out how to split up and how we could possibly reach the forest, we heard his three knocks on the step and then the words, "twenty-five-six". The vulture, Hadzeman, was calling for the girl to come up. After some time she came down, carrying some Pork, and a bottle of milk, with the message: "Happy April fools day. "

Sending pork to a bunch of starving Jews was in itself vicious, adding insult to injury. Only a few people among us would eat it. I think the Triller family and the beady-eyed Max did, since they were not religious at all. No one from our family ate it.

Our money soon ran out. We never imagined that the war would last so long. Soon, Hadzeman threatened again to expel us. This time it was not a cruel joke that he was playing on us. We had no money to give him. In turn, he demanded that we give him everything else we owned. Soon we were sending up the few things we still had, a few sheets and towels and items of clothing. Hating Jews and being a suspicious man, he imagined that we were hoarding all sorts of riches.

Each day, Hadzeman put more and more pressure on us to come up with valuables. He suspected that we were lying to him about everything, but he did not trust us enough to come down into the cellar to see for himself how we lived and what we had left. He was too scared of us and must have thought that we would kill him before he had a chance to report us and have us killed. Who knows, maybe at some point we would have - and it would have been a rational choice.

42

LIFE IN A CAPSULE

On the day the final raid in the ghetto began, Mr. Triller showed up in our cellar. He came in wearing a railroad man's cap, his face smudged with soot. Once he escaped from the ghetto, it would have been easy for him to pass as a Gentile. He was lean, healthy looking and tall, had blue eyes and light reddish hair. By coming to the cellar, he selfishly put us all at great risk. His wife Cilla, her brother, his five-year-old son Heniu, and his old mother-in-law were already there.

A few months after the liquidation, another person came to join us. It was the eighteen year old Mania Sternheim. Her mother and her older sister Selma were also already there. She had been hiding at the home of a Polish man. She was apparently being abused and ran away. Among the people who missed getting out of the ghetto in time to join us in the cellar were Mendel's widow, (white Genia's mother), David Freiman's brother Shlomek, his five-year-old son, the oldest Teicher brother, and my beloved Aunt Laika and her child, little Andzia.

After the executions in the Radlovice forest and the long stage of numbness that we felt, the unbearable pain of mourning turned into anger and alienation from a world that had forsaken us. Isolated and depending only on ourselves for survival, there was no one to ask for help, appeal for mercy, or complain to. We went on living, from moment to moment, one day at a time, as best we could under the most difficult conditions. Each day, we wondered whether it was our last. We could have been easily discovered or died from disease, infection, and malnutrition.

After a few months in the cellar, I put the rest of the world totally out of my mind. Many that I had loved were dead, the others in Sambor were an alien species to whom I could not relate; the rest of the world was irrelevant.

We settled down in our subterranean habitat as best as we could. We considered ourselves lucky to have survived this far and accepted our new life as the only one possible. We lived in our own miniature world. People did their chores grinding the wheat, baking platzki (wheat tortillas), and cooking soup and porridge.

To stay alive, we had to be extremely cautious not to compromise our secret isolation. After the liquidation, many hiding places in Sambor were discovered and their occupants shot. Our Polish and Ukrainian neighbors were only too happy to report Jewish hiding places and claim their reward, a five pound bag of sugar per hiding place.

To become yet more inconspicuous, we thought of a very practical new idea. We decided to turn day into night. We were concerned that someone would smell the cooking and hear the noises we made in the course of our daily life in the cellar. To us, it made no difference whether the sun was rising or setting, because there was no sky; there was no sun, nor moon, or stars. At least we had a ceiling and walls that separated us from the certain death we would have met outside the cellar.

So we slept during the day, when the workers were upstairs in the warehouse and the people in the marketplace were nearby.

The transition from daytime living to being up all night was effortless. Our biological clocks, I suppose, which were set by the sun and the moon, must have been out of phase with the rest of the universe.

Living in our own miniature world, we settled into daily routines, doing our chores, keeping ourselves as deloused as possible, playing cards, reading, talking. We hardly dared to think of a life that could have been different.

People took turns hand-grinding the wheat, and cooking soup and porridge. In the beginning, we had a supply of potatoes, salt, oil and onions, and we could make tasty soup. But that supply was soon depleted and our soup was made by boiling some dirty water with wheat kernels and dry beans. All too soon, a time came when even that became a rare treat.

Whenever he wasn't busy fixing something or other, uncle Moshe would play solitaire on the big dining table, which was simply a sheet of plywood. While playing solitaire, Moshe would whistle.

Sometimes Moshe whistled so beautifully that it could make one cry. This is how he shared not only the music he had loved and internalized, but also how he expressed his innermost feelings. Like his father, Chaim Zacharia, and his brothers Benjamin and Yosef, he was a man of few words. He'd always rather whistle than talk.

His was the only music I heard for sixteen months. It inspired in me a lifelong love for classical music. With melancholy sensitivity he would whistle the music of Bach, Mozart, Beethoven, Grieg, Schuman, Bizet, Offenbach, and others. He whistled all the operas and sometimes also beautiful Italian songs.

The sleeping arrangements in our cellar were simple. Wrapped around the rectangular table, the bed platform was in the form of an L, alongside two walls. We slept one next to another, laid out in a row, like sardines in a can. Starting from the left wall was a space for Mama, Genia and I, followed by spaces for White Genia, Aunt Regina, Yosiu, Uncle Moshe, the Triller family of four, Max with the beady eyes and Luba, whose space was up against the right wall. Around the bend, slept Ester Brenner, with her eight-year-old daughter, Ania, then Moishe Teicher, his brother Heniek and cousin Benek. Together, eighteen people shared this L shaped bed.

In a similar arrangement, eight people slept in the other chamber. Immediately to the left of the entrance, with their heads against the first wall, slept Arco, his sister Mrs. Dachinger, and Luzer Weizengreen. Past these three, and with their heads against the next wall, slept Mania, her sister Selma and their mother, Mrs. Sternheim, Escia, Shlomek's former fiance, and Dudziu Freiman, who later became her husband.

Usually, there would be an ongoing card game on Mrs. Dahinger's bed. I would sit next to Mama, trying to help her out, because I got to be pretty good at cards. Mama would get angry with me, especially when she was losing, because she did not listen to me.

Mania, Escia and Selma would often sing songs. I learned them and sang along. Some people would read, some would tell stories. We had many books and old Hollywood magazines. Each magazine was filled with happy, smiling people. Everybody pictured was so beautiful, which gave me an idea of what one had to look like to be "normal" in America. I decided that I would never measure up and would always be ugly.

Although we brought many books, some people went through them several times. Genia was always immersed in a book, or she would write in her diary in which she would pour her heart out and document our life in the cellar. Genia was known for her writing abilities and her diary would have been priceless to all of us, but unfortunately she was forced to destroy it later when crossing the Polish border to Austria, when we all fled Poland after the war. She and her group had to pretend that they were Greeks returning home after the war. The diary and all Polish writing had to be burned.

There were many romances going on in the cellar. People paired off and consoled each other as best they could. Sometimes, on Sunday afternoons, we'd all go upstairs to the warehouse, where there were many chambers filled knee deep with grain. Couples would disperse and disappear to spend some private moments together. On weeknights or days, couples would have a few private moments in the pitch dark, rat infested tunnel that led to the stairs. Genia and Yosiu would sometimes go there, sit on the damp dirt floor and talk about life and the sadness they shared. I think that Genia was secretly in love with cousin Yosiu, who was a very sweet and a handsome boy of fifteen. But an older girl, Mania, tried hard to divert his attention and to seduce him. According to Yosiu, it never quite happened, but Genia did not know that at the time and she was hurt.

Mania was an olive skinned, long legged beauty with brown eyes and long dark hair. She was eighteen.

I loved Yosiu so much, that when his mother squeezed out puss from the infected boils he developed on his neck, and he cried in pain, I could hardly stand it and I sat in the next room also crying.

Every once in a while, something unusual would happen in

our life in the cellar. Once we got a big and unexpected scare. We heard a big commotion outside the small window in the long brick tunnel. Someone from the outside was banging with a hammer or a crowbar at the window's iron bars, as if trying to break them and enter the cellar. Anxiously listening to the loud voices outside, we understood that one of the peddler women was missing a piece of fabric. She was sure that the fabric had fallen down into the iron barred opening. Of course someone must have stolen it from her because nothing had fallen in.

The banging on the bars continued and sent us all into utter panic. While it was happening, we had to be perfectly still. Had it been easy to remove the bars, it would have been the end of us. Fortunately, after what seemed an eternity, but must have been less than several hours, the banging stopped and it got quiet again. Maybe they had found the piece of cloth, or maybe they were chased away by the guard or the manager of the warehouse. Once again, we breathed a sigh of relief. It was a close call.

Although throughout our whole stay in the cellar we made no demands on Hadzeman, even when we were hungry or had no water to drink, he became more vicious and his threats were more frequent and more ugly. Once again, he said that unless we paid him we'd have to leave.

We were desperate and did not know how we could possibly appease him so that he would leave us alone and let us stay in the cellar. One day, out of the blue, the greatest of all miracles happened to us. My father came to the rescue! Our rescue came to us through the small window in the long brick tunnel.

One night, we heard something fall into the tunnel. At first we panicked, when we heard a sound coming from there. We thought that perhaps someone was curious about that opening and was trying to remove the iron bars to enter. Then it got quiet again. Cautiously, someone tiptoed into the tunnel to check. Lying on the floor, was piece of paper wrapped around a rock and tied with a string. We became very apprehensive. Could there have been other survivors who knew about us and were perhaps looking to join us? That would have been very dangerous. People were desperate and did everything possible to save themselves, even risking the lives of others. When we opened the paper we found that it was a letter from my father.

Up to that point, everyone, except for Genia, had assumed that he had perished in Radlovice, together with the all the others. Genia alone never gave up hope that he was alive. I myself had never been able to mourn him, like I mourned the others. To me it was unimaginable that father had died; he was superhuman and indestructible.

Although Father loved Grzegorz and was sure that he already knew his character, he waited for a long time before telling him anything about our cellar. Finally, after six months he decided to try contacting us, with the help of this good man, who had earned Fathers trust.

Of course, Father had no way of knowing if we were still alive. He knew that our money must have run out long ago and he also knew how vicious Hadzeman was. Father had no money left to help us, but felt that he had to do something. At least he needed to know if and how we are managing to stay alive.

Father had described to Grzegosz exactly where our location was and told him to watch out for the guard.

That evening, Grzegorz went for a walk near the warehouse and when he came near our little window, he bent down, pretending to tie his shoes and threw in the rock with the letter tied to it.

In the letter father told us when Grzegosz would be passing by again. He asked us for a sign or a note to be handed to Gzregorz to let him know that we are alive. Father was very anxious about us because he heard, through Grzegosz, of the many hidden Jews that were caught and shot in the cemetery.

The letter from my father came just in time. We decided to use it as our ultimate and only possible leverage that we would have over Hadzeman. To counter his threats to throw us out, we showed him the letter, which happened to be written in Yiddish. We told him that, in the letter, Father said that if anything happened to us, he would hold Hadzeman responsible for our deaths. Hadzeman understood that to mean that after the liberation, Father would find him and kill him with his own hands. That language he understood.

Still, Hadzeman was very suspicious. He thought that maybe

we made the whole story up about my father living outside the cellar. He could have thought that we wrote the letter and that, all along, father had been with us in the cellar. He also knew that unless he came down to the cellar he would never know for sure. Yet, he would not come down, fearing that we would kill him.

If we had to, I wonder which one of us would have done it? Killing even a chicken was not part of our way of life. But I hated him so much that I think I would have volunteered. To me he was lower than a rat. But I would have deferred to Luba and let her do it, because she had more reason to hate him.

Instead of coming down, he asked us to come up to be interrogated by him, one by one, every one of us. He especially wanted to interrogate the children, and he did that starting first with the youngest, little five year old Heniu Triller.

When my turn came, he asked me every which way if father was in the cellar, or if the letter had indeed come from him on the outside. Of course, I told him how happy I was to find out that he was alive and well, living on the outside.

The letter worked like a miracle, convincing Hadzeman to leave us alone. His harassment stopped, especially since in the last few weeks, the Germans suffered a setback and heavy losses on the Russian front.

Within a few days, Grzegorz came back on the appointed night. Once again he bent down pretending to tie his shoelace and we gave him a few letters to Father. I don't remember how it was done, maybe it was fastened to one end of a long stick that reached to the street.

Genia wrote one of the letters to Father. I can only guess the joy that he must have felt upon finding out that we were alive. For the rest of his life he carried Genia's letter in his wallet. After his death, I found it in his wallet next to Genia's photograph and his and Mama's wedding picture. The paper on which the letter was written was old and the writing was faded.

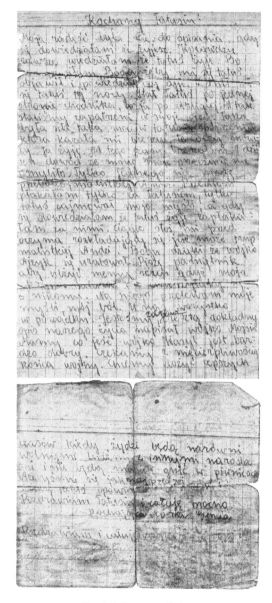

Genia's letter to father

Dearest Daddy,

I can hardly describe to you the joy I felt when we received your letter and I found out that you are alive. Actually, I always knew that you were alive. Because I had asked God to make you appear to me and tell me that you are alive. The night before, I had a dream about you Daddy. You stood on one side of the street and I on the other. And thus we stood gazing into each other's eyes.

Daddy, there was such strength and so much power in your eyes, and they told me to have faith. Those eyes were saying to me "I am alive!" From that moment I had faith. And today I have proof that my intuition did not make a mistake.

But the pain of losing little Andzia I cannot stop. Thinking about her hurts. Before, I only cried for you, Daddy, only you dear Daddy occupied all my thoughts, but when I found out that you are alive, I began to cry for the others. All the time, I see before my eyes, the perhaps already decomposing body of little Andzia.

Thank God, that Uncle Isaak has saved himself. I am writing a diary to ease the pain in my heart, because my private thoughts I share with no one. Into my diary I am pouring my thoughts and my pain. Here, with us, everything is in order. Our health is good. Uncle Moshe will tell you more and give you a detailed description of how we live.

We have food. Uncle "Wasyl" is very good.
We are impatiently awaiting the end of the war. We would like to live to see better times, when Jews will be equally free with other people and with other nations and will no longer be rotting in cellars. I hope that we will see each other very soon and that, you Daddy, will come back.

Wishing you well, and sending you kisses, your loving daughter, Genia

Wishes for health and kisses for Uncle Yankiev-Leib and Aunt Ryfcia. I wish you well and send you kisses, and also for Uncle and Aunt.   Anda

The battle of Stalingrad and Leningrad became major turning points in the war between the Russians and the Germans. America had entered the war, coming to England's and Russia's aid. We got bits and pieces of news from the newspapers that we would find, here and there, lying around upstairs. It gave us some idea of what was going on in the world. Except for Luba going upstairs to service the beast, Hadzeman, and the bits of old pieces of newspaper the men would bring down, we had no contact with the outside world. On market days, one of us would quietly tiptoe up to the window and listen in to the talk among the peddlers. We would find out what they were saying about the war, and where the most recent war front was.

Sometimes the news made us hopeful. Whenever there was some good news from the front, whenever the Germans suffered a setback, Hadzeman would become friendlier and send us something to eat. Once, he sent down a sack of potatoes, and once some cabbage.

Several of our men were heavy smokers and they suffered for it. Every day, after the warehouse workers left for the day, the smokers rushed upstairs, to pick up filthy butts off the floor, They would bring them down to share.

I watched them, as they would nervously rip the butts up, collect the slimy tobacco and re-roll them in pieces of newspaper and then sit back and smoke them with great relish.

Oh, poetic justice! After the war, in bombed-out Munich, I watched as German men and women picked up the cigarette butts that the American soldiers would drop and grind with their shoes into the pavement on the streets.

As the front got nearer, Hadzeman decided to let us stay under the condition that we would each write a letter of appreciation for him for having saved us. He planned to use these letters to protect himself just in case the Germans lost the war. In each letter we had to praise him as our benefactor and protector at the risk of his life. We had to write exactly the way he wanted it written.

43

THE WHITE CAT

The rat population in our cellar seemed to be growing. They were everywhere, openly wandering around. We even gave them names. They were ugly and scary. We worried about the diseases they might carry.

When two of the boys in the Teicher family got very sick, we suspected that they had typhoid, that must have been carried by the rodents, or the lice or bedbugs. We had no medication left. The boys, one fourteen and one sixteen, had very high fever and developed the typical typhoid symptoms. We could not do anything to help them. Some people were already talking in whispers, trying to figure out where to bury the bodies.

As miracles would happen, one day, a white cat appeared out of the blue. Still wanting to believe in God and miracles, it seemed to me that she came to save us from being eaten alive by the rats. She must have come through the bars of the window, off the long tunnel. From that day on she never wanted to leave us. Although she was free to come and go through the small window, she chose to share our lot in the cellar. She became a very important member of our group.

Our bedding and the clothes we wore became moldy from the dampness and they started to fall apart. I made a pair of pants from a coarse burlap sack and wore them everyday. Genia's and Mamma's legs became swollen from malnutrition and the dampness. My legs became weak and my knees were becoming shaky. From that time on, for the rest of her life, Mama suffered from arthritis. My seventeen-year old cousin, White Genia, developed brown spots all over her body and had boils behind her knees. Arco had problems with his vision. Esther Brenner developed a huge boil on her neck. She became deathly ill.

After the cat joined us, the rat population in the cellar decreased somewhat, and they became less bold. The white cat became our hero. She'd kill hundreds of them and she preferred to eat them by my bed. She must have eaten more rats than was good for her, because within a short time she became sick. We were concerned about her because her eyes became runny with puss and even though she ate many rats, she looked emaciated.

Our gratitude to the cat for saving us from the rats was so great, that when once Luba brought back from upstairs a one-liter bottle of milk, most of it was given to the white cat, to help her recover. Heniu Triller, age five and Ania Brenner, age eight, got a cup each. I never got even one sip. At eleven I was too old to get any part of that milk.

The white cat stayed with us in the cellar until liberation and hunted rats till the end. She was my cat and whenever she was not hunting she slept near me.

44

Fantasy
and Reality

Not having quite finished first grade, I was barely literate. Since, in the cellar, there was not much to do and there was no rush, I did manage to get through a few books by reading slowly. One was a thick adult book about the prostitutes of Paris. It was a book by Bruno Jasinski, called "I'm Burning down Paris". In it there was a poem that I still remember: "Magdalenko, Magdalenko, wzruz sie wskruz sie …wierz mej lzie, brna,c w pociemku pod sukienka, zablodzilem Bog wie gdzie."(Maggie, O Maggie have pity, see my tears; God knows where I got lost and wandered off, fumbling in the dark under your dress.)

Another one was a book of poems about the bucolic life in Herzegovina, and one about the flight of Icarus, from which I can still quote: "Lepsze skszydla ojcze trzeba, aby lecic mi do nieba", (Oh my father, I need better wings to be able to fly to the heavens.) Thus Icarus cried out, when plunging to his death, because the sun had melted the wax which his father used to keep his feathered wings together.

I could so well relate to these words spoken by Icarus. Often, in the cellar, I had flying dreams. I would fly, round and round, above the beds and table but I kept hitting the cold and clammy ceiling with my head and never once could I break out into the open sky, not even in my dreams.

In the corner of the hallway, between the two sleeping quarters, twenty sacks of grain were stacked high, almost up to the ceiling. That was our emergency food supply. The men had stolen the grain from upstairs.

I pushed away the top middle sack, creating a perfectly private space where I could lie down and not be seen by anyone. There, I spent most of my time daydreaming and soon I created a fantasy world of my own.

Among the books I read, the two books I loved best were "The Call of the Wild Geese" and "Dan's Daughter". It was these two books that finally opened the ceiling for me and they took me far, far away. My daydreams carried me far beyond the cellar, past Europe and across the Atlantic to Texas. There I rode the wide plains with a mysterious cowboy, the lone rider Dan who spent most of his life in the saddle, and who always whistled at night while riding his spirited black horse.

"At night, Kitty, the girl who loved him, would wait up for him, listening to the sound of his whistling that came from afar and got louder as he would near. Usually, he would mysteriously appear and then leave her just as suddenly, when the call of the wild geese flying above would awaken in him a melancholy restlessness. Then, he would leave the lovelorn Kitty and ride off into the night. Soon Kitty had a child who, with her love for horses and open spaces, took after her father. "

After Dan was shot, I rode with his daughter, Joan, who was also a loner. Soon I was Joan. I had a spirited black horse and a big wolf dog, and at night I would sleep under the stars. The nights under the stars were magical; there, I was at peace.

Within my landscapes of mountains and prairies, walls and ceilings did not exist. There were no people, only roaming coyotes and wild geese flying above. There, I was never scared. With my wolf dog at my side, I rode my horse toward endless horizons.

Whenever I was not daydreaming about my horse and the big Texas sky, I would lie still, up there on top of the sacks, and from my high perch quietly observe my small world in the cellar. People would either ignore me or they would not notice me. I'd listen to Uncle Moshe whistling, to what people were saying, and I'd watch them and observe how they acted. People would fight, cry, gossip, or cuddle up to one another. Once I watched Luba, our "queen Esther", standing near the entrance to the toilet pit holding up a piece of paper to the dim light in the hallway, straining to see something important and confiding in whispers to another girl about something that worried her. She must have been concerned about a possible pregnancy. Although I did not understand it then, that incident stuck in my memory until it made sense later. Once, I saw Triller hit his wife in the middle of the night.

When it got quiet, the rats would come out. I could recognize some of them from the night before and tell them apart as they were parading below. They didn't seem too worried about the cat, which could hardly keep them at bay and eat them all. The cat would climb up and curl up beside me and I'd return to daydreaming about riding my horse under the big Texas sky.

45

THE CELLAR
GOT DARKER

In the summer of 1942, as the front started coming closer to Sambor, bombs began falling above us. Even as the ground shook during the bombing raids, we cheered each explosion because it was a good sign. It meant that the Germans would soon start to retreat. When the electric power station was hit, we were plunged into darkness, with thousands of rats among us. We got more than we asked for. That happened about twelve days before liberation. We had three kerosene lamps, but we only used one because our kerosene supply was small.

When the electricity went out, we could no longer bake our platzki. My mother, always prudent and practical, used to save up, here and there, a few platzki. She would place them in a cloth bag that she would hang to dry on a string above our bed, so that we could keep an eye on them and keep the rats from eating them. This was kept for emergencies, in case we had to leave the cellar or could no longer bake. The platzkis became hard and moldy, but they were all we had to eat, between the time the bombs started falling and liberation. Once a day, we cooked some soup on the small camping stove. It was wheat, boiled with the sparse and yellow water we scraped off the bottom of the well. It was the middle of August, and our well was drying up fast.

Once, as I was sitting in the almost dark room holding a cup of "soup," a bug crawling on the ceiling fell into my bowl. Accidentally, I crunched it between my teeth, but instead of making a fuss about it, I continued to eat the rest of the soup. I still remember the strange taste of that bug; it was nutty and it didn't taste too bad. I think it was a bedbug, or a centipede.

During those two weeks, some people among us ate dry raw fava beans and chewed on hard raw wheat kernels.

Hadzeman asked us one last time for money. Unless we came up with something of value to give him, he wanted us to leave the cellar and go live in the forest. Once again, I'm sure he would have reported us to the Germans if he thought he could get away with it, but at this late stage, he would have implicated himself for having kept us there for a year and a half. It seemed that the letter from my father and the letters of recommendations we gave him were no longer sufficient to make him leave us alone. He made one more effort to extort something from us.

After having given him all our money, clothes, and our last towels, we had nothing more to give him. There was one last resort-- we all knew that Mr. Triller still had a gold watch on him.

Dudziu Freiman called a meeting. Everyone gathered in our chamber and sat down on the bed around the table. The place was dim, except for the small light from the kerosene lamp that stood on top of the table.

We listened to Dudziu as he urged Mr. Triller to give up his watch to bribe Hadzeman and appease him. This way we would buy some time in the cellar. We were so close to liberation, that we could almost allow ourselves to believe that we could last long enough. Judging by the frequent bombs falling, we were sure that the Russians would be coming soon.

Triller refused to give up his watch. Everybody's nerves were strained when a heated verbal fight ensued between Dudziu and Triller. Shouting back and forth at each other, the two men looked like two ferocious animals snarling each other to death.

In the cellar, Dudziu took on the role of an elder statesman. He was well spoken and wise, and now he was pleading with Triller not only for himself but also for all of us. Triller stood his ground. He said that the watch was all he had left in the world and he would need it to pay a doctor to help his five-year-old son Heniu. When Heniu came into the cellar he had an open hole in his head, right behind his right ear. He got injured while still in the ghetto and developed a serious infection. Eventually the infection dried up and left a hole in his head the size of a quarter and it was quite deep. (I understand that little Heniu became a doctor in New York, but I never saw him after liberation.)

The argument between Triller and Dudziu went on for a long time. Suddenly Freiman became so exasperated with Triller's selfishness that he lost his cool and picked up the kerosene lamp and was about to throw it at Triller. Two men quickly grabbed his arms and took the lamp from his hand. Had he thrown it at Triller, no doubt, it would have started a big fire in the cellar. Smoke coming out the tunnel opening would have alerted the guard and the fire department would have flooded our cellar, perhaps after many of us would have first been burned to a crisp. I believe Triller kept his watch.

46

ALMOST FREE

The last two weeks before the liberation were the most difficult ones. We could not bake our tortilla thin-bread anymore, and we were hungry. Without electricity, the cellar was like a tomb, damp and dark. Rats were everywhere, and the white cat was sick and could no longer keep up with their growing numbers. We were afraid that when she'd become weaker, the roles would reverse and they'd kill her. Other than the raw grain, we had no food and the well was almost dry. What little water we could scrape from the bottom of the well was stinky.

Mostly we stayed in our beds, telling stories. Some people would drive everybody crazy, humorously making up delicious menus. Uncle Moshe told stories about his travels. He loved Italy, its people, and their music. He told us many stories about his life in Israel. Once Mrs. Triller talked admiringly about a girl she had known when she lived in Lvov. The girl was studying physics at the university there. It must have made an impression on me, although I was not quite sure what that meant. When, at the age of 15, I found out what physics was about, I thought to myself, I can do that too, it's easy. Ten years later, I also became a physicist.

Hadzeman must have stopped coming to his office when the fighting neared, because to our great relief we no longer heard the three knocks.

One day, the German army swarmed all over the warehouse building above our cellar. In the tunnel by the stairs we could hear German spoken. It was very scary, but we became really nervous when they set down a box full of eggs and other foods on the very step we used as an entrance.

Soon there was chaos in the city. The barrage of artillery shots that were going off all around us was getting more intense and frequent with each day. From then on, hearing the explosions above us made every day our "Fourth of July". Every time a bomb fell above us, we rejoiced and cheered, even though the whole place would shake. Each bomb was a greeting that our liberators were sending us. No other love note ever sounded so sweet.

After a few days, the German soldiers left the building. We listened in on their conversations and understood that the Germans were leaving the city. After they left the building, in our excitement, we ran upstairs to the attic, to see for ourselves that the Germans were indeed retreating. I was standing in the attic straining to look out through a hole in the roof when a bullet pierced the roof no more than a few inches from my left ear.

In the last few days before the Russians came, we kept going upstairs to the attic to see everything we could, straining to see through the small holes in the roof. We saw a city in chaos, with many fleeing together with the retreating German army. We even watched from downstairs, where we could see better through bigger holes in the tin roll–down window covers. The windows looked out onto Przemyska Street, which ran east west, and we were less than twenty feet from the road.

We saw hundreds of trucks and horse-drawn wagons laden with Ukrainian and Polish collaborators and their families, all fleeing with the German army. There were so many collaborators during the German occupation. We feared them as much if not more than the Germans. The Germans were like cold robot-like killers, or like efficient rat exterminators, and sometimes just following orders. The local collaborators were participating in the murder voluntarily out of a hatred they bore towards us for centuries. Why did they hate us so? After all, we used to be their neighbors, their teachers and their students, their clients, doctors and their patients. Above all, we had been their loyal fellow countrymen for centuries.

Among the fleeing collaborators were Hadzeman and his family, including the murderer Holovey.

Thousands of these people headed for Germany, and there they remained when Germany surrendered to the Allies.

After the war, all the Nazi collaborators from east European countries were treated with great sympathy by the naïve and ill informed American relief organizations. All the collaborators were lumped together with the people who had just been liberated from death camps or other rat holes. These fleeing Nazis misrepresented themselves and passed as displaced war victims and refugees. Eventually they came together with us on immigrant boats to the US and to Canada.

Of course, there were some exceptions. Some people from eastern Europe who were political prisoners were also liberated from concentration camps and some from labor camps in Germany.

Hadzeman and his family, including the murderer Holovey ended up in Canada. There, he went around from one Jewish organization to another, pandering for as much money and support as he could get by showing off the letters he forcibly extorted from us under threats.

When the Germans withdrew from Sambor and after the fighting and shooting quieted down, we hastily assumed that the Russians had taken our town over. Here and there a few people began to crawl out from their hiding places. Luba had keys to Hadzeman's apartment. Genia and Yosiu and the Teicher boys got out of the cellar and ventured into the streets, but almost immediately the shooting started again. They barely made it back. Fortunately, because of the chaos in the city, they were unnoticed and were not followed.

It turned out that we were wrong; the Russians had not liberated the city yet. Only the local partisans had briefly taken over the city, but they were soon forced to retreat. During the brief lull in the fighting, Father also got out from his hiding place and he came looking for us. When he finally came down into the cellar, not knowing what to expect, he looked like a mad man. His eyes darting from one face to another, he was seeking the faces of his loved ones. Seeing Mama, Genia and me, he was so overcome by emotion that for a long time he could not utter a word. For me to see him alive was what it must feel like to behold the face of a Messiah. Father remained with us, while above us the fighting went on for several more days.

47

UNCLE MOSHE

Uncle Moshe, my father's brother, was one of the most crucial members in our cellar. Both he and my father had been the original masterminds of the cellar project. My father took charge of getting all the needed supplies into the cellar and Moshe took charge of the work inside to make it livable.

When, as a young man, he lived in Israel as a Halutz (a Zionist pioneer), he acquired many practical skills. Many of these skills came from living and working in a Kibutz (a collective farm) and also from jobs as a builder in the city. Most importantly, he had innate talents and ingenuity. With his mechanical and electrical skills he created for us a place in which we could live for almost two years until the Russians liberated us. Arco, Wizengreen, Shlomek Freiman and Yosiu helped out the most, especially with the digging of the well, and the tunnel. Compared to the conditions in the death camps and some of the other hiding places where Jews were clinging to life, we in the cellar lived in relative luxury.

Moshe was absolutely amazing. If not for his ingenuity, skills and hard work, we would not have survived the war. Uncle Moshe turned a rat infested dark dungeon into an amazing hiding place for twenty-six people; (though it remained rat infested till the end).

Only months before he started to work on the cellar, his beautiful young wife, Elka, and his children were taken away from him. Elka and her children were among the first Jews in our town who were caught by the Germans and sent to a concentration camp where they died in gas chambers.

Somehow, uncle Moshe escaped being caught. He may have

been at work when the raid started. He survived the rest of the Nazi occupation living in the ghetto for a few months helping to create our little orphanage, and then again in the cellar until liberation.

Unlike his three older brothers, Mendel, Benjamin, and Jankiev-Leib, and his younger brother my father Yosef, Moshe was not a businessman. Moshe was an artist and a dreamer. He could fix, build and repair almost anything. He was also very musical. He was a shy and quiet man who loved to whistle.

After losing his wife and children there was an infinite sadness in his dark green eyes. For the rest of his life, that sadness never left him. He blamed himself for their deaths because he listened to his wife's family, who urged them to leave Israel and return to Sambor. After the war, Moshe returned to Israel a broken man.

Just before leaving Europe, Moshe met a widow, Chaika, who had also lost her husband in an extermination camp. Still in Munich, they got married and they had a son, Hayim, who was named for Moshe's father, my grandfather Hayim Zecharia Meisels. They left for Israel right after Chaim's birth.

When I was seventeen, and Uncle Moshe was still in Germany he came to visit us in Munich. I took that opportunity to spend some time with him; I bought tickets for the opera for the two of us and we saw a performance of the opera Carmen. I never did find words to express to him my appreciation for all he did towards our group's survival in the cellar or even for the beautiful music he used to whistle; therefore sharing with him a live opera performance meant a lot to me. It was the first opera he had ever seen on stage.

In Israel, with time, Moshe became reclusive. On a trip to Israel in 1969, my oldest son Jonny who was ten years old, met uncle Moshe for the first time. Young Jonny said that Uncle Moshe was the saddest man he had ever seen and that he had the saddest eyes.

Eventually, towards the end of his life, Moshe went into a deep depression. He became paranoid and soon he lost his mind altogether. He stopped whistling.

The last time I saw him, he was afraid of everyone. All day, he would sit in a chair, , chain-smoking, and staring with a far away gaze, but he was very glad to see me. I spent as much time with him as I could. He held onto my hand, while telling me how everybody was after him. I played for him some of the music he used to whistle in the cellar; I brought him music tapes by Rampal, Galway, and Zamfir. Holding hands, we sat together and listened to the tapes while Aunt Chaika brought us tea and cookies she had baked for me. By that time, she was also sickly, and she had a hard time coping with his depression.

Unfortunately, he was no longer able to even enjoy the fact that his son, Hayim, grew up to become a very intelligent and fine man, who was by then, raising a wonderful new family of his own in Israel. Uncle Moshe died in Israel in 1980.

My last visit with Uncle Moshe in Israel

48

LIBERATION

In September in 1944, we were liberated by the Russian Army. The day was so bright that it was almost blinding. I walked out of the cellar on skeleton-like thin and shaky legs, holding a white cat. I was pale as a ghost, with waist long pigtails full of lice, and was wearing a pair of pants I had sewed by hand from a burlap sack. My arms were all bloody, scratched up by the white cat, because she did not want to leave the cellar, and I would not leave without her. This white cat had been my constant companion and friend, curling up next to me on top of the stack of grain, where I used to escape into my imaginary world.

I always thought that if it had not been for her, sooner or later we would have all been eaten alive by the rats. She had no name. She appeared out of nowhere and willingly shared our dungeon with us.

That first day out of the cellar, I gave the white cat food, but by nighttime she was dead. Weak, or sick from eating too many rats, she fell off the roof and died. Everyone tells me that cats ordinarily don't fall off roofs, but our white cat was not an ordinary cat. Maybe she was very sick and already blind.

Having lived in the cellar for sixteen months, it took me a while to get accustomed to sunlight.

The first week out of the cellar, Arco Velker was blinded by the sun. At first he was completely blind, but within a few weeks, he regained his sight.

Walking out of the cellar, I was stunned. Sambor and its people looked and went on about their lives as if nothing had happened. The place hadn't changed. The Jews had not been missed by our former neighbors, the Polish and Ukrainian inhabitants of

Sambor.

I not only looked like a ghost, I felt like one. The second day out of the cellar I was in the street and as I was walking very slowly on shaky legs, a Polish woman stopped for a moment in front of me and she exclaimed, "Holy Mother of God, child, what happened to you?" She did not wait for an answer and walked on. How could she not have known what had happened to me?

49

FACING SAMBOR ANEW

After liberation, I was supposed to make a fast transition into a mindset that would allow me to fit in and function among others that had not shared my traumatic experiences of the Holocaust.

Finally, I was free to come back to life above ground, to come back to Sambor; but I was a stranger in my own hometown. I was very different from the Gentile people around me, as if I were returning as a member of a different species. It was very disorienting.

How was I to find my bearing? They, the Gentile population of Sambor, still lived in the same homes that they had had for years. Their children never missed a day of school and still had aunts, uncles, cousins, and grandparents. The Polish and Ukrainian children were "normal." They had red cheeks and healthy bodies, they rode bikes, played ball, did cartwheels in the grass, walked to school, teased each other and laughed. At twelve, I was old. I was different. I also felt unwelcome in a town that used to be home to my big extended family for countless generations.

Thinking back, it seemed that before the war, our town's vibrant ambience was shared among all residents of Sambor. Yet in less than four years from the start of WWII, one third of its population was excluded from its life and marked for death. After liberation, many people in Sambor were even heard saying that "too many Jewish bastards had survived" (about one percent). No, Sambor was no longer "home".

Now the walls that separated me from everybody in Sambor were invisible. Like members of different species, we did not relate to one another, although we still spoke the same language and equally knew each square inch of this town.

In a confusing way, the mourning for my family commingled with the excitement of discovering the world anew. Still, questions that I could not answer, like a mind blowing Koan, filled my head. "Why was I alive and my cousin Zosia dead?" "Why, were we Jews so different from other people in the world?" "Why were we so hated?" "Did my uncles in America know what had happened to us during the war? If they had known would they have moved heaven and earth to stop the killings?"

Zosia was not there with me to rediscover the sky, the chestnut trees, a piece of bread or a cup of milk.

All this was going on in my mind for the next days, months and years. I was wrestling within whether to walk over a short few blocks to where the Ghetto had once stood. The mere thought of it was causing me almost unbearable anguish; it rekindled in my mind the horrors of the ghetto, the pain of losing my family, the pain of having survived without them. I was a helpless child facing a cruel world.

I did not go to the ghetto, to face the ruins and the finality they represented. If my parents ever did go there, they never spoke about it.

Years later, I wished I had had the courage to do so. Perhaps I would have found scraps of photographs, and perhaps some closure. For years after, I kept having re-occurring dreams about going there, opening door after door and searching frantically, calling name after name, and crying because no one answered; I never found anyone there, even in my dreams.

Though, emotionally, I was not finished with my childhood, my body was changing, and others began to see me differently than who I felt I was. In time, I learned to play the role of an adolescent, a teenager and a woman. Inside I was none of them. I was neither child nor adult. From a young child I made a quick transition and I became a very old child. For a long time I also remained a displaced person who had a hard time making a transition from being an outcast, living on death row, to becoming a legitimate human being. Though I knew anger and sadness, I did not know how to want and need things. I had to learn how to say aloud the words, "No, you can't do that to us, to me" rather than quietly endure whatever abuse confronted me. What was my birthright?

After having lived for so long in a subterranean rat habitat, and as maladjusted as I was, after liberation I was re-discovering a beautiful world under the open sky. Every new experience felt like a first and was so achingly vivid. At the age of twelve, I was in many ways like a newborn. Everything was new and exciting. Seeing the sky, trees, new people, animals, eating vegetables, eggs, bread, cookies, drinking milk, drinking clean water, hearing music; all of these were all new and very exciting discoveries. Kids and most adults usually take such everyday things for granted. To me, at that time, every experience had the intensity of a miraculous happening.

Still, I was to be more of a spectator than a participant in all that was happening around me. I was old enough to consciously register everything "new" but also old enough to remember the hell I had come from, and I was having a hard time reconciling the two when trying to define my identity and envision a future.

50

IN SAMBOR
WITH THE RUSSIANS

Immediately after leaving the cellar, that same day, we, the twenty-six survivors gratefully presented our liberators, the Russian army, with a gift of twenty sacks of grain. Yosiu, who came back to the cellar to help me get the cat out, brought a Russian officer down with him.

Entering the cellar, the Russian officer was stunned and speechless. Of course, he was taken aback by the stench in the cellar; he kept holding his nose. Beside him, only Yosiu, the white cat and I were there to register his utter amazement at what he saw. When he looked around the cellar, realizing that twenty-six people had survived there for so long, he was overcome with emotion. He told us that someone must make a film about it. I wonder if that officer survived the fighting that still raged west of Sambor.

I often wonder what became of our cellar; could it still be there as we had left it?

My parents soon found an empty place that must have been vacated by Nazi collaborators who probably had left with the retreating German army. We shared the 3-bedroom apartment with many other people, all fellow survivors. There was my aunt Regina and her 15-year-old son Yosiu, Regina's sister Hanka, and her four-year-old daughter Zania.

I think Hanka and Zania had survived living for a time on false "Aryan" papers outside the ghetto. Zania's Aryan-Polish false name was Jancia Pliszewska. (I wonder why I still remember it) I remember Zania as a cute blue-eyed four year-old. She grew up to become a professor at the University of Haifa in Israel.

Uncle Yankiev-Leib, and his wife Ryfcia and her brother Emanuel Langer also shared the three-bedroom apartment with us.

On the first day after liberation, I went with my aunt Regina to get some milk. We took a long walk to a small farm on the out-skirts of town. Aunt Regina knew the young Jewish woman who lived there with the peasant's son who had saved her life and given her shelter after the ghetto was liquidated. It was well known that the young man had been a German collaborator and worked as a Ukrainian policeman and as such, had participated in raids, rounding up Jews for slaughter.

Whenever such survival cases were later talked about, I had the sense that it was to remain a secret to be kept between us, because the poor, humiliated girls felt a lot of guilt and shame. We did not judge them, nor did we fault them for wanting to do everything possible to stay alive.

Not wanting anyone to hear her speak Yiddish, the girl on the farm spoke quietly with my aunt. Apparently, the man she was living with had been abusing her for a long time. We walked out to the large backyard where the young woman was able to talk more freely while she let my aunt milk a cow. After a while, Aunt Regina and I left the girl. We returned home with a big jug of milk.

Aunt Regina boiled the milk, and when it cooled a bit, I walked over to the big pot and drank it all up. No one said a word, no one scolded me, as I lifted the heavy pot to my mouth, tilting it until it was upside down. With a loving expression on her face, Aunt Regina watched me drink the milk, she did not say a word to stop me. I drank the whole big pot. How I loved aunt Regina and how sweet that milk tasted.

The young woman left her abusive man shortly thereafter and joined her brother, Tulek, who was also one of the survivors of Sambor, and they soon left town.

After our liberation Aunt Ryfcia, Uncle Yankiev-Leib's wife, was having a difficult time facing reality. On the verge of losing her sanity, she was still in shock, mourning the loss of her three children. Sometimes she acted strangely. One day she put on a

Russian soldier's uniform and declared to her husband, Yankiev-Leib, that she was going to the front to fight the Germans, to avenge the death of her children. Hard as he tried, Uncle Yankiev-Leib could not dissuade her with words; he had to forcibly stop her from storming out of the apartment and then he locked her up in their room for rest of the day until she calmed down.

After the Russians established a foothold in our town and the front moved a few miles west of Sambor, other Jews who had managed to survive in Sambor started crawling out of their hiding places. The survivors stayed close to one another, sharing empty apartments near our place. People would greet each other with much emotion, expressing surprise at finding one another alive. They exchanged horror stories of what they had witnessed and endured, tearfully talking about the loss of their families and telling amazing stories of their escapes and survival. We were happy to find Mr. and Mrs. Frei and their fifteen-year-old daughter Mela; I don't know how they survived. There was a beautiful young girl Feidzia, who was the only one of her family to have survived. She was saved by a Ukrainian priest who placed her with a Ukrainian peasant family as a Ukrainian orphan. The peasants themselves did not know her true identity; they were very antisemitic.

There were two young sisters, Henia and Adela, from Stary Sambor, who barely escaped being caught during an Akcja in Sambor. Henia who was about fifteen at the time got separated from her sister Adela. She found herself running near the train station looking desperately for a place to hide. She spotted a Gentile farmer at the station platform, sitting on his bundles and waiting for his train. It was winter and the farmer wore a huge sheepskin coat. Henia crawled quickly under the big sheepskin coat. The man took pity on the frightened girl, allowing her to stay under his coat for some time. When it became safer for Henia to crawl out from under the farmer's coat she found her sister Adela, who must have also found a nearby place to hide. Together they headed to the forest, where they lived for over a year. Starving, at night they would steal vegetables from farmer's gardens to feed themselves. On cold nights, they would sometimes manage to sneak into a barn and hide in the hay.

Among the survivors, were a young "Schochet" (a special rabbi who slaughters cows and poultry, according to strict religious law so that they are kosher to eat) and his brother, whom I did not know, and Mrs. Bombach, whom I had known from before and who had survived alone. The Bombachs used to be Aunt Laika's neighbors just before the Germans came. Laika's other neighbors, the Kleins and their daughter Erna, disappeared early on; they must have been taken away during the first Akcja.

A short time after liberation, Mama ran into a blond Gentile woman who also used to be Aunt Laika's, the Klein's and the Bombach's neighbor. The Gentile woman told Mama that she saw Aunt Laika being led to jail during the final Akcja. She recounted that Laika had called out to her, begging her to take the baby from her and save her. Laika told her former neighbor that her sister Sara (my mother) was in hiding and after the war would take the child and reward the woman greatly. Apparently there was an opportune moment for little Andzia to sneak away, had the woman been willing to take her. But the woman was either unwilling to save the child, or too scared to risk her own life. I remember that woman well, although I don't remember her name. She had two teenage daughters. I remember that during the Russian occupation, Laika and the blond woman were on very friendly terms, visiting each other often.

Of all of Laika's neighbors, I remembered the Bombachs best, because they had an adorable little baby boy with big blue eyes and curly golden hair. I always loved babies and I used to play with that child. I saw the mother and baby once again in the ghetto. Later, I heard that during the liquidation of our ghetto, Mrs. Bombach and her baby were hiding in a bunker together with other people. When the boy began to cry, the mother was told by the others to silence the child because everyone's life was in danger. Had they been heard and their hiding place discovered, all would have been shot.

People said that Mrs. Bombach was forced to put a pillow over the baby's face. The baby soon became quiet; it had suffocated. Mrs. Bombach survived, and like us, she was liberated in Sambor by the Russian army. She survived alone. Every one knew the poor woman's story, but no one talked about it much, because we all had our own tragic survival stories. Besides, we were all still in our survival modes, the war was not over till eight months later.

Immediately after liberation, several marriages quickly took place among a few lone survivors. Young Faidzia, Henia, and Adella married older men who had lost their wives and children and who became like father figures to the young women. Mrs. Bombach married the young Shochet.

When Mama bought live chickens from farmers, I would come along with her to bring the chickens to the Shochet's place to be slaughtered. I would see him grab a squirming chicken, bend its neck backward and quickly cut its protruding jugular vein, its blood squirting high in the air.

Though the Shohet was a learned man, and one who held a position of respect and whose services were needed, his job was what it was; killing living things all-day, day in and day out. One moment they were squawking and squirming and the next moment they were all piled up in the corner and all quiet. The Shochet's new wife, the former Mrs. Bombach, would usually stand by in the same room, busy cooking. She was probably too numb from her own pain to care about the poor chickens.

The first evening after liberation, I sat on the balcony observing, from my solitary perch, an unfamiliar world below. I was getting reacquainted with an early evening sky and the sweet smell of clean air, grass and leaves. Across the street, I saw young people strolling under the chestnut trees by the big Catholic Church, laughing and with their arms around each other. I heard a young man who was passing by and whistling a wistful, romantic tune. I still remember it.

That scene and that tune drove me crazy with sadness, because it was so hauntingly beautiful, and because I felt it so deeply, how different I was from those happy and beautiful young people strolling bellow. That's how I would have been also, had I grown up in Sambor without being ostracized and persecuted for being Jewish.

I knew I had not come back from the cellar to "my town," Sambor. I was no longer part of this community, and its "rightful" people. Even the Polish or Ukrainian boy who whistled that beautiful tune would have probably thought that I didn't belong here and hate me just because I was Jewish.

In the course of the following days, my cousin Yosiu and I explored some places nearby. In one abandoned place that was empty of furniture we found lots of books, reproductions of DaVinci drawings, and self-study books. We also found lots of blank paper. I recall wading through the books and papers strewn all over the floors. The place was swarming with fleas. I returned to our apartment with armloads of books and papers, and flea bites on my arms and legs and I sat on the sunny balcony going over them.

I spent the remaining warm days sitting on that balcony from morning till dusk, soaking up the sun and relishing in seeing the sky. I couldn't stand walls and ceilings. I also drew and copied some of the beautiful pictures I had found.

Only miles away from us, the fighting was still going on and in the distance, shooting was still heard. Not too far from where I was sitting under the sun and drawing pictures, people were still dying and they were still killing each other; beautiful, healthy, young men were dying and getting maimed. For that magnificent prospect, they did not even have to be Jewish.

Perhaps out of revenge, knowing that most local Ukrainians had been collaborating with the Germans, immediately after entering Sambor, the Russians started grabbing young Ukrainian men off the streets and sending them to face German artillery as a line of first defense. These men were totally untrained.

I remember seeing Ukrainian mothers standing in front of the fence of a large field, where the Ukrainian men were being detained before they were taken to the front. Wrapped in their head-scarves, they brought for their sons some food and they cried a lot. Many of the captured were mere boys.

I also saw the Russians lead a large group of disheveled and hungry Hungarian prisoners-of-war through the center of town. I saw one bend down to grab a dirty apple core that was lying on the ground. The Hungarians had fought alongside the Germans. I hear that the Hungarian people themselves were less vicious towards their Jewish fellow citizens than the Poles and the Ukrainians.

I saw German prisoners-of-war, staring vacantly from behind a barbed-wire fence just a few feet from the cobblestone steps where Aunt Dvorka's candy store used to be. I stood there with clenched teeth, looking at the caged Nazis, remembering a smiling Dvorka behind the counter of her candy store. Looking at these cold, hungry, and sad bastards in their tattered green uniforms, I should have liked to have see them dying the way I remembered them, at the height of their murderous arrogance, before it was too late for Dvorka and the others. I was all confused and churning inside; I choked on my feelings and on the words I could have shouted at the Germans, but did not, because it was all too much for a child of twelve to make sense of.

While standing there, I saw a local woman attempting to give some bread to one of the German prisoners behind the fence and I called the Russian guard over, and pointed at the woman as she was trying to squeeze a slice of bread through the wire fence; the Russian guard chased her away. Such was the rage I lived with then and for many years after.

The German prisoner, human enough to feel his own fear and hunger, the woman who pitied him, the Russian guard who chased her away, and I, who told on her, all shared that same silent moment on a winter evening in 1944. Though we stood there, close enough to touch, we would each remember it differently and never once hear one another out. Then again, what would be the point of that-- Dvorka and her children were already dead. I couldn't have envisioned then, a time when I would want to reach out to all people, for the sake of my children, and make an effort to bridge the history, the misunderstandings and the hatreds that divide us and could cause so much destruction and pain.

The Russian soldiers were everywhere. I loved the Russian soldiers; they were my liberators, and I found them to be good people. They were friendly and related to us as fellow victims of Nazi atrocities. They shared with us what little food and whisky they had, and they had very little. They drank a lot and would often sell their coats for a bottle of whisky. Perhaps the whisky dulled the fear of having to face the next round of bullets on the front that was not far away.

The Russian soldiers camped out just below our balcony; even in cold weather they washed up in the open, with ice- cold water from the well. Later, when winter came, they scrubbed down their bodies with snow. They were amazingly hardy. They usually hung out there on a patch of grass or snow, and talked, laughed, ate and drank whisky. At night they sang beautiful, sad, Russian songs, all in minor keys. The strong smell of machorka, their rough tobacco, would fill the air all around them.

The Russian soldiers loved children. I liked hanging around them. They taught me their songs and once they even gave me a little dog named Sharik, who had been their pet mascot. Some of the soldiers were as young as 16, and many of the young Russian boys were already wounded. I was in love with most of them. I too wanted to be a Russian soldier. I especially admired the Russian girl soldiers. They were strong and tough, they fought alongside their men and they drove tanks. I also wanted to wear a Russian uniform and begged my father to get me one. Thinking that it was cute, my father, who could never say no to me, got me a uniform which he probably bought from a soldier for a bottle of vodka. The tailor next door fixed it to fit me. Father also got me black boots to go with the uniform. I wore the uniform all the time and I refused to wear anything else. Now, I wonder if the soldier he bought it from had taken the uniform off a dead comrade, because I saw soldiers on the street peddling uniforms and coats that were still bloody.

Grateful to our liberators and fearing that the Germans may come back, I begged my parents to leave Sambor immediately after liberation and move to Russia. I idealized our liberators, who I knew, in theory, aspired towards creating a more just world. I no longer wanted to live among the Poles and Ukrainians because they did not want us.

I totally believed the Communist propaganda, as I heard it and kept repeating it when singing the Russian war songs I learned from the soldiers. Some songs were about "Our beloved father Stalin who will lead us to victory." Other songs were a mixture of wartime romance, its losses, victories and more propaganda. Through the images that these beautiful, heartfelt and romantic songs projected in my heart and mind, I would visualize my future life in Russia.

One day, I met a tall, thin, and pockmarked Russian air force officer. His eyes were deep-set and somewhat slanted. I think he was a Tartar from the Ural region in Russia. He seemed overly friendly, but he did not scare me, and I was happy to talk to him. I told him that I also wanted to become a pilot so that I could bomb the Germans and kill them all. He asked me if I would like to go to Moscow and go to school there. I said yes, that was my dream.

The tall, pockmarked officer was probably a bit drunk, because he took me seriously, and he went to my parents to tell them that he wanted to take me back to Moscow and enroll me in a military air force school. In the meantime, he wanted to marry me. He then grabbed me, pulled me into our family's bedroom and locked the door. Immediately, my parents and my sister started frantically banging on the door, pleading with him to open it and let me go. They told him that I was only twelve and still a child.

Somehow, they may have made a false promise to him which he apparently believed, because he finally opened the door a crack. I pushed it open and bolted out and hid in the attic until nighttime. The man was not rough with me, and at first I was not at all frightened, but then I smelled his alcohol and the banging on the door got frantic; everyone sounded as if they were pleading for my life. Only then did I realize that this might turn into something serious and scary.

That episode did not make me think less of Russian soldiers or love their songs any less. Nor did it diminish my desire to move to Russia. In Russia, I thought I could become a "normal" human being. Communism promised equality, and that's what I longed for, above all. Where else would I go to be just a normal kid and not a dirty Jew, as the Polish kids still called me in Sambor, even after liberation.

For a few months, I tried going to school in Sambor. The girls made fun of my Russian soldier uniform and moved my coat over to the boy's section. The local people mostly disliked the Russians.

Some kids called me dirty Jew and some told me that they

liked the German soldiers better than the dirty Russians. After school, on the way home, I'd beat up these kids mercilessly. Although I was small and not in good physical shape, I beat them up with such passionate anger that they would later cross the street and walk on the other side to avoid me. I was going to become as tough as the Russian soldier girls and I had my start fighting back, right there.

I had only one friend left-- beautiful, delicate Stasia, who lived nearby and was very poor. Her mother was a house cleaner, and she did not have a father. They lived in a tiny place. Her mother was a tall, quiet and friendly woman, and she reminded me of my Aunt Dvorka. I liked spending time there, especially since their dog had new puppies. At Christmas time, Stasia and I made little paper angels from colored paper and I helped her decorate the tree in their one-room home.

One winter evening coming back from Stasia's place, a Russian soldier grabbed me in the street and pinned me against a wall. It was getting dark and cold and the streets were empty. Somehow I freed myself from his grip by wiggling frantically, and I ran home as fast as my legs would carry me. I don't think I told anyone about it. To think that I was old enough to attract a soldier, and even find that exciting! Still, I was ashamed of my femininity, and the soldier's forcefulness scared me.

Sometimes, some Russian officers would come up to have some drinks and food with us, and only behind closed doors and in strict secrecy would they disclose to us that they were also Jewish. Apparently, anti-Semitism was rampant within the Russian army too. To me, who romanticized and loved Russians, learning this, was a terrible blow. Here we go again, I thought.

A few months after liberation, my parents befriended a handsome young Russian officer by the name of Voskovboynikov. He was a very friendly man and would visit often. He liked my parents and would bring drinks and food to share. Voskovboynikov was not Jewish but he had a Jewish wife back in Russia.

Within a few months after liberation, most of the Jewish survivors started to leave Sambor. One could not do it legally because the Soviets did not let people out. Sometime in January 1945, we got out of Sambor forever.

Aunt Regina, her son Yosiu, Uncle Yankev-Leib and his wife Ryfcia also soon left Sambor. After a brief stay in Poland, they managed to go to Israel. Only White Genia remained in Poland, after the rest of us moved on to other countries. She married Edmund Hebenstreit, a bright and handsome Polish Jew who had been a Polish officer; he survived the war in Russia. Edmund was well educated, and upon his return to Poland assumed a prominent teaching position. They lived well for a few years, but when their little daughter started school she was bullied daily by other kids because, unlike her blond parents she had black hair like her grandfather Mendel, my father's middle brother, and she apparently looked more Jewish than Aryan. Still bemoaning the loss of his beloved Polish language and culture, Edmund and and White Genia promptly picked themselves up and moved to Israel for the sake of their daughter. Not knowing the Hebrew language, they had a hard time adjusting. However their daughter, Renia, grew up to become a well adjusted and a proud Israeli.

Edmund, White Genia,
and their daughter Renia, in Uniform

51

LEAVING SAMBOR

Our Russian friend, Voscovboynikov, happened to have a big Studebaker army truck at his disposal- courtesy of the American army. With his truck he helped us get out of Sambor and into Poland, which lay beyond the western shore of the river San, and less than a hundred miles west of Sambor. At the border, the Russian guards waved us on. Most likely, our handsome officer friend must have bribed them with bottles of vodka.

Voskovboynikov continued to visit us in Poland. Soon he proposed a business arrangement to my father. They became good friends and business partners. They would travel to Hungary by truck, where they would load up on good Hungarian Tokay wine and then bring it back to Poland and sell it locally. At that time in our region, the black market was the only market.

Voskovboynikov had a mattress on his truck bed. I overheard that he would often pick up women on the road and bed them in his truck. In time, there must have been scores of gorgeous little Voskovboynikovs running around between Hungary and Poland.

After we left Sambor, we lived in Przemysl for a short while, before moving on, further west, to Krakow. The wine trade continued for some time.

In Przemysl, we found a two-bedroom apartment which we shared with a Jewish couple, the Schors. Mr. Schor was short and rotund, with black hair and a "Chaplinesque" mustache. He could have been handsome if he were not so fat. Mrs. Schor was tall and well built. She was almost pretty, but she painted her face too much and dressed provocatively, fixing her long hair like a teenager and wearing little pleated skirts that were way too short. Mrs. Schor had once been Mr. Schor's sister-in-law.

From listening to gossipy talk I found out that before the war Mr. Schor lived with his wife and kids in a small town and that his wife's younger sister had been his lover for some time. Somehow, the two of them managed to go into hiding together after the wife and his children were caught and taken to a concentration camp where they were killed.

I don't know how my parents met them, but we all moved into a two-bedroom apartment that Mr. Schor found and together with the Russian officer, he and my father became partners in business. Eventually my parents talked the two of them into marriage, and they became Mr. and Mrs. Schor. Mrs. Schor always waited on her man, hand and foot. He was lazy and he bossed her around as if she was his servant, but I think that she had an eye on the handsome young Russian officer, Voskovboynikov. We all did, young and old.

Our apartment in Przemysl was confiscated from an older woman who had lived there with a daughter and her infant baby. Apparently, a German soldier had fathered the baby. Because of that, the young woman had become an outcast in the neighborhood and the three of them were literally thrown out from their apartment by the Polish housing authority. Apparently, Mr. Schor found out about the available apartment from a Polish official, whom he had known and had probably bribed.

I watched as the mother and the young girl packed their belongings; they were leaving the apartment just as we were moving in. Without saying a word, and looking very sad, the older woman carrying a suitcase and the young girl, with the baby in her arms, meekly walked out of the apartment. Recalling that scene is like hearing the screech of chalk on a blackboard. It was nauseating, even though these women had been wrong to associate with the enemy.

Out in the streets, Russian soldiers returning from the German front were peddling stuff they had looted and brought back from Germany, attracting crowds that were starved for merchandise that was hard to get during the war.

The Russian soldiers stood on top of the heaps of stuff that were piled up high on the beds of their American-made trucks, and they peddled clothing, umbrellas, and household items. The jolly, half-drunk soldiers were raking it in. A mob of people surrounded the trucks and the Russians were selling their stuff as fast as they could reach the money that the people were waving at them.

In Przemysl, the apartment house we moved to was close to railroad tracks. At first, the passing trains were uncomfortably noisy. Within a short time, I got used to the trains, coming and going around the clock. I even got to love their klikety klick klatter, especially at night. The passing trains would spark my imagination, and they made me restless and want to go to far away places.

I watched open railroad cars filled with looted machinery and equipment going from Germany to Russia, and often the trains were filled with wounded Russian soldiers returning from German front lines. Some of the returning soldiers were sitting in the open doors of cargo cars with their legs playfully dangling off the sides, and singing and playing on their looted accordions. Sometimes I saw transports of German prisoners of war on their way to Russia. Seeing them defeated and looking dejected in no way lessened the pain of remembering what they did to my family en route to war fronts.

The apartment house we lived in was nice and modern, but across the way there was a bombed out and abandoned apartment house which people from the street used as a toilet; it was full of feces and garbage.

I found a little white dog that I named Ciapush. Mama let me keep him; I also spent a lot of my time sitting, once again, on a balcony and drawing. This time I drew with my ten-year-old Jewish neighbor Hesiu who also loved to draw. Sometimes Hesiu and I wandered around the city together. Like in Sambor after liberation, here too, I did not feel that I fit in with the local population. Although we spoke the same language, we had nothing else in common.

Shortly after we had moved from Sambor to Przemysl, we came to experience Polish anti-Semitism from members of the Polish underground. One afternoon, as I was coming out from the bathroom and calling for my dog, I suddenly felt someone grab me by my throat from behind; a big hand was squeezing my throat so hard that I began to choke. Then the tall man who was choking me, noticed in the bedroom a framed picture of Stalin and it made him furious. He asked whose it was. It was standing on my night table. "It's mine," I naively answered, and the big hand around my throat tightened, and I was choking again. I kept Stalins picture because I considered him to be my liberator, and felt that only the Russians were as angry with the Germans as I was. I also believed that they were fighting the Germans in revenge for what they did to us Jews.

Shoving me in front of him, the man held on to my throat with one hand, while using the other to push open the door to the Schor's bedroom, where he threw me to the floor. My mother, both Schors and a middle aged Gentile lady who was their visitor, were all lying on the floor, face down. A second man stood over them with a pointed gun, ordering them not to move or he'd shoot. Cursing and shouting anti-Semitic expletives, the two men were demanding money. They were members of the Polish underground, known as the A.K. (Armia Krajowa) and considered themselves at war with the Soviets.

My mother and the Schors looked terrified while the Gentile Polish lady was whimpering and begging for mercy. She kept saying "please don't kill me, I am not Jewish, I'm a Pole".

After what seemed a long time the underground men left. They ransacked the place, but they could not find any money. We were all left shaking. To this day, I often have a feeling that someone is about to sneak up from behind and grab me by my throat and whenever I'm being seated at a restaurant, I'm always the first one to grab a chair in a corner so that my back is against the wall.

Soon after that incident, we left Przemysl. Father and Genia left first, they must have gone in a truck with Voskovboynikow, taking all our stuff. Mama and I took a train to Krakov. I had my little dog, Ciapus, with me, hiding him under my coat from the conductor. Mama always let me have a dog.

In Krakov, once again, we found and shared an apartment with the Schors. I attended a small Jewish school for several months. Almost all of the children in the school were Jewish orphans who had lost their parents in the Holocaust.

Kracov was a beautiful city. By the spring of 1945, I was a mature girl; I was almost thirteen years old. I enjoyed wandering around town and discovering new things. Often, I would take the trolley to the "Sukkennice," which was a well-known folk Bazaar in Krakov. Once I bought some chewing gum in a small store. I read the instructions over and over and still could not figure it out what to do with it. I had never seen anyone chew gum before.

The downtown trolley in Krakov used to pass near a big church and all the passengers would cross themselves as soon we were passing in front of it. Sitting there in the trolley, I always felt that all the passengers were starring at me with anger because my hands would remain in my lap. Once, I remember feeling so uncomfortable that I brought my hand up to fumble with the buttons of my blouse so as not to stand out and be stared at with disdain. Polish people did not tolerate diversity.

In Krakov, my father made enough money so that we lived comfortably, though apartments after the war were scarce and our family of four still had to share a three bedroom apartment, sharing the kitchen and the one bathroom with the Shors and a single Gentile woman.

Although Krakov, with its medieval castles, universities and a cultural aura was the pride of Poland, its population was still quite backward as far as being tolerant of people who were non-Catholic. I found the people there, in 1945, still virulently anti-Semitic, no less than were the people in our small eastern town, Sambor.

One Saturday morning in the spring of 1945, as I walked down the stairs with Mama on our way to join my father in the Synagogue, our janitor intercepted us in the hallway and warned us, "don't go near the Synagogue because Jews are being beaten there." He said, "go home and lock the door." Hearing that, Mama grabbed my hand and we ran back to our apartment. As Mama bolted the front door behind her, I ran back down through the fire escape. I knew that father was attending the Sabbath services at the old Synagogue, which by coincidence was on Rabbi Meisels Street , and was near the marketplace in the old part of town. I was worried about my father and ran towards the Synagogue as fast as I could.

As I neared the Synagogue, I saw Jews being beaten by the people in the street, and some Jews were being escorted by a couple of Polish soldiers. Nearby, in the middle of everything, the military band was playing loudly, as if trying to stage a distraction from the frenzy of violence that was erupting all around. It was a bizarre, surreal scene. Why didn't these men in Polish uniforms put down their drums and trumpets and act like one might expect soldiers of the newly liberated Poland to act?

Soon, a "kind" elderly lady, seeing me in the crowd and mistaking me for a Gentile child, grabbed my hand and pulled me inside a store, which was packed with fleeing Poles, apparently hiding from bloodthirsty Jews. Holding on to me, she said to me in a concerned and grandmotherly manner: "Child, don't go out there because the Jews are catching Christian children to use their blood for Passover." She held on to my hand firmly and would not let go. I was shaking with fear and anger, but kept quiet about being Jewish. The crowd would have instantly lynched me. In her other raised hand, the "kind" old lady held a torn fragment of the Torah scrolls from the Synagogue, as she passionately declared, "This will be a souvenir of this day when we finally get rid of the last Jews in Poland". The store was packed with angry people who were ranting and shouting anti-Semitic slogans. Terrified of the mob, I escaped the old lady's grip and ran out to look for my father, fearing the worst. I could not find him. I wondered around the streets for a while, still looking for him, and then in late afternoon I went back home, hoping that maybe I'd find him there. He was not.

Mama, realizing I had ran off, had been concerned about my disappearance. I told her what happened, where I went, and what I had witnessed near the Synagogue. Of course, she then got very worried about Father.

After escaping the beatings in the Synagogue, my father had hidden in a nearby house and returned home later in the evening, after the frenzy in the streets calmed down. Late that evening, our janitor came over to our apartment. He was drunk. He said that he came to apologize. He proceeded to tell us that the police had detained his thirteen-year old son for a couple of hours because he had started the whole riot near the synagogue. Apparently, somebody had paid him to run out of the Synagogue, covered with some kind of animal blood, and scream: "Help, the Jews in the Synagogue are using me and other Christian children to draw blood from us for Passover."

After that incident, we started looking for ways to leave Poland, once and for all. Poland had been a home to Jews for centuries. Historically, a Polish king invited the Jews over one thousand years ago. Still, the Jews were never considered by their fellow citizens to be "real" Poles, even after years of living together. Even before 1939, the children in my neighborhood and in my first grade class shouted at me "dirty Jew, go to Palestine." During the Nazi era, we were just as afraid of the local Gentile Poles and Ukrainians as we were of the Germans. Our neighbors pointed us out to the SS, and then while we were running away and hiding like mice, they would pillage our apartments.

All this saddens me because I still love to speak Polish; it was my childhood language, and I still sang Polish lullabies to my children because they were part of my childhood too. I feel a sad nostalgia when I hear Polish music, read Polish poetry, watch a Polish film, or see Polish folk costumes. I feel a sense of betrayal by these people who were so inhospitable to us, their fellow citizens. After the extermination of Polish Jews and after the few survivors migrated to Israel or the West, there are practically no Jews living in Poland. Yet I recently read in a magazine that the city of Krakov is now inviting tourists to celebrate an exhibit of "Jewish life and culture in Poland." What blatant sugar-coating of a disgraceful history of intolerance!

We stayed in Krakov until December 1945.

Within six months after the "Pogrom" I had witnessed in postwar Poland, my parents decided to leave Poland and head to where the Americans were. The war had just ended and the Americans were occupying Germany. Father bought some false papers for my Mama and I, so that we could cross the Czech border. He and my sister each took different routes to Germany and arrived in Munich within a few weeks after Mama and I got there.

52

LEAVING POLAND

With false papers in hand and only the clothes we had on us, Mama and I crossed the border from Poland to Czechoslovakia by walking across a small bridge in the divided border-town of Szczecin. When asked by the border patrol where I was going, I was told by Mama to answer that I was going to visit my aunt on the other side.

Once on the Czech side, Mama and I boarded a train for Prague. We had the address of two men who lived there, who we had met when still in Sambor, shortly after the liberation. The two men were Czech–Hungarian Jews. During the Nazi regime in Hungary, the two men apparently missed deportation to death camps where their fellow Jewish countrymen were taken, by passing as Gentiles and as such, taken to serve in the Hungarian army. Their wives, who I believe were not Jewish, had, in the meantime, moved to Prague. The two men were taken as prisoners of war by the Russians and held over in Sambor. They must have been among the captured Hungarian soldiers I saw being escorted by the Russians right after our liberation. Somehow word got around to my father that among the prisoners of war held in Sambor were two Jewish men. With bribes and with the help of a Russian officer he knew, my father helped free them. These men had not been voluntary collaborators.

After they were freed, the two men stayed with us for a short time before leaving Sambor to go home. Grateful to our family, they gave us an address in Prague where we could find them, if ever we came their way and needed help.

In Prague, Mama and I stayed with them for one week, and they treated us with much hospitality. They had reunited with their wives, who were both very elegant and pretty, and wore lots of make up and diamond jewelry. After a brief stay with them, we went on towards Germany. On the way, we stayed with their relatives in Karlovy Vary (aka Carlsbad). Although we kept our mouths shut while traveling through Czechoslovakia without proper papers, we got into trouble on one occasion after boarding a bus from Karlovy Vary, to continue on our journey towards the German border. As soon as I boarded, the people on the bus started screaming at me. They left Mama alone but they threw me off the bus, insisting that I was German. I could not open my mouth in self-defense because I did not speak Czech and we had no identity documents. I would have been probably better off saying something in Polish, because in fact, I did not speak German at all, but Mama had told me not to open my mouth. Fortunately our Czech friends intervened. They had come to see us off and were still standing at the bus station; they vouched for us, that we were not German, and we were allowed to get back on the bus.

We traveled to our next destination, a small town near the German border, staying with relatives of our hosts in Karlovy Vary. With their help, we got a paid guide to take another couple and us across the Czech-German border. We met up with that couple, a Mr. and Mrs. Eimer, in Carlovy Vary. They were also from Sambor.

To get to the German side, we traveled on foot, in the middle of the night and in deep snow, for many hours, crossing a thick forest. By dawn, we reached a train station on the German side. It was still dark when we got there and it was freezing cold. The station was filled with refugees. Hundreds of tired and cold people were sitting on the floor huddled together with children and crying babies, all waiting for a train. After a few hours we boarded a crowded train for Munich.

My mother had an address of a Jewish couple, a Mr. and Mrs. Reinstein, who lived in Munich. They were friends of friends, and had left Poland before us. The war had ended in May 1945; we arrived in Munich on a bleak winter day in December 1945. All around the railway station we saw nothing but ruins. American bombs had reduced that area of Munich to rubble.

Mama asked for directions and soon we found the Reinsteins.

It was early in the morning and when we knocked on their door; they were still in bed. They lived in one small room. We were cold and very tired. Mrs. Reinstein asked us to share her small bed. Mr. Reinstein moved over to the floor and Mama and I, still in our clothes, crawled into the small bed with Mrs. Reinstein.

The Reinsteins were total strangers. In those days, it was normal for Jews to help each other in this way. We were, together, one family of survivors. Many refugees in transit had also stayed in our place and we kids would give up our beds to them and sleep on the floor.

* * *

Yosiu joining the fight for Israel's independence.

53

STUCK
IN GERMANY

In 1945, we went to Germany, not to stay there, but to get away from Poland; we preferred to be in a place that was occupied by the American army. We went to Germany, not to live among people who had treated us as if we were less than human, but with the hope to emigrate to either Israel or America. As it turned out, we got stuck in Munich for five years, where we were rootless transients without passports. In fact, we were being designated and referred to as stateless persons, or displaced persons-- DP's for short.

Our roots in Poland had been severed. We left behind not only the old and desecrated graves of our ancestors, but the ashes and mass graves of our contemporary Jewish community, family and friends. We did not leave behind even one living relative, however distant.

Ready to give up on Europe, my parents at first planned to return to our roots in Israel and start a new life in our ancient homeland. However, thanks to British politics, which at the time was trying to appease the Arabs, immigration for Jews to Israel

---

*On the date of British withdrawal the Jewish provisional government declared the formation of the State of Israel, and the provisional government said that it would grant full civill rights to all within its borders, whether Arab, Jew, Beduin or Druze. The declaration stated: *"we appeal... to the Arab inhabitants of the State of Israel to preserve peace and participate in the upbuilding of the State on the basis of full and equal citizenship and due representation in all its provisional and permanent institutions."* Thus, upon creating the state - any inhabitants inside the newly formed State of Israel became Israeli.

became "illegal". The British kept turning away boatloads of Jewish immigrants from Israel's shores, while Arabs from the surrounding lands were free to come in and settle, to take advantage of the shortage of workers, and the equitable wages being paid by the socially minded early pioneers of Israel. Undeterred by the British, family members, like Yosiu and cousin Meniu Langer, managed to get through in leaky boats. They went on to fight in the war of Israel's independence and then defended Israel in several more Arab- Israeli wars.

I often try to explain to my American friends who wonder why on earth the Jews so desperately needed a sovereign nation of their own. Historically, the Jews were an anomaly, because no matter how many hundreds or thousands of years we had been in Europe and other parts of the world, and no matter how much we tried to assimilate and contribute to the various local cultures, we were never totally accepted and always the subject of persecution.

Before WWI the territory that was then called Palestine was an Ottoman-Turkish colony. After WWI "The League of Nations" placed all of Palestine (both sides of the Jordan River) under a British protectorate and gave it mandatory power. "The League of Nations" recognized the historical connection of this territory to the Jewish people (and vice versa), designated the territory of Palestine to become once again a homeland for Jews. Many already had lived there for generations and many wanted to emigrate there to escape antisemitic persecutions. Recreating their national Jewish homeland anew, they would fulfill their two thousand years of prayers, dreams , hopes and longing to end their exile. There they would rekindle their nationhood, cultivate and adapt their ancient language to contemporary life, extrapolate their cultural heritage into the future, and defend themselves from racial and religious persecution around the world, so that they would have a future. At that time, Palestine was mostly a desolate wasteland of deserts and swamps. In 1922 Great Britain proceeded to divide the territory under their mandate in the following way: 80% of Palestine was cut off and awarded to the local Palestinian Arabs, to become the so called Palestinian homeland, thus establishing the "Arab Emirate of Trans Jordan" (now

Jordan).*(The Toronto Star, june 1,1991, k12) Less than 20% that remained of the Palestinian territory was to be allocated to the Jews.

The controversial issues of Arab Palestinians who presumably were disenfranchised by the mere existence of Israel only arose after the surrounding Arab countries got nervous about a non-Muslim Democracy arising in that region, and they began exploiting them for political gain. They should have recognized the realities of population shifts and exchanges that take place whenever territories are divided to form separate states, like in the case of India and Pakistan, or East Poland and Russia who each had to give up land to the recently created sovereign Ukraine.

The Jews had consistently maintained a presence in Israel since biblical times, and even before the formal reestablishment of the state of Israel in the twentieth century the Jews were transforming the deserts and swamps they were buying up from Turkish absentee landlords, that had little value to anyone else, into blooming farms and forrests. While it is true that there had been many old Arab families who had lived in the Israeli territories for many generations, they were welcomed as citizens with equal rights*, while native Jews in Arab countries were not welcome in Jordan and in the other surrounding Arab states. Over five hundred thousand Jewish refugees from Arab countries alone had not only found refuge and shelter among their brethren in Israel, but were welcomed as fellow citizens without the perpetual stigma of having to live as "refugees" for generations and remain the responsibility of the United Nations.

At the time he left us for Israel, Yosiu was seventeen. I saw his picture, taken by a newsman, as he was riding in a tank wearing a helmet, and looking tough and very handsome. Oh, what a sight that was for me! Looking at the picture, I thought of cousin Bunek, who would have been the same age, and who was so defenseless when they were leading him to his death in the forest of Radlovice, at the age of thirteen. I thought of Yosiu's eleven-year-old sister and Ryfcia's three children, and the millions of others who never lived to see such a sight; a Jewish kid in an Israeli tank. In that tank, fighting for Israel, Yosiu silently spoke for them the words: "Never again!"

After Israel's statehood was established, all other members of our surviving family eventually moved there, and they have lived there ever since.

To my great disappointment and upon my mother's urging, we applied for immigration papers to the US. My mother, who had been very traumatized by the war, was afraid of the ongoing wars with the Arabs. She also wanted to reconnect with her two American brothers who left Poland when she was very young. Her big American family also included a very rich aunt in the Catskills, an uncle of modest means in Brooklyn, an Aunt Ida who no one knew anything about, and many, many cousins, whose names we did not even know.

Even though we had a large family in the US who could have helped us come to America sooner, they did not know us, and would not accept the responsibility of guaranteeing our support, once we arrived. Ironically, we really didn't need any financial help from them, but only a formal guarantee of support or employment. That was all that was necessary to obtain papers quickly. Apparently, they refused to help us because we received no response to our letter for help with expediting our immigration from Germany.

We ended up stuck in Munich as "Displaced Persons", waiting our turn for five years, just like any other immigrants who had no special family connections in the USA.

Although our American family were "good" people: decent, hardworking, friendly, and kept in touch with members of their American family through "Cousins Clubs," they were not too interested in their European family; either in the ones that perished during the Holocaust or in us, who had survived. If they were, they did not communicate it to us.

Although Mama's older brother, Phillip, never wrote to us in Munich, after we arrived in the US, we maintained a rather affectionate connection with him. By that time, he was quite sick with a heart condition. Between 1945 and 1950, both Uncle Benny and Uncle Phillip suffered heart attacks and Benny passed away. I never got to meet him.

I should like to forgive my American family for not helping us get out of Germany, because they really are good people. At first, it was hard to shed the bitterness, because the first five years after the war were precious years of my teenage youth and could have been happily lived as an American teenager. Instead, for five long years, we were stranded in Germany, the source of the evil that had destroyed our universe. In the course of each day, for five long years, I had to interact with a people who had supported Hitler , and daily, I choked on my anger. The anger always overshadowed all my experiences of learning and of discovering cultural events, be it concerts, operas, plays, or even when reading great books in German. How does one open one's heart and mind to the exquisite German classics or watch a moral play by Lessing, when even hearing the German language while buying a pound of potatoes made me sick to my stomach? German happened to be the language in which I was learning beloved subjects, and in time, it was the language I knew best. The young man who was my tutor in math and science was a former Hitler Youth member and was still convinced that Hitler was right. He was a brilliant university student, and had taught me enough in seven months for me to catch up from first grade to the university entrance exam level. His name was Helmut. I admired him greatly and I hated him just as much.

Mama, who had desperately wanted to fill the vacuum created by the loss of her family in Sambor, was hoping that her American family would help her fill it. I wish that she had given up on that idea before her disappointment set in later. It would have been better to have cut our stay in Germany short and gone to Israel, even on a leaky boat. The fact that we did not, was heartbreaking for both Father and me. However, we were destined to go to America and in time we came to fully appreciate and understand what America stood for and we all became truly proud Americans.

54

MUNICH

My mother and I came to Munich in late December 1945. Within a few days after our arrival, my mother turned to the Jewish community center that had opened on Mehl Strasse. She needed help finding a place to live. They helped us find a room near the outskirts of Munich in a place called Borstei.

Borstei was an exclusive and modern housing project, most of whose elegant and distinguished tenants were former Nazis. Borstei had its own shopping center, library, and a park, where each Sunday, a concert of classical music was presented. Maids polished the hallway stairs and a laundress would pick up dirty laundry and deliver it back a couple of days later clean, starched and ironed. Only a few miles from Borstei, close to the main road, was the notorious death camp Dachau with its gas chambers and crematoria. Dachau had been liberated by the American army only eight months earlier. Had its privileged Nazi staff once lived at the Borstei? Probably.

Mama and I moved in on Voigt Strasse 12, with an elderly German couple, Herr and Frau Moebius. The first thing I noticed in the three-bedroom apartment was a picture of an SS officer on the old man's desk. It must have been a picture of his son. From the start, the old lady was kind and made small friendly gestures towards us. We shared the kitchen and the one bathroom. Always very polite, the old lady, Frau Moebius, would hand me a towel whenever I washed my hands, so I that wouldn't drip water on her spotless kitchen floor. The old man always walked around with his teeth clenched, looking like an angry, mad dog. I hated the old man with a passion, but it wasn't easy to hate the plump old woman, who looked like sweet grandma. Soon, I was very happy to have found something that would annoy Herr Moebius. The old man was superstitious and he hated to hear me whistle, so I whistled all the time as loud as I could. Pathetic as my revenge was, it was lucky that I had found some harmless ways to vent the anger that was churning within me each time I saw Germans and heard German spoken; be it in the street, in shops, on trolleys, or at home. Once, I was angry with Mama for days because she stopped a German woman in the street to tell her that she had dropped something. How could she?!

Out of necessity, I myself had to start learning to use the German language when my mother would send me to the store. She would instruct me to say: "I would like to buy a bottle of milk or a pound of onions".

Soon Father and Genia joined us. Genia traveled alone with a group of Jewish refugees pretending to be returning Greeks. First Genia travelled from Poland to Austria. At the border, they all had to destroy all papers written in Polish and, unfortunately, Genia had to burn her wartime diary in which she had so thoroughly documented our life in the cellar.

Father traveled separately with another group of people. Among them was a nine-month pregnant woman. The group went illegally from Poland to Czechoslovakia crossing the Carpatian Mountains on foot in deep snow. At one point, during the strenuous climb, the woman and every one else in the group had to stop. Lying down on the snow, she gave birth to a healthy baby boy and then within only a couple of hours after giving birth, mother and baby and the rest of the group continued their journey and proceeded to cross the snow covered mountain range on foot.

When they got to the Czechoslovakian town of Bratislava, the local Jewish community gave them a big welcome and made a big circumcision party on the eighth day of the boy's life. After a brief stay in Bratislava, my father made his way to Munich, where he found us. Within a short time my cousin Yosiu had also arrived from Poland and came to live with us.

Now that we were a family of five, we had to exchange bedrooms with the old German couple, because they actually had two rooms, a bedroom and an office-sitting room, and they also had the larger bedroom. Our one room was too small for us.

In Munich, I dove into my new life head first. There was so much to do, to catch up with the "normal" world. At thirteen I was quite illiterate, having missed five years of school.

Even in the bombed-out city of Munich, there were many things for me to discover. Genia had many friends as soon as she enrolled in the Hebrew school that was soon organized among the survivors. I did not go to school and I had no friends.

I spent my days wandering alone through the city or riding the trolleys from one end of town to the other. Once, a middle-aged man pressed himself against my body inside an almost empty trolley car, but I was able to free myself and escape. I loved hopping on or getting off moving trolleys, running as fast as I could to catch them mid-street, as if it were a sport.

Wandering about the city, like a curious alien from another planet, my mind was open and uncluttered by society's or teacher's opinions of what and how I should be thinking, what I should be seeking out, and how I should be seeing the things that were in front of my nose. Because I had no friends that were my age, my daily excursions were not limited to "a common denominator" of shared interests with others. My loneliness, far from crippling me, made me want to explore more of everything. I discovered museums, art galleries, parks, concerts and lectures.

The transitions from childhood wartime experiences and the limiting cocoon-like life in the cellar, to an open world unfolding before me as a thirteen-year-old, were rather sudden. Wandering around Munich I was voracious in my drive to see, to discover and to learn.

One day, I discovered talks on psychology that were being held in a newly established Jewish adult school. Although the people in the audience were all much older than I, I found the talks fascinating and could relate to much that was being covered in the lectures and discussions. The lecturer, a Dr. Peisachowitz, would talk about the things I was also struggling with. The topic I most related to was fear. I lived with fear all the time. When I was a little girl, I was afraid of ghosts and dead people. The open-casket Catholic funeral processions terrified me; even the sight of black-veiled widows gave me the creeps. It seemed to me that ghosts were hovering about them. Later, at the onset of the war, I was terrified of bombs. Of course, my fears grew exponentially as I was being persecuted and hunted by the Nazis.

One day, in my wanderings about Munich, I found a swimming school. As soon as I walked in, someone handed me a swimsuit and a towel, and told me to join the other girls who were already wearing the one piece tank suits and were all lined up on the side of the pool. The swimming coach probably assumed that I was one of the enrolled kids and was just walking in late.

This looked like a great opportunity to do something new and exciting, and I did want to learn to swim. I changed into the swimsuit and lined up behind the other children. One by one, all the kids in line started jumping into the pool. When I watched them swim to the other side it looked so easy and natural. Soon it was my turn; there was no time to think or hesitate. I jumped in. Immediately water flooded my nose and mouth. I nearly drowned and they had to pull me out of the pool.

I never told anyone in my family about what happened that day. After that incident, I did not learn to swim until I was twenty-one, and I still have a fear of deep water.

Further exploring Munich by myself at age thirteen, I secretly looked for a ballet school. I had wanted to take ballet lessons since I was two, ever since I used to come along and watch my sister in her ballet classes.

One day, I came across a ballet school. Eager and excited, I walked in and inquired about enrolling and taking ballet lessons. "How old are you child?" asked a skinny tall woman with tightly pulled back, dark hair. "Thirteen," I said. The tall woman shook her head and simply said: "Child, you're too old." I was crushed and felt like I had missed my true calling forever because I was already too old. I was simply too old for everything and there was no catching up; life had already passed me by, I thought.

Some time later, at the "Deutches Museum" of Munich, which I visited often, I saw an announcement that the Russian Ballet of Monte Carlo was coming to perform in Munich. This was very exciting. To see a professional ballet performance would be such a prewar luxury, and now it was almost within my grasp. I found out that the tickets were expensive, but it never occurred to me to ask my parents for the money to buy a ticket. I walked into a pawnshop and inquired if they would buy the coat I was wearing. It was a nice American coat that I had received from the UNRA relief organization. I had fished it out from a box of used clothing that had been donated by Americans for refugees.

The man in the pawnshop offered me 17 D-Marks for the coat, which I happily accepted. That was just enough to buy a first row ticket to see the matinee performance of Swan Lake. It was all a secret, and fortunately Mama never asked about the coat.

I also loved music and wanted to learn to play an instrument. My father bought me a small, secondhand accordion and Mama found an accordion teacher who lived a few houses down from our room on Voigt Strasse. The teacher was a very polite gentleman. My problem was how to reconcile his good manners and the beautiful music he played, both on the accordion and the piano in his living room, with the framed picture he proudly displayed on his grand piano, in which he was wearing a Nazi uniform.

It was all so confusing. For a few months, I took a few joyless and conflicted lessons from him. I did enjoy disturbing Herr Moebius with the accordion noise when practicing scales.

By 1946, there was large Jewish community of refugees that had gathered in Munich. Some had been liberated by the American army from death camps, and some, like our family, had escaped from Russia, Poland and other countries that had been previously overrun by the Germans, where the Jewish communities had been destroyed forever and one could not go home again.

The Jewish community center was aided by Jewish American organizations, like the Joint Distribution Organization, UNRA, and ORT. When a Hebrew school was established, Genia was immediately enrolled, but I refused to go. I was 13 years old and illiterate. I figured that I would have had to start from first grade all over again, with small children, except that this time it would have been in either Hebrew or in German. I told my parents that instead, I would like to go to an ORT school, learn a trade and then work and earn money and become independent. No amount of talking by my parents could change my mind; I was very strong headed. I thought that I would like to study auto-mechanics and learn all about cars and motors and be tough like the Russian soldier girls who were tank drivers and pilots.

The women I knew during the war were weak; they were always helpless, wailing, and crying. They were handicapped by their monthly periods that were so embarrassing and difficult to manage during the war. When, soon after liberation, I got my period, I was so upset that I wanted to jump into the well in the yard and kill myself. I did not know what it meant or how to manage it. It happened one morning when I was still in bed and I felt something gush out of me. I panicked. "What's that?!" I screamed to my mother. She shoved a wad of cotton up my legs and never said another word about it, that day or anytime later. From then on, I was always very secretive about my periods, never knowing what they meant and always wondering why women were afflicted with that terrible burden. I heard boys make crude jokes about it and I was so afraid that anyone would find out that I was also one of those "weak" and handicapped girls. I never talked to Mama or Genia about my agonizing thoughts about it. I took care of it by using newspapers to pad my underwear, because that's what I saw the women in the cellar do. The coarse paper chafed my skin, and showed thorough my clothes. I hardly had a chance to wash and dress in privacy, and I was utterly miserable. I resolved to use my will power to put an end to that horrible ordeal. Sure enough, by the time we left Poland, it had mercifully stopped. I felt very pleased with myself for being in control of my body; I was proud of my strong will power, and I even tried to flatten my budding breasts with a bandage, so as not to invite smirky and embarrassing questions or comments from anybody. I was not ready to be an adult. Then, within a few months after our arrival in Munich, I was checked by a doctor who asked all sorts of questions. He gave my mother some pills for me to take to regulate my period. Thus ended my reprieve from this terrible by-product of being a girl.

I did enjoy the romantic side of being a girl. Secretly I was always in love with one boy or another, and usually with some-one from among my sister's many friends. At best, her friends never even looked at me, but at worst they thought that I was a weird kid and did not even bother talking to me.

My greatest love at that time was the great French film star Jean-Louis Barrault, whose three-hour film "The Children of Paradise" I saw three times by the time I was fourteen.

Eventually, my parents agreed to let me enroll in the trade school. The Ort schools were created by a Jewish American organization to retrain and rehabilitate Jewish war refugees so that they would learn new trades to enable them to support themselves when they eventually resettled. The Ort school was a school for adults. Mama decided that she would also enroll and learn to become a corsettiere.

When my father went with me to enroll, the director of the school, Mr. Lapidus, said to me in a very patronizing way "Why would a pretty girl like you want to crawl under a dirty car and soil her pretty dress?" I disliked him instantly for being so condescending and I told him that it would not be a problem because I did not like to wear dresses anyway.

In the end, I had to compromise and I was allowed to enroll in a radio-technical class, since I did not need to crawl under a radio to fix it. At age thirteen, I started going to a trade school with the goal of becoming a radio-technician and getting a job.

The first classes met in a huge hall in some deserted school building. There were about fifteen students, and most of them were in their twenties and thirties. At thirteen I was, of course, the youngest, the only girl, and just a naïve kid. The other students and the teachers must have all wondered what that pale and skinny girl was doing there. They left me alone; sadly they all ignored me.

Day in and day out, I would come to class, always on time, and I would sit in the furthest corner from everyone, neither speaking nor being spoken to. Our wrinkled old professor, Herr Hoffman, who wore thick glasses, was bald, and had one leg shorter than the other, kept limping back and forth in front of the class, from one side of the blackboard to the other, lecturing to us. I did not understand a word he was saying, nor did I understand the diagrams and equations he was constantly drawing and writing on the blackboard. Somehow, I never gave up, thinking that I would eventually understand it all. At one point, when he talked about magnetism and a "hysteresis" curve, the men in the class started roaring with laughter, because "kurva" in Polish, and "kurve" in Yiddish meant, whore.

The men in my class were very crude. Each morning, they would talk and joke among themselves in Polish or Yiddish about the encounters they had with whores the night before, and about their girlfriend's messy periods. They paid no attention to me and made crass jokes all the time. It was very embarrassing and I felt like a nobody, being so ignored and disregarded.

It was not a happy situation and I was not a happy kid, but then I did not expect "happiness". That was an unfamiliar aspiration. It was already a lot to be given a chance to be alive, fed and free to roam about the city, free to learn and explore. War children learned early on not to whine, not to complain, and not to expect much.

I went to this Ort school for the next nine months and most of the time, I did not understand anything the teachers were saying. Each day, I would come to class, stare at the blackboard and listen to the incomprehensible lectures in German, understanding only the dirty jokes of my fellow students, spoken in a language I knew. Neither in school nor at home did anyone ever ask me how I was doing. Everybody left me alone. There was one handsome blond eighteen-year-old boy in my class who sometimes talked to me politely. Sometimes he smiled at me and once he even stroked my cheek. I would go home and daydream about him. Everyone called him by his last name, Bakstansky.

We had one other German teacher for the lab part, who was about twenty-five and very handsome. Georg had beautiful blue eyes and was patient and good-natured. He always laughed and joked with the other students who were about the same age, but when he talked to me, while trying to help me with the lab tools he would always blush. Only with me was he shy. He'd turn beet-red and be so nervous that he could hardly talk to me. To this day, it's hard for me to admit that I had a major crush on him. After all, he was German and had probably served in the German army. Hating him as a man was as difficult as not hating him for being German. Every time I had to interact with him, I had a hard time dealing with that conflict. It was impossible to reconcile the excitement I felt when he would come around to talk to me, with my memories of the sadistic German Nazis. They were still so fresh. I hated myself for being a girl and for having these kind of exciting feelings for the young German teacher and I was embarrassed for being a girl like the ones the men in the class talked about so disrespectfully. I knew that at least I was tough and independent and did not act like the other weak girls who did what their parents told them to and who went to schools for children, like nice little girls.

Soon, there was talk about a final exam. A bit apprehensively, I went to the library that was located within our housing project and took out a couple of thick and heavy radio engineering textbooks. Since our one room was noisy and crowded I read the books in the bathroom that we shared with the old German couple. That really annoyed Herr Moebius.

I would stay in the bathroom for hours, reading the incomprehensible sentences over and over again until one day, they started to make some sense. It never occurred to me to give up. Since there were seven people sharing the one bathroom in our small apartment, every few minutes someone would knock on the door, interrupting my studies.

I would not fail. I assumed that, had I failed the radio school, everyone who had told me to go to a regular kid school would have been proved right. Not having participated in the classroom the entire time, and not having ever experienced a "test," I was worried and I shared that concern with my father. Shortly, he arranged for me to meet with a neighbor, a German engineer who was in the radio business. Mr. Frenzl said that he'd be glad to help me out by testing me on my knowledge of radios. He was a very kind gentleman, and he invited us to come over to his house in the evening.

He was about thirty years old. His pretty wife, holding an infant in her arms, opened the door and let us in; she was very gracious.

Mr. Frenzl was waiting for me in his office. They seemed to be such a beautiful and happy couple. As I looked around the peaceful and orderly apartment, I noticed several photos of Mr. Frenzl in a German officer's uniform.

The sight of the green uniforms with the boots and high hats had once filled me with dread. Now, once again, that evening, like so many other times in my daily life in Munich, I was to experience the nausea-like feeling in my gut, because I was unable to reconcile the incongruence of my two perceptions of Germans. While always aware of the anger inside, I would act politely to the "nice" people I would come across, because they were often genuinely likeable. It was all so confusing and so complicated because the two pictures in my mind did not jive; my constant inner conflict made me serious and withdrawn.

I sat down next to my father and across Mr. Frenzl in his comfortable office and he started asking me many technical questions. I was shocked to discover that I knew the answers to most of his questions. By the end of the evening, Mr. Frenzl offered me a job in his company. He told me to contact him after the exam.

My interaction with Mr. Frenzl gave me the confidence I needed to take the test. I did not find it difficult and passed the course, surprising my teachers and fellow students as well, because they did not expect much from me. Shortly after the exam, before starting to work for Mr. Frenzl, I went to Switzerland for three months on a special rehabilitation program for child survivors.

55

SWITZERLAND

In late 1946, Mama found out about a program for Jewish survivor children that was being made available by a few Swiss Jewish families. These families offered to invite about two dozen children, all Holocaust survivors, to stay with them for three months. I think that it was meant to give the war-scarred children a taste of normal life and perhaps a bit of rehabilitation from the trauma they had experienced.

Actually, I did not qualify for this program. It was intended for very young children under seven, and I was thirteen. But my mother was convinced that such an experience would be good for me, and she would not give up; she was very persistent. After knocking on many doors at the Jewish Agency and talking to several people in charge, she succeeded after all, to get me accepted.

And so the trip to Switzerland, when I was thirteen, became an important junction in my life.

To everyone who has seen the film "Heidi," Switzerland had always seemed like a fairyland place of beauty and wholesome living. During and immediately after the war, compared to the rest of war- ravaged Europe, it was like an oasis of peaceful, "normal" living and uninterrupted prosperity. Yet Switzerland was only a short train-ride from Hitler's death camps. To me, Switzerland appeared even less real than a mirage of a lush oasis in the middle of a desolate landscape; at times it also looked to me like an odd relic from a lost civilization.

There were about twenty children in our program. We were to travel by train under the supervision of two American UNRA ladies who wore American military uniforms. The train compartment we boarded was in a third class car with cold and hard wooden benches. It was December, and during the trip, all the children were cold.

Throughout the nighttime journey, the American ladies, whose faces were heavily painted and who spoke to us children in English only, were nowhere to be seen. I tried to find them, especially at night whenever the younger children would be crying. Sitting or lying down on the hard, cold benches, we were very uncomfortable. Throughout the night children were fidgeting; They were scared, or wanted a drink, missed their mamas or had to use the toilet. I was up all night, taking care of them. Early the next morning when we arrived in Switzerland, the two women finally showed up looking fresh and rested; the coat of paint on their faces appeared to be perfect and not a hair was out of place. It turned out that the two American ladies had been traveling in the first class sleeper cars.

Our first stop was Basel. It was still dark when we arrived there. After getting off the train, we children were all taken to a bathing facility, supposedly to be deloused by a bunch of women who were dressed like nurses wearing little white and blue caps and aprons. We had to strip and together get into steaming vats of soapy and "disinfectant-smelly" water. Our clothes were taken from us to be washed and sterilized.

Though I was thirteen, my privacy was not respected; After all, I was one of the "poor" refugee children, who mostly met each situation with a wide-eyed silence.

I found the so called de-lousing procedure very humiliating and insulting. It's not as if we had just come out from a concentration camp or the ghetto. By that time, we had been free for one and a half years, and although food and spacious living quarters had been scarce, we valued opportunities to bathe more than people who had taken them for granted all their lives. Though we were not living in luxury yet, we did have bathtubs, showers, soap and water, and clean clothes.

After the obligatory "sanitization" ordeal, we got back on the train and continued our journey to Luzern, where our "adoptive " families met us at the train station. There, we were met by a bunch of smiling couples; each family came to claim their "child". It was a weird scene. Although they were there for us, they were not like family beaming with recognition and joy at us as when greeting a beloved grandchild, niece or nephew. The patronizing elements of pity that I felt or imagined coming from these well fed and well dressed smiling people set me apart from them. We children met them with solemn and apprehensive faces. Where I came from, people did not smile so readily at strangers or in general, and for no good reason. One would perhaps smile seeing a puppy or a kitten, but not at strangers until one got to know them and love them. It would take me almost fifty years before I would spontaneously smile at strangers.

My adoptive family, Franz and Inge Wiener, looked surprised and greatly disappointed to be greeting and taking home such an "old" child, but they were very nice about it. I liked them immediately and probably would have chosen them out of all the other people who were meeting us at the station. Mrs. Wiener, in particular, seemed to project a shy and quiet sensitivity. She was very warm but did not say much; Mr. Wiener did most of the talking. He insisted on taking from my hand the small suitcase I was clutching, but upon lifting it, he wondered why it was so heavy. I told him I had many books; I lied. In fact, I was smuggling a set of silverware which I was hoping to sell somewhere, so I would have some money to travel with and for emergencies.

In those days in Germany, things were bought and sold on the black market. It was a necessary and accepted way of life. We would receive rations of cigarettes and food and exchange the things we did not need for the things we wanted. A carton of cigarettes could pay the monthly rent on a big and beautiful apartment. Indeed, our family had moved into one. A cleaning woman was paid with a pound of sugar for a day's labor.

Luzern was beautiful beyond my wildest expectations, especially in winter. The town was clean and well lit. There were no ruins and it was full of merchandise-filled stores, but best of all, I loved looking at snow-covered mountains that surrounded the city. The Swiss people were well-fed, well-dressed, cheerful, courteous, relaxed, and "pre-war" normal. I would watch them as they would often stop to exchange smiley greetings with acquaintances and make pleasant small talk. Where I came from, when people would meet in the street, they would express surprise to find each other alive and exchange terrible stories of survival and losses, and they would talk about their plans to emigrate, or how best to buy something or make a buck in the black market.

There was such an innocence and naiveté about the Swiss, I thought. I could hardly believe that Mr. Wiener would accept the story about "books" weighing down my suitcase. Next to them, I felt shrewd and cunning and I gloated inside, because I managed to smuggle something across the border, and then fool him. (Against my mother's pleading, my father gave into my wishes to smuggle the silver set, so that I could have some pocket money.) My parents gave me a telephone number of a surviving distant French cousin, whom they had not met personally, but knew of from cousin Fanny in America. He now resided in Zurich. I imagined that somehow this cousin would help me exchange the silver set for Swiss franks, perhaps by taking it to a pawnshop. I was hoping to get $20 for it. Within a few days after my arrival in Luzern, I contacted our cousin by phone and soon took a train to Zurich where we had arranged to meet in a small kosher restaurant that looked like someone's apartment. Mama's cousin treated me to some soup and then took me to meet his two small daughters, who were living in an orphanage for Jewish refugee children who had managed to escape from France. His wife had died earlier, during their transit from France. The frizzy-haired, blond and blue-eyed girls were between five and seven years old. I left the silver with our cousin. He was a young man, but looked sad and serious. After our first meeting I never heard from him again and never got any money from him for the silver. He probably needed it more than I did.

I returned to Luzern the same evening. While traveling and all through the day in Zurich, I had to report to the Wieners by phone every couple of hours. They really cared about me but they also understood me enough to cut me some slack; they let me travel more than once. For that and for so many other daily gestures, large and small, I really got to appreciate them and love them dearly.

Actually, there were two families who shared the burden of having me for the three months of my stay. Both of my adoptive families, the Wieners and the Lepeks, turned out to be wonderfully good and pleasant people. Though Mr. Wiener was in his forties and Mrs. Wiener was not much younger, they were expecting their first child.

When I arrived I noticed that Mrs. Wiener looked "very" pregnant. Apparently Mr. Wiener must have been concerned that the stress of having to take care of a refugee child would be too much for his wife in her delicate condition. They had made an arrangement with another family, the Lepeks, according to which I would spend the day with the Wieners and every day after dinner go to sleep at the Lepeks and have breakfast there as well.

Mrs. Lepek, was a widow; she lived with her eighteen year old son Michael and her twenty year old daughter Janet not far from the Wiener residence; about ten minutes walking. She was a heavy set old lady and she must have had a thyroid problem because her eyes were bulging, giving her a bulldog-like expression. She was a sweet and kind old lady, nonetheless. Every morning, she sent me to a small bakery nearby to buy delicious fresh rolls, she called "mueschli." Then she would make everyone a breakfast of rolls, cheese, preserves and hot ovaltine, which she would also make for me at night before going to sleep. It was the best ovaltine I have ever tasted.

The Lepeks had a mail-order business which they ran from home; it was a photograph framing business. They lived modestly. Their spacious upstairs apartment was old and musty, with dark walls and old dark brown furniture that was heavily upholstered with faded-dark fabric. I was to sleep on the couch in the dining room. Each night, I would stare at the many family photographs on the wall above my bed. The ones of Mr. Lepek would scare me the most, because I knew that he was dead and I feared his ghost. The whole house was dark and spooky, but especially the room where I slept. At night, I would curl up into a ball and pull the covers over my head.

Janet worked in another town, but she would visit often. She was warm and friendly. She was pretty, but it was the kind of "pretty" that doesn't last past twenty five or thirty. Michael was a jolly boy. He was tall, well built, and in spite of his severe acne, handsome. From all I heard about him, I understood that he was girl-crazy; running around, he would often come home very late at night.

They were all very nice to me, especially Janet. She was such a sweet and naïve girl. She even confided to me one night, over a hot cup of ovaltine, that she had once met an American soldier and went out with him briefly and that he had even kissed her. When he left he promised to write and to soon return. Innocently she would talk about him with a thirteen-year-old girl, smiling shyly and looking dreamy. Apparently she never heard from the American again, at least, not by the time I saw her four years later. I found out many years later that Janet never married, although she had a great personality and had once been pretty. I heard that she became overweight and started looking a bit like her mother.

I loved being in Switzerland, and grew to love the Wiener family as if they had truly been family. Inge Wiener, especially, was the sweetest person in the world. Franz Wiener was caring and interesting. He genuinely wanted to share with me his knowledge of books and music. In the war torn world I came from, full of rootless refugees, in physical and emotional transit, their friendship was very reassuring. Observing daily their calm demeanor and sharing with them a stable environment and a pre-war way of life allowed me to reconnect emotionally with our own prewar lifestyle and security. For me, that sense of continuity was important, especially because they too were Jewish. I found myself on a rock island in the middle of a turbulent sea, and I was well cared for.

The Wieners second story apartment in Luzern was on Himmelrich Strasse #2; it was very cozy and pleasant. Even their stuffy, antique furniture exuded a sense of stability. Their massive wooden furniture had carved animal claw legs; there were upholstered easy chairs and dining room chairs to sit on, lots of books and a big black grand piano that no one ever played that was covered with a silk shawl. My favorite place was a round space near the window, with an easy chair on each side of a bookcase and a record player that stood on top of it. Nearby was a stack of classical and semi-classical records. There was a white lace tablecloth on the oversized table. At mealtimes the table was always beautifully set, with crisp white linen napkins rolled up inside silver napkin holders.

When I first came into their home, I was offered yummy things to eat, things I had not eaten or even seen for years. On their massive dining room chest of drawers, there was always a big bowl filled with oranges and bananas and other exotic fruit. The Wieners would offer me fruit, chocolates, cheeses, fresh buttered rolls, sour-cream and cakes, and I would stare at the food and salivate, but I was too embarrassed to show how much I wanted to eat it. I would always say, "no thank you," or eat just a bit, but never nearly as much as I wanted to.

Each morning, after breakfast at the Lepek's I would walk along the old narrow streets, to the Wieners. It was fun walking in the snow; the air was cold and crisp, and from everywhere there were spectacular views of the snow-capped mountains. Luzern was such a cozy and beautiful town. The people were friendly, the houses untouched by bombs, the store windows displayed beautiful merchandise, the likes of which I had not seen since I was seven. There were stores full of shoes, clothes, watches, jewelry, flowers, furniture and skiing gear. The grocery stores were stuffed with incredible food. There was tropical fruit, an incredible variety of cheeses and baked goods, and an unbelievable selection of chocolates. At that time in Munich, all the stores were bare and even basic food was scarce. In Munich, in the beginning, we lived on rations that were handed to us refugees weekly by the UNRA. I did not like the canned food. It tasted rotten, and the powdered milk and powdered eggs tasted grainy, lime-like and smelled strange. Everything else, like fresh fruit and vegetables and normal eggs, was hard to get, even on the black market. Once, during a meal in Munich, to everyone's disgust, I chose to eat my share of butter all at once, so I could fully taste it. But it soon made me sad; it made me think of my young cousin, Eli's son, who once did the same at our table during the war. He never lived to taste butter again.

Mrs. Wiener took me along to do her errands and for walks. Usually, we would also stop at a coffee shop and get some amazing pastry and coffee or hot chocolate. Inge Wiener was a beautiful person. She was not considered pretty, only because of her protruding upper front teeth but she had beautiful light blue eyes and she was built well. She was gentle, quiet and very ladylike. Just by personal example of her exquisite manners and character, she taught me much. She was originally raised in Berlin, but was orphaned early when her parents died in a car accident. Because of that, she would not allow her husband, Franz, to buy a car. Being a traveling salesman, he was forced to lug around suitcases full of samples, and travel by train.

Although the house was kosher, they were not overly religious. On Saturday afternoons, we would take walks near the lake and always stop off at a cafe for coffee and pastry. Mr. Wiener never paid for these on the Sabbath. The owners knew him and trusted that he would eventually pay.

Seeing the Alps daily, with all that beautiful snow, gave me a passionate desire to go skiing. I hoped that the $20 I would get for the silverware set would enable me to do so. I must have talked about skiing a lot, because one day the Wieners made arrangements for me to go on a one week long ski trip with a group of Swiss Jewish scouts, or "Pathfinders". They were all a few years older than I.

These young people were all well dressed and well-equipped with ski-gear. I was very self-conscious about my shabby and unsporty clothes. I was given Mrs. Wiener's skis and boots and I soon found out that they were way too big for me, because she was a tall lady.

The day came when Mr. Wiener brought me to the train and I joined the group of young pathfinders on their way to the mountains. We traveled by train to Gstadt and then trekked up a mountain on foot carrying all our supplies and gear. Soon we reached an Alpine chalet, which must have been a youth hostel. Early the next morning after breakfast everyone put their skis on and went outside, to ski down the hill. There were no lifts near our isolated chalet. After skiing down everybody would trek up the hill and then ski down again, or we would trek up the big hill above the chalet and then ski down towards our hut. I watched everyone, closely observing their moves and maneuvers and tried to do the same; it all seemed so easy. All day I was euphoric sliding down the hills, walking up and sliding down. Soon I was becoming very bold, each time going a bit farther and a bit faster. I knew nothing about skiing and I never asked for help, I was too shy to approach others and no one offered to teach me or ski with me; I was on my own. But then, at one point, I found myself going down too fast, and I soon lost control. I knew that I had to stop, but the loose shoes gave me no support and the skis were too long for me, and they were hard to control. I saw how others would stop by bringing the tips together, but I must have done it the wrong way, turning my ankles out instead of in and I fell hard. My ankle hurt and I could not get up. Suddenly a gorgeous blond skier appeared and lifted me off the ground. While holding me close in his arms, skis and all, he skied down with me to our chalet. I was so enraptured with the man's looks, his closeness, and the romantic setting of this moment that I stopped thinking about the throbbing pain in my leg. Within a short time my ankle became swollen and turned purple. It was also very painful. Someone bandaged my foot but it did not help much. We were far from any town and any medical facilities. All I could do was hobble around on one foot.

I stayed with the group in the chalet for seven days, until the camp was over. For the next six days, I sat by the window and watched everybody else skiing outside and having fun. Everybody felt sorry for me and I hated that; it made me feel like a charity case, an object of pity. I never felt like a part of that group of carefree young teenagers anyway. They all knew each other and they were much older. They seemed to come from well-to-do families. They were carefree, and playful with each other. I was an odd, shy and an unsmiling outsider.

There were a lot of flirtatious interactions going on among the participants who were between fifteen and seventeen. The group leader's assistant was a very handsome dark-haired boy of about 19 whose name was Hanania. He always hung out with a short, plump, and freckled redhead, who was one of the scouts. I was totally in love with Hanania and wondered why he hung out with that ugly girl. He was very nice to me but treated me like a pitiful child; not only was I the youngest in the group, I was small for my age and wore two pigtails that made me look even younger than I was.

On the last night, before the camp was over, we had a party. After dinner, the scoutmaster had us all sit on the floor in a large circle. Then the lights were turned off and everyone sat in the dark singing songs together. Afterwards, we listened to recorded music. Sitting in the dark, together with a bunch of happy kids and listening to beautiful music I almost felt like I was one of them. For a serious and lonely kid that had no friends, this was a beautiful and novel experience. I got so swept up by the romantic setting and the music, that, when the Blue Danube started playing, I spontaneously began to whistle along with rare exuberance, forgetting myself and momentarily shedding my shyness and self-consciousness; the whistling just popped out of me. Being in the pitch-dark room may have helped that to happen.

Upon hearing whistling in the room, our group leader became furious and he abruptly stopped the music. In an angry tone, he said that whoever the impertinent "Laus Bub" (worse than rascal) was, he must leave the room immediately. I thought I'd die of shame and humiliation, as I hobbled out in the dark on one leg. There was a gasp in the room and everyone felt sorry for me and begged me to stay, but I proceeded to hobble out in the dark and up the stairs to my bunk bed. It was not the first time that I had been shamed for my exuberance; it used to happen often when I was a lively little girl and my mother would shout at me to quiet me down.

Some time later that evening, Hanania came up and tried to make me feel better and talk me into going back to the party. Though I refused to go back, it was nice to have Hanania's exclusive attention for a few minutes.

We left the ski chalet next day. Hanania carried me into the train compartment, with the ugly redhead right behind him. When we arrived in Luzern, Franz Wiener, looking concerned, was waiting for me with a cab. The next day, I was taken to a doctor's office and X-rayed. It turned out that my ankle had been fractured and I received a cast that reached up to my knee.

Because of my cast, I no longer walked to the Lepeck's for the night. I got to sleep at the Wiener's from then on, and that was very nice. I got the royal treatment, and I spent a lot of time talking with Mr. Wiener and playing chess with him, especially while Mrs. Wiener was busy in the kitchen or resting. He played opera and operetta records, talked to me about his interest in psychology and the books he had read, and told stories about his travels. We listened to the great operatic voice of the famous German tenor, Josef Schmidt.

One day, Mr. Wiener told me the story of what had happened to Josph Shmidt during the war, and I found it very upsetting. He was a Jew, and during the war was forced to flee from Germany. He made it to Switzerland, but there the Swiss detained him in a detention camp together with other Jewish refugees who also managed to escape from Germany. Like the Vatican, Switzerland wanted to maintain neutrality at all cost. In camp, Joseph Schmidt lay sick with pneumonia. Though, apparently, prominent members of the Jewish community in Switzerland tried to obtain his release by appealing to the Swiss government, to enable him to receive proper medical care, they were unsuccessful. The Swiss government would not release him. And so, Josph Shmidt, the once famous German tenor, died in a detention camp in Switzerland.

Every morning, Mr. Wiener would come into my room carrying hot ovaltine on a tray to wake me; he was genuinely concerned about my well being and I felt loved and welcome in their home. In the afternoons, he spent time playing chess with me and talking to me about life and growing up. I was his rehab project. I no longer remember how our conversations went. I do remember that at no time did we talk about my wartime experiences. I never talked to him about my fear, my anger and hatred towards the people I blamed for the Holocaust that robbed me of my family, a normal childhood, and my home. I never spoke about hating to be me, an ugly lost girl who did not have friends who spoke her native language and shared or understood her background. I never spoke about hating to be a girl. But among the good changes that happened to me in Switzerland was coming to accept my girlish fate and body and my girlish tendency to find handsome boys like Hanania very attractive. It helped to observe the girls during the ski trip, and in town. I started looking more in the mirror and getting interested in nice clothes. Once, I was very embarrassed when Mr. Wiener caught me looking in the mirror. I was wearing my tight lilac sweater and was squaring my shoulders, sticking out my budding chest.

I loved going out with the Wieners. Once, they took me to see the operetta, "Die Fledermaus". It was an amazing experience; I had never been to such a theater performance before.

In Switzerland, I learned to speak German fluently and managed to read a few great books that Mr. Wiener had recommended. I read several books by Stefan Zweig, and the book,"Casper Hauser," by Feuchtwanger, which I loved; I could well relate to poor Casper, who had been hidden away like an outcast and suffered from loneliness. Only in Switzerland could I enjoy reading and speaking German without simultaneous feelings of sadness and anger.

In Switzerland with Mrs. Lepic (left)
and Mrs. Wiener (right)

Franz Wiener was a distributor of ladies sweaters. Sometimes I helped with the sorting, the folding, and the packing of the sweaters, getting them ready for shipment.

Soon, the cast came off and it was time for me to depart. Upon leaving, the Wieners gave me a beautiful yellow sweater as a present. I never wore it. I saved it, and gave it to Genia as a present when I returned to Munich. She loved elegance, and I thought that it would look more beautiful on her. Perhaps, by now, she forgot all about that gift.

Although three months does not seem like a long time in a person's life, my short stay in Switzerland had far reaching positive effects on my further development. It felt wonderful not to hate the people around me for three whole months. To this day, I feel very connected to the Wiener family and keep in touch with them. Even my children feel the family-like connection.

Later in life, Franz became much more observant and rather conservative on all levels. Their pretty and bubbly daughter, Jenny moved to Israel at the age of eighteen and became orthodox. Their handsome son, Harry, was at one time a ski instructor, but later he became a brilliant and successful student and teacher of industrial psychology. When he was a young student, he came to stay with us in Los Angeles. A few years later, my sixteen-year-old son, Jonny, spent a summer as a councilor in Harry's private school. For many years, the circle of friendship continued to roll between the Wieners and us. Most recently, Harry's and Kathrin's daughter Tamara came to study in Los Angeles, staying over often. Tragically, we lost beautiful Tamara in an accident at home, at age twenty-two. Her pre-existing diabetic condition may have contributed to her accidental death.

56

WORK AND STUDY
IN MUNICH

After returning from Switzerland to Munich, I started working for Mr. Frenzl. He was becoming very prosperous, as he now owned a radio factory and a small laboratory where new radio models were being designed, developed and tested. I was given a job in the small laboratory, which was located in a little town called Mosach, just outside of Munich. Each morning, I would ride on my bike to work, passing the Dachau extermination camp on the way. The sight of Dachau would gel the blood in my veins, but I would cycle on to do what I set out to do.

I would arrive at the home of the chief engineer, Herr Doctor, (he had a doctorate in engineering), and I'm sure must have been a Nazi who was hiding out in the little lab, which was set up in a shed in the garden behind his mother's house. That was the sense I had of him. He was tight lipped and serious, but never showed anger or rudeness towards me. He never went anyplace other than to the house and the lab in the back. There were five of us working there. There was Herr Doctor, and Hans, who was a nice red haired boy of nineteen who was very bright and helpful to me. It would have been hard to imagine Hans as a Nazi. Then there was Herr Liebl, a strange looking man of about thirty-five, who had a very small head and almost no chin. He was a good mechanic and he taught me how to use all the machine shop equipment: the saws, the drills and the lathe. He was very kind and patient. Working in the lab was also a tall, very pale, and shy boy, Herman. He was an apprentice, and was delicate and effeminate in his mannerism.

As was polite custom in Germany, each morning, everybody would come in and make the rounds, shaking everybody else's hand and saying,"Gruess Gott", which was like saying good morning and meant God's greeting. This same ritual was repeated in the evening before leaving. Before going to lunch, even if only stepping into the garden with a sandwich, or remaining in the lab, everybody would say, "Malzeit" to everybody else; it meant more or less, have a nice lunch. The people who worked in the lab were extremely formal and always spoke in hushed tones.

I liked the work assigned to me. First, I would cut a large sheet of 1/8 inch thick aluminum and construct a chassis for a radio by cutting off the corners and bending the sides so that it became an aluminum box. Then I would drill holes in it, large ones for the radio tube sockets and smaller ones for the bolts to fasten the sockets in place. Then, Herr Doctor would hand me a schematic diagram for wiring a radio and I would put it together, soldering the wires to all the various circuit elements: the resistors, the capacitors, and the solenoids and to the appropriate tube socket terminals. I would then proceed to test, calibrate and tune the radio to the various stations, using an oscilloscope. When it was all done, I would hand the finished model to Herr Doctor. He seemed pleased with my work, always acknowledging it with a cold nod of his head.

In the lab, all day, very little was spoken. There was no small talk, no chatting, no personal questions asked of me, as to who was I, or where I had come from. I was paid thirty Marks per month and worked there for over a year. I still had no friends. Genia had lots of friends, and she traveled with them on outings and to summer camps. She seemed to have a very exciting social life. Sometimes I would visit her for a weekend in her summer camp but I felt very lonely, because they all had such a good time with each other. I, on the other hand, was an oddball outsider.

Often, I would go on outings with my parents. Bavaria is full of lakes and castles. We would travel by train. Once, in the spring of 1946 I went with my father on a day trip by train. Food was still scarce, and we took a few slices of bread and a few hard-boiled eggs with us. Along the way, I looked out of the window and saw a black American soldier looking out the window of the next compartment. Flashing a broad smile, he asked me how old I was. I lied and said sixteen, though I was only fourteen. I lied, because I enjoyed the attention and wanted to meet an American in person. I did not think that he would look at me twice if he knew my real age. In a flash, the soldier came over to our compartment. My father who knew how to count in English asked me why I said sixteen. It was very embarrassing.

Being very polite, my father invited the young soldier to join us for lunch. European etiquette would have dictated the young man to say, "No, thank you," or at most, take a small symbolic bite. Instead, the soldier ate most of our food. He was very friendly and had a big appetite and apparently did not realize how scarce food was for us. Being strictly kosher, we wouldn't have bought food along the way, even if it had been available. We were hungry for the rest of our trip and I felt very guilty for having lied about my age and being caught flirting. My father was nice about the whole thing, though.

My parents let me do pretty much what I wanted. Once I traveled by myself to visit my sister in her summer camp. When I got off the train, I found out that the camp was far from the train station and I set out on foot and hiked for miles until I found it. I walked through picture-postcard villages and countryside that were completely unscathed by the war. The scenes were so picturesque that they looked almost unreal.

Genia's camp was beautiful. There were many boys and girls her age. They had organized social activities, and they danced and flirted. It all made me very sad because I was considered a mere "kid," an outsider who did not participate. Adding injury to insult, the next morning, as I sat by the lake below the camp house, I was suddenly struck on the head by a sharp rock. I felt a sharp pain and blood started gushing from the top of my head. In a panic, I ran to the nurse in the camp house, counting numbers to stay conscious. Finally, I got some attention; everyone was very concerned. My head got bandaged. It only looked bad, but I was fine. Later that day, we all went on an outing in a truck. I sat between the driver and a visiting man who was very interesting and who told me he was a journalist. During the whole trip going and coming back, we talked for hours about serious stuff. When

I told him about my philosophy on the futility of life, he was intent on cheering me up and telling me about life's positives.

Fifty years later, I sat next to him at a luncheon in Israel. I remembered him well, but he did not remember me at all.

I worked for Mr. Frenzl for over a year and saved up one hundred dollars. I gave the money to Genia as a wedding present.

Though I used to read a lot on my own, when I was almost sixteen, I decided that I was very ignorant.

I found out that it was possible to study for matriculation exams outside of official schools and then take the final with the graduating class at a gymnasium (junior level, high school). As I found out, there was a problem with my age, and they rejected me in the gymnasium where I applied. Apparently, one had to be eighteen to have permission to take the matriculation exams. Such were the rules of the Department of Education.

Being very naïve, I went to the offices of the Department of Education and asked to see the Minister of Education. To everyone's surprise, I got an appointment and soon saw him in his office. The distinguished looking gentleman behind the desk said to me: "But child, you are so young, and you have lost so many school years; it will be impossible to catch up so quickly with eighteen year old students who had uninterrupted schooling." Not realizing the amount of work I had ahead of me, I assured him that, if he granted me permission to take the exam, I would be ready by June, which was about seven or eight months away. The kind old man granted me my request and gave me written permission to take the tests. I was to take all the written tests with the German students and, because I was "an externist," I would have to take oral tests in all the subjects as well.

The next step was to find teachers to teach me all the material I needed to learn. My mother became my biggest champion in this endeavor. She never doubted that I could do it and she helped me find qualified tutors. I had one tutor for math, physics and chemistry, one for English, another for history, and one for classic literature: Greek, Latin, French, English, and German. In June 1949, I took the exams and I passed them all.

During the written portion on German classical literature, we were given a specific topic to write about. The theme assigned to us was: "What legacy did our German poets and philosophers leave us to live by, today?"

The topic ignited a storm in me. I started writing and pouring all of my bitterness into the essay. I wrote about the Holocaust and how the Germans had learned nothing from the humanitarian classical German writers, whom I came to love so much. How could the heirs to that great literature have been so immoral and bestial, and pervert their legacy so? Sadly, while discovering the exquisite beauty of German classic literature, I was also remembering having heard that same German language during Jew-extermination raids. How this language used to fill me with terror!

Writing the essay I must have dug my nails into the palms of my hands, because when I finished they were bleeding. Later that afternoon the professor who read my paper called me outside. He was all red in his face and livid with anger. He crisscrossed my paper with a red pen and gave me a D. I'm sure he would have wanted me to fail, but my grades in history and the old Greek and Latin classics were good, and in math and science they were excellent, so I passed. Immediately after matriculation, I applied for admission to the Technical University of Munich. I took the entrance exam with sixteen hundred other applicants. Fortunately I was among the eight hundred students who had passed, so I could enroll in the school of electrical engineering.

Math and science brought a welcome order into the chaotic world around me. My view of the world was that each nation, each community, and each person was fighting everybody else, to enhance only their own survival, without regard to the human cost. I saw neighbor denouncing neighbor to steal an apartment, and everything inside. I saw that the Poles hated Ukrainians and Germans, Ukrainians hated Poles and Russians, Russians hated Germans and they all hated Jews.

I loved mathematics and physics, because these subjects consistently followed simple logical steps that made sense and did not tax me emotionally. At first, I was convinced that the reason that there was so much hatred, cruelty, and killing in the world was because people did not communicate logically, like scientists and mathematicians do. Then, I realized that among the German

Nazis, there were many very good scientists, engineers, mathematicians, and doctors. Did they, in a perverted way, all come to a "logical" conclusion that it was okay to exterminate Jews and enslave millions of others? Had their scientific logic been superimposed upon an old and rotten belief system based on racial and religious discrimination, one that they never thought to question?

57

THE BLUE DANUBE

How I loved the music of Johann Straus! It made me want to dance and take off into romantic reveries. This music was indelibly fused, in a bittersweet way, with my own history. It evoked not only images of formal social events in Europe's elegant ballrooms, but for me, it also brought up memories of of pre-war Sambor and the resort places my parents used to go to in the summer. There are memories of well-dressed, well-fed people, solidly embedded within opulent lifestyles, strolling in resort parks in pre-war Poland. There each day, musicians sat in the center of green, well-manicured, parks in white gazebos and played beautiful semi-classical music. I remember the strolling vacationers, sipping mineral waters and socializing, exchanging trivia and social gossip, politely nodding and tipping their hats in greeting as they would pass others of like status.

After the war when we lived in Munich, once again I would hear the music of Strauss, but this time in Bavarian parks. This time, it would fill me not only with joy, but also with a sadness.

In the Summer of 1950, as in the olden days, before the war, Mama decided to spend a few weeks in a resort. Once again, I found myself watching people strolling in a resort park to the music of Johann Strauss. This time they spoke German instead of Polish, or Yiddish.

I watched the well dressed, well fed, German resort guests, their faces pink, from massages, healing mineral and mud baths and elegant lunches, strolling in the park, and enjoying the music.

I watched the well-mannered ladies and gentlemen, with smiling faces, speaking German in the sweetest, diminutive tones. How pleasantly they conversed, how polite they were, and how beautiful their language could be! And yet how dreadful that language sounded to me during the war. How could I ever listen to it without hearing the voices from the past: "Rauss, verfluchter Jude!" ? (Words I used to hear during Akcjas: "Out, you cursed Jew!")

The sound of the Blue Danube would churn in my head, mixing with images from the past.

Strolling with Mama among the other resort guests, I watched the laughing faces, and sounds of light-hearted blue-eyed German teens. It seemed that their laughter was unspoiled and unpolluted by images of Nazi uniforms, curses, shouts, the sound of bullets, screams, and frightened, desperate faces. Most likely, their father's Nazi uniforms, wartime memorabilia, and copies of "Mein Kampf", were well stashed away in their attics in locked trunks.

Mama, well dressed and well-rested after a daily mud bath and massage, would sit on a park bench with me, perhaps remembering the romantic ball-room dances she used to attend when being wooed by father. She would politely exchange words with people who would sit down next to us. She used to love to speak German and to waltz to the Blue Danube, but now, how could she stand to be part of this scene?

I, well dressed in a brown and white checkered suit and a crisp white blouse (all tailored by the finest tailor in Munich for the post-war going price of a carton of American cigarettes) did not look much different from the well-dressed German young people, who were strolling past me with their polite and distinguished looking parents.

I often wondered why I was made to endure that trip. Made to endure by whom? Perhaps, by some of my own choices. I was, supposedly, privileged to spend that summer with Mama in the posh Bavarian vacation place. As soon as I got there, I remember feeling that I needed to run away somewhere, but where? I know that I should have had, somehow, the chance to express what I was feeling. I was so confused. I needed to protest, to scream, because I was choking on the feelings that were being stirred up in me daily, with no reprieve.

That summer, on beautiful afternoons, I usually remained sitting next to Mama, an unread book in hand, listening to the music of Johann Strauss, and often feeling that I was losing my grip on reality. Where could I have run away to?

The distinguished looking Doctor, who had a practice in the resort and whom Mama and I saw for a check up, had a son in Munich, studying at the same university in the engineering department I had been attending. He told Mama that he wanted his son to meet me. Having perhaps ascertained my virginity during the thorough examination, he thought that I was a very nice girl, unlike the many he had examined in his practice. Apparently, after the war, with so many GI's everywhere, VD was rampant among many young German girls. The doctor gave me a book to take back to his son.

Soon after returning to Munich, I met his very nice and handsome son, when he came to our house to pick up his gift. The boy suggested that he and I soon get together at school; but even though he was very nice and I liked him, I did not want to meet with him again. He never knew why.

58

AFTER
MATRICULATION

While I was on a one-on-one basis with a tutor, I was able to learn fast. In contrast, I did not do well at the university. I felt lost in the huge lecture halls and I was too shy to ask questions. Aside from two nuns, I was the only girl among the eight hundred freshmen in my class, and it bothered me that the male German students were so nice to me and paid me so much attention. It was the kind of attention that I would have ordinarily craved, had it been in another country. Often they would pass notes down to me from the higher tiered benches above, asking me to meet them after class. I never responded. Soon, I started skipping classes and missing assignments.

Wanting to learn more about everything, I tried to build my new life on an intellectual foundation, but at the same time I lacked emotional grounding. I still didn't know how to bridge the past and the present. I was constantly plagued by nightmares, and lived in a constant state of anxiety, fear and tension. When alone at night, I was afraid to close my eyes to go to sleep, no matter how exhausted I was. In the dark, whether indoors or outdoors, I would be totally overcome by so much fear that I would leave all the lights on in my bedroom, all night. Walking or sitting alone, I would struggle with the urge to keep looking back. I would wash my hair with my eyes open, no matter how much the soap and shampoo would sting my eyes. Going back into my own memories made me feel out-of-touch and detached from the world I lived in.

Still in Munich at seventeen, I sometimes sat in on psychology lectures at the University of Munich where my friend, Jacob Stern studied medicine. Once he suggested that I attend with him a lecture on fear; he thought I'd find his professor of psychology, Dr. Bumke, interesting.

My young friend, Jacob whom we all called Kuba, was the sole survivor from his whole family. One day Kuba shared with me his own amazing story of survival; his story was far more gruesome than mine. Kuba told me that when his Jewish community was liquidated, all the Jews from his town were taken outside his town and machine-gunned into a mass grave. Kuba, who was twelve at the time, was there, with his parents and siblings standing at the edge of the huge ditch and facing the German machine guns. Just then, when he was to be next in line to be killed and hit by the barrage of bullets, he threw himself into the mass grave, pretending to have been shot.

By nighttime, he dug himself out from under a pile of bodies and escaped into the forest. After the war, at age fourteen, he supported himself by selling cigarettes the American soldiers would give him. He found odd jobs and began to study. Soon Kuba got a scholarship at the University of Munich and he enrolled to study medicine. Still in Munich he completed his studies and by 1951 Kuba became a medical doctor. Later, in America, he worked at the Montefiore Hospital in New York. I often think of Kuba and other survivors of the Holocaust, who after the war put their energies and feelings of sorrow towards rebuilding a new life. Since they had no country, home or family left to go home to, they relocated as best they could, got jobs, acquired professions and started new families. They became productive and grateful members of society. Kuba's personal experience with death and human suffering drove him to become a healer.

What a contrast between Holocaust survivors like Kuba and Palestinians refugees. While I would not belittle the trauma of displacement, it is tragic that many Palestinians remain stuck in their victim mode. While other refugees went on with their lives, many Palestinians turned their suffering into hatred and terrorism, exploding airplanes, trains, and bus-loads of innocent people. Stagnating in refugee camps while being supported by the

United Nations, their victimhood mentality has been exploited by Arab politicians for over 50 years to vilify Israel.

After attending several of Dr.Bumke's lectures with Kuba, I decided to approach him. I found him to be warm and friendly. One day at the end of a lecture I waited for Dr. Bumke outside the lecture hall. I spoke to him; I asked for his advice in dealing with my fears. The frail old professor was very kind. He was very attentive and genuinely sympathetic. He asked me to come see him in his office.

The address he gave me turned out to be that of his beautiful home, which was a big, spacious private Victorian house in Munich's best neighborhood. I rang the doorbell and his house-keeper showed me to his elegant office. Dr. Bumke made me feel comfortable and welcome. I was there for a long time. He did not seem to be in a rush, and we talked a lot; he asked me many questions. He said that he wanted to see me again. I came back several more times and he tried to treat me with hypnosis. I'm not sure whether he succeeded in hypnotizing me, but I remember that in the course of the hypnotherapy-sessions he would make positive suggestions. From the first moment I met him, I loved the old man, he was like a loving old grandpa.

Soon the visits with Dr. Bumke had to stop. Our immigration papers arrived and we were finally able to leave Munich for America.

A few months before our departure I had applied for a scholarship to a college in the US, but had no response by the time we were leaving.

59

THE SLOW BOAT
TO AMERICA

It was winter 1950. We packed up and left for Bremer Haven, the sea port of Bremen, where we would later board our immigrant ship. Before departing to the US we first needed to stay in Bremen in a quarantined environment for an extended period of time and undergo thorough medical examinations. This procedure was to make sure that we are fit to come to America. We lived in army barracks, dormitory style, in which men and women were separated.

Finally, the day came when we boarded a small, ten ton army transport ship, called "General Balou."

On the day of our departure, I saw the sea for the first time. On board of our ship, we were assigned bunk beds below deck. Men and women were once again separated.

The trip took ten days. It was December and the sea was rough. From the first day of our sea voyage on, at least ninety percent of the immigrants on board got seasick; most remained sick throughout the trip.

I never got seasick, perhaps because I did not know much about sea voyages and did not anticipate getting seasick. The rougher the sea got, the more the small ship rocked, the more I liked it. It reminded me of amusement park rides.

With so many sick people on board, the one American nurse on board had a lot to do. I volunteered to help her. My job was to prepare baby bottles and tend to the many small babies whose mothers were too sick to care for them.

Genia spoke some English and could type, so she got to share a cabin with another woman above deck. The bunk-bed accommodations below deck, where I was staying with Mama together with many other women, were miserable. It was hot, noisy, and the place reecked with the stench of vomit. The sea was especially rough as we were crossing the English Channel. On most days, the cafeteria was almost empty, and our food trays, filled with scrambled, smelly powdered eggs and cotton-like slices of white bread would slide all over the place and fly off the tables.

The deck was full of miserably seasick people. Wrapped in blankets, they'd be lying or sitting around the deck from one end to the other, complaining, moaning and wrethcing. When I found my seasick father on the deck, looking pale as if about to pass out, I panicked and barged into the nearest officer's cabin, looking for a glass of water in the bathroom. where the startled officer was sitting on the toilet and reading. Undeterred, I proceeded to fill the glass with water. This was an emergency; I had to get a glass water for my father. I was gone before the startled man could utter a sound.

Whenever I could slip away unnoticed, to escape the miserable scene on deck and below, I would crawl into one of the lifeboats hanging over the side of the ship, enjoying the rocking, the mist, and the roar of the stormy sea. I was sure-footed and naïve; it never occurred to me that I could have fallen into the rough ocean. My fears were of a different nature. Most of the upper deck was off limits to the immigrants, but sometimes at night, I would sneak in to see the movies that were being screened exclusively for the ship's crew. A handsome Jamaican sailor, who wore a gold earring and knew me from the cafeteria, would offer me his lap. He was never crude, and never took advantage of my naivete. Nor did anyone ask me to leave.

Towards the end of our journey, we docked at Halifax for one day. It was exiting to see land again. While the sailors were busy docking, I climbed the highest mast on our boat to better see Canada. I probably also did it because it was against the rules. I was spotted only after I had reached the top. Then, all hell broke lose on deck. Below, I saw a bunch of sailors screaming at me to get down. I pretended that I did not understand what they were saying. It was true that I did not know English well, but I understood what the fuss was all about. When I came down from my great vantage point, no one was really angry with me. Even though I was eighteen, I still looked like a kid.

Within a short time, we left Halifax, and the voyage continued to New York. In the middle of the night, there was a lot of excitement; everyone went on deck to see the Statue of Liberty and the New York skyline. I went below deck and cried. I knew absolutely nothing about America, its history, its promise, or its reality. I only knew that we had a large family there who never had much interest in us. I had wanted to go "home," once and for all. Here, I thought, once again, we would be strangers, and as Jews, probably unwanted ones at that. While everybody on deck was cheering at the sight of America's shoreline, I asked myself, "Why am I on this boat?" I was angry with everybody for not coming to our aid during the Holocaust, at the American pilots who bombed city dwellings and churches, but not the railroad tracks to Auschwitz and other death camps. I thought of the refugees that were turned away from America's shores, back to the gas chambers. I was angry with my mother who made us come here. Why was I on this boat? What did I have in common with these people?

60

NEW YORK, USA

We docked in New York on January 1, 1951. Uncle Phillip, a tall handsome man, smartly dressed as if stepping out of a fashion magazine page, came to meet us upon arrival. I liked him immediately and felt close to him, because he looked amazingly like his brother, Uncle Isaac. Wearing a long mink coat, his wife Tillie, a small pretty woman with a soft and kind face, stood next to Phillip, smiling at us. Benny's son-in-law, Adolph Shapiro, a wonderful, warm, young man, also came to greet us. I also spotted a stooped, gray-haired little woman, Fannie, whom it seemed I had known and loved all my life; she was definitely my family.

Having arrived on the Sabbath, my father, being orthodox, would not get into Phillip's shiny car. Father, Adolph and I took a long walk across Manhattan to Adolph's apartment where we found more members of our family, waiting for us. They had gathered to welcome us with lunch.

Our cousins spent some time admiring our clothes, which, to their great surprise, were quite fashionable. We had also brought some expensive gifts. It seemed that we did not fit into their idea of refugees.

61

A REFUGEE
IN AMERICA

The first thing that amazed me about the United States was the variety of its people. Here, the full human spectrum was represented, forming a unique nation unlike any I had ever seen or imagined. In this American melting-pot, comprised of people of all races and ethnic backgrounds, its citizens were living together as one people, Americans, committed to the ideals spelled out in the American Constitution and the Bill of Rights. Their diverse and not-too-distant ancestors had left their countries of origin, which were torn by wars, hatred, poverty, and social injustice. As an immigrant and Holocaust survivor, I understood that on this American soil, a new kind of society was evolving. America was way ahead and beyond Europe's petty chauvenisms, racisms, rabid anti-Semitisms, and all the other "isms" that have plagued Europe and other places throughout the world for thousands of years.

To everyone who has lived under dictatorships and in war-torn countries, having lived through long periods of depravation, lacking security, food and opportunities, coming to America became a dream come true. And I also soon embraced the American dream, in spite of my earlier reservations. Although far from perfect, more than any place on the planet, America was the cradle of democracy that became a refuge for so many immigrants who longed for freedom, justice, and security.

I liked the idea of a melting-pot of people from different ethnic and racial backgrounds where they each would contribute from the cultures of their origin and choose to live together with mutual respect for one another. I was looking forward to getting to know Italians, Irish, Puerto Ricans, African Americans, Asians and Native Americans.

I also assumed, that this new world, America, would be a rational, intelligent society, one made up of people who, because they themselves fled from persecution and slavery, would be thus sensitized to human suffering at the hands of others.

Because of my idealistic expectations, it was hard to adjust to the realities I started confronting daily in my new life in America. I found New York divided into separate ethnic and racial communities who rarely socialized with each other.

In Europe, we had heard so much about Harlem Jazz. Naturally, when I came to New York in 1951, I wanted to go to Harlem to listen to jazz. I was told that white people don't go there. When I invited Charlie, a black friend from college to my birthday party, all windows in our brownstone Bronx apartment house opened and all heads shook disapprovingly. My poor mother never heard the end of it from our neighbors. What kind of melting pot was this?

One day, Charlie invited another mutual white friend, Arno, and me to his party and once again, windows in brownstone houses opened, this time, in Harlem and we were stared at, as if we were part of an alien invasion, or had taken a wrong turn.

I was also horrified to see dirty people in rags, sleeping on the pavement in New York's Bowery district, which in those days was a dirty slum. No one had told me that there was poverty and homelessness in the USA.

As a survivor of deadly racial prejudice, I was sensitive to things that "normal" people in the U.S. generally seemed to ignore. In the fall of 1951, the night I arrived in Alabama to go to college in Jacksonville, I noticed "White" and "Colored" signs on bathrooms and water fountains. I was totally confused as to which bathroom to use or what water to drink. I did not know that the color references applied to people's skins. When I got off the train in Aniston, Alabama, I boarded a bus to take me to Jacksonville. I remember everybody staring at me when I chose to sit in the back of the bus. Blacks looked at me as if I was crazy, whites looked at me in anger. I did not deliberately sit down in the back to make a political statement of protest. I simply liked sitting in the back so that I could see better; it also made me feel more secure to have no one sitting behind me. Strangely enough, I did not know anything about segregation between Blacks and Whites and the rules in the South about where one was supposed to sit on a bus or toilet.

The first few weeks after we arrived in New York, we stayed at an old hotel on 27th St. in Manhattan. Then we stayed in Uncle Phillip's apartment for a few days, until we found a place of our own.

I was struck, not only by Uncle Philip's resemblance to his brother Isaac, but even more so by how much Phillip's two daughters looked much like Isaac's two daughters. Rhoda, the oldest, looked like our common cousin big Andzia, and the blond Gloria looked like Zosia.

I so wanted to talk to my beautiful American cousins about our common European family, cousins, uncles, aunts and grandfather. My American cousins, who were in their twenties and thirties, dismissed it all with a few words: "Let's not talk about it, it's too sad," and then proceeded to show us their wedding pictures from June, 1943. I saw pictures of smiling faces, long gowns, tuxedos, a band, dancing couples, and banquet tables laden with food. Little did they realize that on June the ninth, 1943, that same year and month that they were celebrating so exuberantly, the Sambor Ghetto was being obliterated, the Jewish population of Sambor wiped out, together with the whole Polish Glickman family that was common to us.

Our first few months in New York were bewildering. I felt like I had taken a wrong turn on the way out of Europe. We, the new Jewish immigrants, definitely felt unwelcome. The people in the street, and even our neighbors and employers, were rude and impatient with our broken English. They looked down on us refugees. I, in turn, having retained traces of European snobbishness, made general judgements about Americans. I thought them uncultured. Often, I still think that the kids here are primitive, as far as education goes. Many have bad manners, use bad language, waste their time watching TV, read trash, and dress sloppily.

Initially, for me, communication was difficult. People here knew only one language; rarely did they even know their own ethnic language.

Within a week of our arrival In New York, I started work, while attending City College at night. The Jewish agency who arranged our immigration was staffed by mostly rude people. They looked down on us, the new immigrants, even though their own parents had also been immigrants. Within days of our arrival, they gave me a job. They expected us to be very grateful, no matter how unmatched the jobs were to our skills and education. First, I worked on an assembly line in an electronic factory somewhere within the downtown slums. Later I worked in a sweatshop near Fourteenth Street in Manhattan. All the people working there were immigrants from different countries, and spoke different languages. It was a sweaty tower of Babel. The sweatshop was in an old building without elevators and without fresh air. It was hot, crowded, and full of sweaty workers; it was a staff of men and women who were being paid by the number of items they finished, cutting, sewing, or ironing. Many ate their lunch as they ironed with the other hand at the same time. They hardly took the time to use the toilets. My job was to cut pockets for military coats that were manufactured there. A supervisor timed us in the bathroom. She would knock on the stalls and tell us to hurry. I worked there all spring and summer. At the same time, I was going to night school at the City College of New York on Amsterdam Avenue. and 125th Street. Every night, I would take the subway to and from Harlem, walking alone late at night to and from the subway stations. It was only later that I was told that it was not a good idea for a young girl to do that. I suppose ignorance helped me do what I had to do.

At first, we were given a two-room place in Brooklyn, in the house of an elderly Jewish couple. Mr. and Mrs. Cohen were in their eighties; they spoke mostly Yiddish and some heavily accented English. They had come to the U.S. many years before and looked down on us "green horns," as they called us. They were of very modest means, and it seemed that they were both illiterate.

One night, after night school, when I was returning home by

subway, the ride seemed unusually long. Soon the train emptied out and stopped at an above ground depot. The conductor told me to get off. I was totally lost, and I did not know which way to turn. My English was not good enough to get the directions right. It was a very cold night and the streets were forsaken. With newspapers and street garbage flying in the wind, I walked through the dirty and slummy streets. It was spooky and scary. Fortunately, it was so cold that not too many people were out that night loitering in the streets.

I did not find our place until four o'clock in the morning. After that experience, on the nights I had school, I slept at Uncle Phillip's in Washington Heights.

Uncle Phillip and his wife Tillie and their 20 year-old son Stanley, lived in a modest apartment. The Washington Heights area was not too far from from the City College. I slept in Stanley's room. He was rarely home, and when I got there late at night, everybody else was already asleep. Nor did I see anybody when I woke up very early in the morning to leave for work.

My cousin, Stanley Glickman, was a very talented artist. His room was full of his drawings, watercolors and oil paintings. To me his room was magic. It smelled of paint and reflected Stanley's life, his personality, and his esthetic sensitivity. I loved the ambience, I loved his art, and I was in love with Stanley. Like all my other crushes on boys, this was also my secret. Of course, no one, not even Stanley, knew about it.

Stanley had the sweetest personality. He was over six feet tall, slim, handsome, quiet, and mysterious. He had curly, already graying hair, and he had the most beautiful dreamy blue eyes.

Once, he waited for me downstairs and invited me for a cup of coffee. I was shy and awestruck. Besides, I did not speak much English, so there was hardly any conversation between us. After coffee, we returned to the apartment. He disappeared, and I crawled into the bed in his room. That night, he must have slept on the couch in the living room.

62

ALABAMA

One day, a few months after we had already moved from Brooklyn to Knox Place near Moshulu Parkway in the Bronx, a letter had arrived from Alabama. It was addressed to me in Munich and forwarded to Brooklyn. My brother-in-law, Joseph Tenenbaum, who, with my sister, still lived in their rented room in Brooklyn, came running to me one afternoon, holding the letter in his hand, having sensed that it contained something very important for me. Indeed, I was being offered a full scholarship from the International House in Jacksonville, Alabama for one year. The scholarship covered room and board and tuition at Jacksonville State Teacher's College, in Jacksonville, Alabama. Long before we left Munich for the USA, on the advice of a friend,I had applied for a possible scholarship to study in the U.S. for a year. I did not follow up on it, neither was I contacted about it by anyone in the USA, so I forgot about it.

As soon as I read the letter, I wrote back to the college in Alabama, accepting the scholarship, even though I knew nothing about that particular college. I had no idea where Alabama was. I knew neither the geography nor the history of the USA. I welcomed a chance to get out of New York, where I felt trapped. Within less than a year of my arrival in the U.S., I was off to Alabama.

I had seen a film with Jeannie Crain about life on an American college campus. I did not understand the story, but the girls were all beautiful and the male students were all handsome. The girls wore flat shoes with mid-calf skirts, tight sweaters and cardigans, and they all danced the jitterbug. They were so different from the intellectual and serious students I had known in Europe when I was a student at the university there. The students in Munich, aspired to be very sophisticated, and the young women in my circle placed much emphasis on dressing elegantly. As students, we had discounts to theaters and the opera. It was cheaper to see plays and operas than to go to movies. We'd get together to discuss Sartre's existentialism, modern art forms, go to classical concerts, dance in elegant nightclubs, or take off on excursions in the Alps. These American students seemed childish and unsophisticated, but they were physical, healthy, good-looking, simple and sweet.

Early in September 1951, my parents took me to the train station and saw me off. I arrived in Anniston, Alabama, late at night. There was a bus that took several people to my new school, Jacksonville State Teacher's College. I was dropped off at the girl's dormitory. It turned out that my scholarship was part of the International House program at the college. I was sponsored by a well-to-do philanthropic couple. At the international house, there were other foreign students from many countries: Cuba, Venezuela, France, Belgium, and Switzerland.

We, the International Students, were all given full scholarships and were expected to travel as a fund raising group and attend all sorts of ladies clubs, Rotary clubs, and church groups, representing our respective countries of origin. The French girl and the Belgian boy would sing "Frere Jaque", the Venezuelan and Cuban students would sing "Cielito Lindo, ay, ay, ay" etc. Then there was a very intellectual, Swiss student, Ernst Schwartz, who seemed totally out of place in this small Hick-town college, because he was very sophisticated, even by European university standards. All the international students, including Ernst, seemed to have a great time with each other and with other students with whom they mixed and often dated. We made our presentations to the ladies with the blue-gray hair, who wore ill-fitting, gaudily colored clothes and the men in funny, tasseled Shriner's caps. All of my international friends smiled a lot and told heart warming and humorous anecdotes about their countries. They all were so "cute" and "precious". I was neither. What cute stories could I have told them about my life in Poland, about the wonderful people there, the ones I was now asked to represent, but who had never considered me to be real Pole? I refused to sing Polish songs for the nice folks.

Dr. Jones, whose brain child that international program was, always led these fund raising trips. I think he was very disappointed in my not being Polish enough. He was a good man, and I hated to appear ungrateful, failing to fulfill his expectations. Dr. Jones was a professor at the college; he had a doctorate. Why, then, was he so ignorant about Poland's bloody recent history? Why did he never ask me, "How was it, being a Jew in Poland?"

Although I did not speak Hebrew, I would have liked to sing Hebrew songs; I even offered to learn some. That idea was not received favorably. Even in the International House, it seemed that I did not quite fit in, or belong.

I certainly was an oddity on campus. I was extremely shy, serious, innocent, and at the same time very "old" for my age. As far as I knew, I was also the only Jewish student at the college. There certainly was not even one Black student at the school there.

One year later, among all the International House students, I believe I was the only one whose scholarship was not renewed for another year. Dr. Jones was polite, but rather cold. He was not too happy that his son Bill always wanted to study math with me and sometimes take me out for a walk or a soda.

Mrs. Jones ran the dining room and the kitchen in the International House. She was the kindest person on campus. She was very kind to the black cooks and helpers. She always picked them up and drove them home. I once went along with her and was shocked and amazed to see the shacks they lived in. Their whole community was a shantytown. Although I had been looking forward to listening to black spirituals in churches, I soon gave up on that idea.

I did not know of any other Jews on campus I could celebrate Jewish holidays with. On Yom Kippur I went to a little forest nearby, where I spent the whole day alone, fasting. I took with me a small prayer book with an English translation that father handed me before I left new York. Neither English nor Hebrew was easy for me to read.

When I returned to the international house that evening, Mrs. Jones served me the meal I had missed; she had saved it for me in the oven.

Math and physics were very easy for me because I already knew the fundamentals well and I knew how to study by myself. In these subjects my poor English was not a big handicap and I was getting high grades. I developed a great learning strategy. The day the class began a new chapter I'd work through it from beginning to the end, and do each and every problem at the end of the chapter. For the rest of the week I'd sit back in class, enjoy the review and I was able to volunteer doing problems on the blackboard, that other students had trouble solving.

Socially things did not go so well for me. I was lonely and did not date; no one asked me out. The college was not too far from Fort McClellan, which was an army base. Every Thursday evening, the army sent out a bus for girls who wished to spend the evening dancing with the soldiers at the base. Thursday night thus became the highlight of my week. I danced with the soldiers every dance, until I was exhausted.

Some girls actually started dating some of the soldiers, and one soon got married. None of my dancing partners ever asked me for a date. Maybe it was my poor English, or my shyness away from the dance floor. When they heard my accent the first thing they would ask is, "where are you from?" I would say, "From Poland."

"Oh, you are Polish? "

"No, I'm not Polish, I'm a Jewish refugee from Poland. "

At that point, the questions would stop. Still, I continued to dance every dance because there were many soldiers there and only one bus-load of girls. At all times, the soldiers acted like gentlemen towards me-- maybe because our dormitory housemother was chaperoning and ever-present near the dance floor.

My first roommate in Jacksonville was Betty. Blond, with big blue eyes, she was the prettiest girl on campus and she had the morals of a bunny rabbit. Guys were nice to me so that they could get close to Betty. Betty never studied. Often guys would sneak in and out of our dormitory room through the ground floor window.

Jacksonville was in a "dry" county. One time on a Saturday night, I got to go out with a bunch of students. We drove for some time until we arrived at a mountain of beer cans. I was told that we had arrived in Georgia.

Betty always kept a bottle of whisky under her bed. Eventually, she trusted me enough to offer me a slug. All that fuss about alcohol was very strange to me. In Europe, alcoholic drinks were always kept in the house. There were bottles of wine and liquors on the table on Friday nights. On a hot day, guests would be offered cold beer. Even as children, when we had a cold, we were given hot tea with whisky, lemon, and honey. After I left the school, I found out that Betty had gotten pregnant and was kicked out of college.

There was a Jewish family in Anniston, Alabama, who contacted me after a few months and invited me for a holiday on several occasions. Mr. and Mrs. Henry Nathan were very hospitable. Though they were very nice, they also never asked questions about my wartime experiences in Europe.

For Christmas, the couple who had sponsored my scholarship had a surprise for me. I got to fly home to New York for the holidays. The lady, who was a pretty and pleasant woman in her early forties, picked me up before the trip and took me on a shopping spree to a small clothing store in Anniston. I was amazed at how cheap looking and ill-fitting the clothes were. She also bought me a pair of cheap flat shoes, made of velvet cloth and rubber soles. In Europe, before and after the war, our clothes were made to order by the finest dressmakers in Sambor and in Munich, with lengthy consultations and numerous fittings. I owned only four dresses, but they were all exquisite. My high-heeled shoes were made to order.

When my sponsors picked me up to take me to a small private plane to connect to a commercial airliner in Birmingham, I wore one of my European dresses, a Dior copy, and high heel shoes. I remember the look the rich lady gave me. Something did not add up for her.

I never had any lengthy conversation with the rich couple; they never asked personal questions, like "who are you, how did you live, or survive Europe, or how come you are so well dressed?" I was a token refugee, or a token foreign student, and was of no personal interest to them. They must have felt very good about their tax-exempt, but impersonal, generosity.

I arrived at Moshulu Parkway in the evening, taking the train from the airport to the Bronx. Hoping to surprise my parents with this unexpected visit. I soon spotted them and for a few minutes I walked quietly behind them as they were taking their evening stroll; and then I suddenly greeted them. It was a joyful reunion.

Spending a school year at the Jacksonville State Teachers College was an interesting experience, even though I felt very "different" and lonely there. I had a chance to learn English and get very good grades in math and physics, which later helped me get into the day school at CCNY, (The City College of New York).

My sister, who married a fellow Holocaust survivor when she was very young, had many Jewish and European friends in New York, some she had known from the Hebrew high school she had attended in Munich. Because of that, she was perhaps spared the loneliness and alienation that I had felt during my first years in the US. Only on my visits with my immediate family or with the people living in Israel did I feel a sense of connectedness and belonging. With them, I had a shared history and we knew each other's sensitivities and emotional language. For example, many survivors shared my attitude towards food. I could never throw out old leftovers. I'd eat bread that was almost moldy, or eat chicken down to the bare bone and then proceed to chew on the bone until it was all gone. At home or in restaurants, I'd race everyone to grab a chair at a table, where I could sit with my back against a wall.

In the United States, for the rest of my life, I lived among and with people who knew very little of World War Two, and even then they knew it only from history books, the evening news, and from perspectives that were only relevant to their lives in America.

Because I did not live among other survivors in the U.S., my experience was perhaps different than my sister's. My wartime identity was locked up inside me. When reading or thinking about the Holocaust, I'd feel like I was about to be sucked back into the past and into an emotional abyss.

At such times, I would feel such anger that I could almost hear myself scream, blaming everybody, faulting them for not having done more to stop the systematic murder of six million European Jews. But I kept the screams in. I lacked the eloquence and the courage to express myself verbally. Going back into my own memories or reading about other Holocaust survivors, seeing documentaries about the raids, the executions and the concentration camps, seeing movies like "Winds Of War," "Schindler's List," or "Sophie's Choice", etc., made me feel like I was losing my mind. I would sob uncontrollably, asking myself, "What am I doing here? I should have been there with them..." For a few days afterwards, I'd feel totally alienated even from the people who were now my new family, my new friends, and neighbors. At least, my nightmares and my anger were somehow keeping my slaughtered family still alive in my own life. Besides, any expressions of my feelings would have been out of place and out of sync with everybody else.

I was especially angry with those American Jews who had lived relatively normal lives in safety during the Holocaust, and never raised a voice of protest loud enough to have made a difference. After all, we did have a common history and common issues to deal with in the future. Neither my loving Jewish friends in Switzerland nor my aunts, uncles and cousins in America asked me even once: "Child, what happened to you during the war? How did you live, how did you survive? What happened to our family? How did they live, how did they perish? Why are you so shy and so fearful?" Not even my history or humanity professors at colleges and universities asked me these kinds of questions. Neither did my American friends, and later, even my American husband of 29 years. Neither did the Rabbis at the temple I have attended for 25 years. My husband, who was raised in the US, was Jewish by birth and raised by almost-orthodox parents. He had joined the U.S. Navy at seventeen to fight the "Japs"-not Hitler.

How is one to become rooted among strangers who don't care to know who you are?

I kept my feelings of anger and alienation in. Besides, I rationalized, now that I was safe and well fed, what was "I" doing, to ease the suffering of others? How was I reaching out to help the abandoned kids, the poor, the abused, and the homeless? These people were having their own private and lonely wars, and what was I doing to help them? How much would I want to dwell on other people's sad history and issues? Would I risk my life and that of my family, to save them?

63

MY SISTER GENIA

After graduating from Hebrew High school in Munich Genia went on to study medicine at the University of Munich until we left for the US in late December, 1950. Genia married early. When still in Munich she met a fellow Holocaust survivor, Joseph Tenenbaum, who had miraculously endured and survived years of brutal internment within several Nazi concentration camps, where his parents were murdered alongside thousands of others. Being a strong youth, Joseph had lied about his age and skills so that he would be assigned to the group of prisoners who were used for hard labor. The alternative would have been joining women and children who were herded into gas chambers. When he was taken to the camps he was only fourteen, and when he was liberated he was eighteen.

Although he was very young when he lost his parents, and when the community he grew up in had been destroyed, young Joseph never forgot the lessons of traditional values and the love of learning that his family had infused in him since childhood. His is an amazing story of resilience and courage which he has written about in his autobiography, " LEGACY and REDEMPTION -A Life Renewed" published by the Holocaust Museum in Washington D.C.

One of the camps where he spent a long time was depicted in the movie Schindler's list. After liberation by the US army, Joseph spent a few years in Munich where he met my sister Genia. Joseph followed Genia to the US and they soon got married. After a difficult start in New York, they went on to settle in Canada where they raised three children, Sidney, Gary and Tamara. Genia created a beautiful home for her children, and they in turn, are raising their own beautiful families. With hard work, perseverance and integrity, Joseph became a successful builder, entrepreneur and well respected member in his community. Genia went on to pursue a brilliant career in art. Her sculptures are shown in galleries in Canada and abroad. Yet beneath the shiny veneer of their success and achievements, the memories and scars of their childhoods linger.

Genia beside some of her sculptures during an art exhibit

My five beautiful sons in 1970

Portrait of our growing family in 1965

64

RAISING A FAMILY

The best thing I have done with my life was to raise my five sons. While they were growing up, I was fortunate to have had their father as a partner. He was a good person and was very intelligent. A teacher and a very rational person by nature and a scientist by profession, he shared with me a lifelong love for learning and the love for our children. I quit my job as a research physicist to stay home and raise my kids. Later in life, I struggled, and was unable to catch up with my career and get a job in my profession. Nonetheless, I consider leaving my job to raise my kids a good decision. I have no regrets about that and I am still reaping the rewards from having chosen to do so. My five sons are intelligent, secure, and creative. They have high moral and ethical standards and they love to learn and exchange ideas. We have a great friendship.

In our family, we all shared a love for nature and animals. In the spring we planted trees and flowers in our big yard. Even though we lived two blocks away from a busy main street in the San Fernando Valley, in Los Angeles county, our large backyard was home to horses, ponies, a sheep, chickens, many dogs, cats, birds, snakes, and even a pet tarantula. When the boys got older, there was a full basketball court up front. Kids from the neighborhood always loved to visit and play. There was always a lot of music in our house. The kids were all very musical and all played various instruments. My children were bright and healthy; my husband, who was prominent in his field of space physics, had a good job and afforded us a comfortable lifestyle. Our house was always open to friends and family, especially on Friday nights when we celebrated the Sabbath with festive dinners. On Sunday mornings we also held a traditional brunch. Life was good.

We almost never went on vacations without the children. I did not like leaving them with baby-sitters. The imaginary scenarios of accidents and other disasters would fill me with anxiety, so it was hard for me to leave them - even for a few days.

We eventually bought a big camper and travelled up and down the West Coast and throughout the national parks. While camping, I was reminded of how a simple life could be beautiful, and how little we really needed. When the boys were off fishing with their dad, I'd be busy cleaning the camper, preparing meals, reading, and quietly enjoying the forests, the mountains, deserts, the lakesides, and the rivers.

65

LOSING
MY PARENTS

My father who had never been sick a day in his life died within a year of being diagnosed with prostate cancer. Although he initially underwent surgery and radiation, the cancer soon spread throughout his vital organs. He died on March 15, 1968. Six months later he would have been sixty-six years old.

I saw him last in December of 1967. He was already looking very gaunt and haggard, and often moaned in pain at night. He could not hold his food anymore but still followed his daily routine, almost till the end. He would still get up at 5 am in the morning, spend an hour at the synagogue praying, and then take the subway to his business, on 27th Street, downtown New York. When I came to New York to see him, wanting to spend more time with him, I went with him in the morning to his small store. At the store he wanted to tell me something very important; he reached in his pocket and took out something he wanted to show me confidentially. It was an airline ticket to Israel. All his life he had longed to live there, but after W.W.II, he made a concession to Mama to come first to America. Now, he said, he is not waiting any longer. He would go there alone. He longed to see Israel and his only two living brothers, Yankiev-Leib and Moshe, who settled there after the war. Father had also had many cousins, all fervent Zionists who had moved to Israel in the early twenties. Father said that he would no longer wait for Mama to come with him. She was afraid of Arab terrorism and refused to go there even for a visit, but she had also been afraid to stay home alone in the Bronx; so he could not leave her alone at home. Now, resolute, he said to me: " God willing, this Passover I will be in Israel"

At the time of my visit with my parents in New York, I was six months pregnant with my fifth baby. My second son David who was six at the time came along for the trip. He had been going to Hebrew Parochial school, and already at that young age he was excelling in his religious studies. In the morning, during our visit, notwithstanding the cold climate to which he was unaccustomed, David would wake up at five and insist on going to prayers with his grandfather "Josy". Although that made my father very happy and proud of his grandson, he worried about the child catching cold; but David would not be talked out of going to prayers with his grandfather. Father told us, that during the prayers David would bury himself in his grandfather's prayer shawl and kiss it's fringes. Father was deeply moved by the child's sincere reverence in the way he prayed and his love for a grandfather he barely knew. He was brimming with pride when the rabbi and the other worshippers came over to meet the child that behaved in such an unusual manner. It was Hanukkah; in the evenings David would sit on my father's lap and both would light the Hanukkah candles and sing.

Soon David and I had to return to Los Angeles. I wasn't allowed to come back to New York till after the baby's birth. My doctor would not let me travel by plane in the last stages of pregnancy. During the next two months I was anxiously awaiting the birth of my baby. I was worried, impatient, and frustrated because I was unable rush back to New York to be with my ill father. To please him, I asked him over the phone to choose a name for my new baby. It is a Jewish tradition to name a baby after a well-respected and beloved ancestor. (I never had an ultrasound so I did not know whether it would be a boy or a girl.) Father's direct, matter of fact answer astounded me. He said the baby would have two names. One will be Pinhas, after his beloved Rabbi Pinhas Tversky, and for the second name I needed to wait. He must have known that the baby will be named after him, after his his death, but he also wanted to spare me.

On Monday, March 11, 1968, at six o'clock in the evening I

called the doctor and drove myself to the local hospital. The contractions had started and they were becoming intense. At 3:52 a.m. on March 12, my fifth beautiful boy was born. Mama told me by phone, that upon hearing of the baby's birth, father raised his arms in prayer and gratitude.

By next morning I began to inquire about immediate airplane reservations to New York. No airline would allow a one-day-old baby on board. I came home on Thursday and packed my bags. Next day, Friday at 5 PM, Genia's husband, Joseph called from New York; Father had passed away. Joseph, who had a close relationship with my father, based on mutual love and respect, stood with Mama at father's bedside till the end. Father could only whisper to Joseph his last words. Father's last words were, "take me to Israel". All religious Jews want to be there when the Messiah comes. Genia had gone back to Toronto for a few days to check on her kids. By the time she got back to New York she was too late to say goodbye to our father, his body had already been taken out of his hospital bed to the morgue.

On Saturday morning I was on a plane with my new born three-day-old baby who now had the missing first name. His name would be Yosef. I was heading to New York to be with Mama. I needed to be close to the people and things that still bore traces of father's life: his prayer books, his Yiddish newspapers, his favorite reading chair, his ties and his fine hats. I needed to surround myself with the people who knew and loved him. My father's casket was taken to his synagogue where a large group of fellow worshippers had gathered. Friends came from all over New York and some flew in from Canada to honor him and share our grief. The synagogue was so packed that many stood with umbrellas outside in the pouring rain. The young Puerto-Rican man who had worked for my father called and cried like a baby. He said that he had also lost a father. An older Ukrainian man who had attended evening school with father stopped me in the street to talk to me about father; he was crying.

On the eighth day of his life, my new baby boy, Yosef, who inherited his grandpa Josy's luminous turquoise eyes, was circumcised according to Jewish tradition. During the circumcision and naming ceremony I had a strong feeling that at that very moment Father was being laid to rest. Indeed, as I later found out, Father was being laid to rest at the Mount of Olives in Jerusalem at the time of the baby's naming. My sister Genia and her husband Joseph took him there for the burial, honoring his last wish.

As father had already known in his heart, four months before, by Passover, he was in Israel, the land he turned to three times daily during each of his prayers, for all of his life. Each day in his prayers he would repeat: "Next year in Jerusalem". Although he lived to witness from afar the miracle of Israel's rebirth and the liberation of the "Western Wall" during the six day war, he never got to set foot in the land that to him was indelibly and intimately connected with his God and his very own being. From high on the Mount of Olives, overlooking the terraced hills of Jerusalem he is probably watching over and blessing the land of his forefathers and now, the land of his Israeli grandchildren and many great-grand children, as he is awaiting the coming of the Messiah.

After my father's death, Mama moved from New York to Toronto, Canada to be closer to Genia and her family. In August 1976 Genia called me to come to Toronto. Mama was very ill, there was no hope for her recovery; by the time they diagnosed her cancer it was already inoperable. Amazingly enough, two weeks before her death she was still seen at a bar mitzvah celebration, all dressed up and dancing. No one at the party suspected that she was gravely ill. When I got to Toronto one week later I found her in bed. That night she was moaning in pain.

In the morning she came down to the living room. I played for her Strauss waltzes, the music I knew she loved. Listening to the music she used to love to dance to, she looked sad, saying to herself: " I think the game is over, I lost."

Next day, we helped her get dressed to go to the hospital for a check up. Before leaving her apartment, she insisted on putting on lipstick, and for the first time in her life she applied some rouge to her face, not to appear sickly. Stepping into the elevator we held on to her, but she pushed our hands away when a neighbor entered the elevator, not wanting to appear sick and helpless.

After her examination she was told to remain there. Mama thought that perhaps they would perform surgery on her. But Genia and I were told that it was too late for that. One week later she was dead.

For seven days I stayed with her every day, all day. Mama lay there, cancer stricken, helplessly living with a failing body. Her existence was defined by pain. Each of her body functions, that are usually so simple and often automatic or unconscious, were now painfully performed and engaged the mind to be a witness. I saw her face contorted with pain but not fear. I saw her acceptance of her distended, painful body, but not resignation.

Ever since the war, Mama had lived in fear. Her door in her Bronx apartment had three bolts and chains on it. Until she was widowed she was too fearful to go anywhere alone or stay home alone at night. Now on her deathbed she amazed us with her courage. This very person whom I remember to have always been almost hypochondriac, endlessly dwelling on her common aches and pains, be it headaches, heartburn or arthritic leg pains, who was swallowing daily aspirins as if they were candy. Now riddled with cancer, she did not complain. She was informed enough to understand the prognosis and her imminent fate. She was perceptive enough and attuned to her body to feel the rapidly progressing stages of her illness. Yet she hoped. She hoped without drama and self-pity. She hoped for a cure as she sipped, through a straw, carrot juice and other healing fluids, and patiently watched the drops of IV fluid entering her veins.

By the seventh morning in the hospital, she suddenly said, "Will I die yet this week?" It was as much a statement as it was a question. Genia and I, who kept constant vigil at her bedside, heard her. We neither confirmed nor denied it.

By noon she became edgy. An inner battle seemed to be taking place within her. Acceptance and hope gave way to impatience and anger. She asked us to speak to the nurses and doctor and tell them to stop all medication. She no longer wanted to medicate and feed the body that had betrayed her, that has caused her so much pain and had refused to mend.

In the course of the last few days, she had been anxiously watching the clock. Literally shaking with pain, she would ask if it were time for her next morphine shot. Now she came to the realization that there is no recourse. She said in Yiddish, I thought I'll make it, but now I see that there is no way out, "Es geht nisht".

She refused even a sip of water, or even to have her lips moistened.

Having made her decision to surrender to her fate, she became very calm; her face took on a peaceful aura. She gave up her fight and was ready to make her exit. In her own way she made it very clear to us that she no longer identified with her body.

Late that afternoon Genia's daughter, Tammy, who at the time was twelve, came to her grandma's bedside. Mama became concerned about Tammy's safety, when going back home, travelling alone in the subway. She told Tammy to hurry home before it got dark. Even when on her deathbed, Mama was still concerned about other's welfare. Walking Tammy downstairs I noticed a magazine on the newsstand that featured an article by Margaret Kubler-Ross, the Doctor who has written the book, "On Death and Dying". I glanced through it and was grateful for the timely message. Dr, Kubler-Ross wrote about how hard it was for a sick person to die when surrounded by loved ones. Genia also read the article.

By dusk Mama closed her eyes; she appeared to be asleep. I touched her face and kissed her lightly. She responded, whispering, "I know". She had tears in her eyes and they commingled with mine as they ran down her face. She found my hand and touched it with her lips. All my life I used to bicker with her. Now I felt total love for her. Watching her amazing inner strength in her moment of ultimate helplessness, I was proud to be her daughter.

Moments later she seemed to be talking to someone; to a nurse it would have been no more than some delirious words of a dying person. But Genia and I understood what she meant. She spoke in Yiddish, clearly speaking to someone only she could see. She was saying wait, wait for me, I'm coming with you. She talked of going out, of going through, of coming down. Then, without drama, directly and with the utmost honesty, she asked us to bid her goodbye and leave her; because, she said, she can't die while we were looking at her.

The lady that once gave us life and to whom her two daughters were the crown jewels of her life was now asking Genia and I to leave her to be alone and allow her to die.

I simply said, Mama, I am letting you die, it's OK. Goodbye Mama. Then Genia talked to her, and kissed her and said goodbye to her.

Genia and I shared this moment; it was Mama's last gift for us, a final and most poignant lesson in dignity. Upon entering life, Mama had taught us our first lessons in life and now she taught us how to exit.

We did as we promised; we left her and went home. I lay down in my room and closed my eyes; for the first time death ceased to be the sinister mystery that used to evoke in me bottomless fear. Unlike the other losses of loved ones that I have endured in the past, Mama's death was a natural departure, a final transition and it was ultimately on her terms. It was part of her life cycle and mine.

A shrill phone ring woke me up; Mama had just died.

I lay there feeling an icy void inside, but also accepting that the one who bore me was now dissolving irreversibly into an endless Universe. With my thoughts I spoke to her ; It's OK Mama, it's OK. Thanks for all the love and all the things you have taught me. Go in peace.

Early next morning, before the funeral, I went to Mama's apartment and began to clean it with a fury. I took notice of the things in her apartment that reflected her life, her interests, her taste, her lifestyle, the framed plaques lauding her active participation in charitable causes, and her history. Her walls were covered with the pictures of her children and her grandchildren. I noticed the two round green velvet chairs she had bought twenty-five years ago on my advice, even though everyone else thought them to be ugly. The crystal vases, our old silver candelabra, and the elegant Rosenthal porcelain dishes and figurines seemed just right in her gleaming china closet.

I cleaned the floors, scrubbed the bathroom, emptied and washed the refrigerator, and dusted the furniture. I seemed to have lots of energy. Soon, my niece Tammy joined me. Quietly, we both kept busy. Growing up, Mama was always on my case, not to mess up the house, to keep things in their place. She taught me to clean, to sew, to iron and to cook. Mama was a great housekeeper, she always loved her home to be squeaky clean, and I knew that she would have wanted to leave it that way.

After the funeral, we gathered at Genia's house where Genia and I remained in mourning for seven days, sitting on low seats - close to the ground. "Sitting Shiva", is in accordance with Jewish custom. All the mirrors in the house were covered with white sheets and lit candles stood on the low table near us and flickered around the clock. A constant stream of friends and family kept coming around, bringing food for us, because, according to tradition, direct-family mourners are not supposed to prepare food. Food is life, preparing food is partaking in sustaining life; the mourners, on the other hand have another task to fulfill. They are to find closure by fully acknowledging the death of a loved one. They are to keep their attention on the deceased person, remembering his or her life and acknowledging the loved one's final departure. Sitting with us, the visitors reminisced about Mama.

After seven days Genia and I left the house. Our brief walk signified the end of the "Shiva" stage of mourning.

Outside the August sun and sky and the colors of the trees and flowers seemed more vivid and brilliant than when I had last seen them, the week before...

66

MY BELOVED
AMERICAN COUSIN FANNIE

My mother's American first cousin Fannie, uncle Mechels daughter, was the only American relative who had made an effort to search for and find us after the war. She was the only one that wrote to us, in the course of the five years, when we were stuck as "Displaced Persons" in Germany. I later found out that she alone, ran from one family member to the next, travelling by subway after work, up and down New York, pleading with them to get us visas and help get us out of Germany after the war.

One day Fannie told me that one night in June of 1943, she had woken up in middle of the night and told her father that something terrible was happening to their family in Sambor. That was exactly the moment when the mass execution in Radlovice was taking place. Fannie had a remarkable intuition and a big heart.

Fannie had a difficult life in America. All her life, she worked hard, mostly in garment sweatshops, while at the same time raising a son, alone. She spent her weekends inside the 42nd Street library in New York, and dreamed of one day becoming a writer and owning a small bookstore. I loved Fannie even before I met her in person on the day we arrived in New York as immigrants.

In 1961, when I already lived in Los Angeles and was expecting the birth of my third child, I received a "Holocaust – reparation" check of $5000 from the German government. I invited Fannie to move to Los Angeles. With the money I received, I wanted to give her the opportunity to fulfill her dream. She had spent forty years behind a sewing machine and was still poor.

Within less than six months, Fannie had a beautiful bookstore on Ventura Blvd. in Sherman Oaks, and I think that it made her happy for a year. Unfortunately, the bookstore was not viable, because Fannie was already old and tired, and not the least bit a businesswoman. She refused to deal with customers she did not like, or sell the kind of books that she thought were vulgar and trashy. She loved kids and Hippies who hung around, sitting on the floor reading but not buying.

With three children under the age of four, I was unable to spend much time at the store. So, after a year, Fannie's "dream" bookstore folded, but she remained a dreamer.

With her baggage full of books, she went off to Oklahoma and New Mexico to be with Native American people, whom she loved. As a Vista volunteer, she wanted to help in any way she could. She taught the women sewing and helped the children with their schooling. She especially loved the members of the Kyowa tribe in New Mexico, who welcomed her into their community and eventually honored her with membership of the tribe.

When she retired and got to be very old and almost blind, I flew to Albaquerque, New Mexico, rented a U-haul truck and brought her and her many boxes of mildewed books back to Los Angeles. Within a few years, at 85, Fannie died of a heart attack; to my regret, I had stepped away from her bedside in the hospital for a couple of hours, when she suddenly died. The nurses said that she was calling for me. I did not get back to her in time, but I hope that she knew how much I loved her.

Fannie

Riding Fiddle in the Topanga Hills

67

HORSES

Fiddle Play

Come on Fiddle, my four legged friend
Let's gallop up the hill
You and I will this day live
It's spring and I can't sit still

M y first horse, Black Beauty, and the last one named Fiddle, looked just like the one in my daydreams in the cellar.

Although, in my twenties, I sometimes rode rental horses with friends, I did not have a horse of my own until I was thirty-seven. When, on his fourth birthday, my son Robert asked for a pony, I thought that it was a great idea. We looked in the yellow pages and found a ranch that was advertising ponies for sale. On a beautiful Sunday in California, we packed the kids in the car and set out to get Robert a pony for his birthday.

A sweet "hillbilly" stunt man, Sonny Jones, and his very nice and pretty wife, owned the small ranch we found in the phone book. We called and told them that we were coming out there to look for a pony. The kids were all excited, but I was probably more so.

My kids loved Sonny's place. It was not only full of ponies and horses, but also their open home was full of happy children, dogs, and many other animals.

After showing us a pony for Robert, Sonny wanted to show me a horse he kept in the back. He insisted that I see that horse which he said he knew I would love. He was sure about that.

I walked over to the back fence and I saw a beautiful big black mare with the sweetest face. I stood by her side for a long time, stroking her face and neck. I was in love. Sonny must have watched me standing there, near the horse. He came out and told me to take her out on the trail. I did just that and when I came back, I'm sure Sonny could tell that I wasn't going to leave without buying her.

That same afternoon, Sonny arrived at our home with a horse trailer loaded with the big black mare and a small white pony for Robert.

The first time I took my beautiful black horse out on the open trail, I cried the whole time, and that night I cried myself to sleep, in my thoughts thanking Sonny Jones, who sold me that horse for a hundred dollars. For a hundred dollars, Sonny Jones gave me something of my childhood back.

Black Beauty was a well trained old horse who made riding easy for a novice rider. To ride my next four horses I needed to acquire greater riding skills. Sometimes I would train, and share corrals with young teenagers; and I took grooming a horse, raking the corral, and exercising, just as seriously, as if I too, were a kid. I seemed to have more in common with them than with their mothers who would drop them off at the corrals.

For the next thirty years, some of my happiest moments were riding in the Topanga hills in California. I could never get enough of the open spaces. I rode for hours, at least three days each week. After dropping the children off at school, I would head for the hills in Topanga where a dirt road would take me to the open trails in the Santa Monica Mountains. After riding, I would get back in time to pick up the children from school.

Usually, I rode alone, so I could take in with all my senses, the spaciousness, the sounds, and the intoxicating smells of sage, along the way. Riding the trails, I would forget that I was a busy housewife and a mother, or an adult who normally would have many other things to do. Out in the hills, riding my horse, was the best way I knew to give expression to things I could not put into words, but were always churning inside of me. It was the best way I knew of to cope with my restlessness.

Just as it was once in my fantasy world, when I was on the trail with my horse, I was at peace and totally unafraid to ride alone, even though I would sometimes come across rattle snakes, bobcats, and other animals that would often spook my horse. By contrast, in most social situations, I rarely felt at ease. On my horse out in nature, I was able to be authentic, relaxed, and simple.

My last horse was named Fiddle Play, he was the grandson of the great racing horse, Foul Play. He taught me much and we shared many a beautiful day in the ring and on the trail. Often it seemed that we could read each other's mind. After riding him for twenty years, he was retired in my backyard to wander around freely on four acres of adjoining pasture. Sometimes he would stick his head in the door to receive treats.

One day Fiddle fell and could no longer get up. He was almost 35. He died, surrounded by my children and grandchildren. My daughter-in-law, Rebecca, remained in the house, crying. My son Mark, who had ridden him often, held Fiddle's face, comforting him. I heard him whisper in his ear, "Thanks Fiddle, for all the rides". Soon after, Fiddle died. There was sadness, love, and thankfulness. This happened on Thanksgiving day, in the year 2001. While we all sat around on the ground near Fiddle, a big turkey was roasting in the oven, and the table in the empty dining room was laden with holiday food. After Fiddle died, the attending veterinary and animal regulation officer who answered our emergency calls, came into the house and joined our family at the Thanksgiving table.

Exercising Fiddle

Rafting the Colorado River

68

A HEALING PROCESS

World War II broke out when I was seven years old. When I was twelve, I was liberated physically. I was finally liberated from invisible emotional prisons when I was in my late fifties.

My education as a physicist and my brief work in research was of no help to my emotional well-being, although it was intellectually fascinating,

While living in New York, Alabama, and Los Angeles, I was outwardly like any other American. I felt differently inside, though. Gregarious and friendly on the exterior, inside I was always a lonely alien. Constant fear was entwined in every aspect of my life. I was still troubled by nightmares. While I was in New York, back from Alabama, I talked to my father about it; he consulted with his cousin, Dr. Litman, for a referral to a psychologist. I made an appointment with one but had only one session with him.

The first thing the good Jewish therapist asked me was: "How do you feel about the male penis?"

He also asked me if I had consulted with a psychotherapist before. When I mentioned to him that in Munich I had several sessions with Dr. Bumke, he gasped. He walked over to his bookcase and opened a thick book to the page where extensive mention was made of Dr. Bumke's work and about his Nazi background. The sweet, grandfatherly professor at the Munich University whose help I had sought, had been a prominent supporter of Hitler's racial policies. Apparently, he held a special position of prominence in Hitler's circle of racists.

My search for relief from fear and from my frequent nightmares led to a quest for understanding the workings of the human mind. This, in turn, led me to psychology and philosophy classes, lectures, and workshops. Here and there I'd have an emotional breakthrough; a little window would open to let in some light. While on a river-rafting trip through the Grand Canyon, I experienced many a moment of spiritual and emotional awakening. These amazing glimpses of inner peace and joy inspired me to seek healing from fear and anger through greater consciousness. That path made more sense to me than escapism, repression and forgetfulness.

Just before the trip, I had come across a small book by Alan Watts, and I brought it with me. At first, learning to be meditative seemed self-centric, if not self-indulgent. Then again, I was reminded that a journey through life, from moment to moment, is like any other journey. One begins from where one is at. Meditation is the process of focusing on one's reality, in the most fundamental way.

Two weeks on the Colorado River with a book by Alan Watts became, for me, the start of a long process of transformation. With time, and many enlightened teachings later, I learned that it is through consciousness that one becomes aware of the life within us and how it relates and responds to the life and everything else outside of us; living takes place only in the present and is not to be confused with memories, so that the past, though well remembered, need not obscure the experience of the present moment. Otherwise, our memory inevitably would lead us to relive the emotional pain of past traumas, over and over again. And so, rooted in reality, I began to confront my past and work through my fears.

In time my fears abated, though the memories are and always will be wirh me; but I can now talk about them, and still be able to treasure each moment of my life, perhaps even more so, because of what I remember.

* * *

R-L Genia and I in 2006

69

Epilogue

"Rabbi Tarfon said: the day is short, the task is abundant… you are not required to complete the task, yet you are not free to withdraw from it…"

From Pirke Avot, the Sayings of our Fathers

It's a cold November day, winter is approaching. A small bird is sitting on a low branch outside my window. Did he forget to fly south? A big gray cat, sitting on my patio is poised to pounce on the cold and weakened bird. Who will mourn it? Are we to hate the cat?

Animals are not evil. Nature is not evil, though sometimes it is hard to accept it's cruel ways. It would seem that all of nature, the whole universe, from the biggest stars to the smallest atoms, was complicit in creating the physical conditions where a Holocaust of such cruelty and magnitude could have taken place. But I cannot blame our bloody human history on the cruelty of nature. Specifically, the decisions or non-decisions made by those who perpetrated the Holocaust or by those who allowed it to happen were *human*. The Nazi ideas were conceived in sick human minds and tolerated by those too cowardly to speak out against them.

Jewish tradition is based on the fact that, unlike animals, we humans have free will to choose between good and evil. Humans have a capacity for evil, but they also have an awesome potential for greatness; and it would seem that the choice between good and evil is simple.

People could be taught, that a good life, one of mutual respect, is possible and within their reach and is worth pursuing. Yet, no matter how educated we are, or how masterfully we navigate the material world, we humans often succumb to insecurity and self doubt. Whenever we attempt to relieve our anxiety by blaming our shortcomings on others, we allow fear or anger to guide behavior. In such a state of mind people begin to behave like barbarians.

Taking into account man's nature, I think we can define an objective standard of morality, that should be acceptable to all people who want to coexist with others, no matter how diverse they are. Such a morality will have to be based on reverence for human life, mutual respect and individual freedom.

Given the fact that today's military technology enables evil tyrannical governments to unleash weapons of mass destruction upon the rest of the world, I hope that in the next few decades a common morality of this sort will be shared by most people, even the descendants of those who today hold on to hate in their hearts and threaten to destroy the free world and all of our western civilization. Even then, we would still have to remain vigilant.

It takes courage to honestly look at ourselves and measure our actions against our fundamental morals; it takes consciousness to recognize evil and yet more courage to name it and condemn it.

To me, the scariest aspect of our post WWII society is the ignorance of history and the indifference on the part of the so-called "good" people. We must remember that less than seventy years before this book was written, politicians were willing to appease Hitler and negotiate peace with him at all cost, even while he was making murderous speeches to enthusiastic throngs of followers and advocating the destruction of all Jewish people.

Today, in 2006, we face a disturbingly similar situation. Radical Islamic and other fascistic rulers (and the terrorists sponsored by them) are openly calling for the destruction of the State of Israel, which is equivalent to calling for a second Jewish Holocaust. In spite of that, many politicians, especially European ones, are ready to negotiate with and appease the murderous terrorists and their sponsors.

Those of us who are lucky enough live in a free society, need to be aware of what it takes to guard freedom and do whatever it takes to preserve it, so that evil does not take control of our world and destroy the amazing achievements of creative, industrious, and freedom-loving people.

Much suffering still exists in the world and so far our educational as well as our religious institutions have not done enough to make the inhumane among us more human. There is a lot of work yet to be done and it would be easy to get discouraged. In response to that, one of my sons brought to my attention a quote from a book of rabbinical teachings, called Pirke Avot:

> *"Rabbi Tarfon said: the day is short, the task is abundant? you are not required to complete the task, yet you are not free to withdraw from it..."*

For all of us on this planet, our shared "each-moment-of-life" connects us to one another in an intricate balance. Therefore, everyone's brief stay on this earth should be welcome and become a blessing to all. We breathe the same air and rise to the same sun, and are nourished by the same earth. Ultimately, we return to the same earth and give back our borrowed molecules to pool them all together for new life to be born and once again blossom or suffer. For the sake of our children, let us make our choice clear.

And so, I will end my story. I will share it with others and move on to a new day.

* * *

Epilogue

Good morning life. Let's see, what can I do today? What can I learn and what can I teach?

I awaken and look out my window. I see the sky, trees and mountains and I am grateful to have eyes. Dear God, there is so much beauty to behold! I will play some music and maybe dance, because I have legs. I take a deep breath and I am grateful for the sweet mountain air that fills my lungs. I am grateful for the heart my grandparents and my parents gave me, a heart that always knew how to love and one that knows how precious life is.

Middle Andzia

ACKNOWLEDGEMENTS

In addition to thanking my family and friends, for helping ponder and edit this book (especially through those very hard hard-to-face passages and chapters), I wish to acknowledge the following text that allowed me to place dates, check facts, and cite other survivor's accounts:

The Book of Sambor - and Stary Sambor

Edited by Alexander Manor (Published in Israel, 1980) (cited on pgs. 111, 150, 183)

Made in the USA
Lexington, KY
10 March 2013